BULLYING

EPIDEMIC

Not Just Child's Play

LORNA BLUMEN

CP

Camberley Press

Copyright © 2010 Lorna Blumen

Library of Congress Cataloging-in-Publication Data (US)

Blumen, Lorna.
Bullying epidemic: not just child's play / Lorna Blumen
[ ] p. cm.
Includes index
Summary: A look at the crucial role adults play in children's bullying and what parents, teachers, and children can do to reduce and prevent bullying
ISBN-13: 978-0-9810589-1-7 (pbk)
1. Bullying. 2. Bullying in schools. 3. Parenting. 4. School environment.
5. Interpersonal relations. I. Title.
649.64 dc22   BF637.B85B576   2010

Library and Archives Canada Cataloguing in Publication

Blumen, Lorna
Bullying epidemic: not just child's play / Lorna Blumen
Includes index
Issued also in electronic format
ISBN 978-0-9810589-1-7
1. Bullying. 2. Bullying in schools. 3. Bullying-Prevention. 4. Bullying in schools-Prevention. I. Title.
BF637.B85B58 2011   302.3   C2011-901233-2

For bulk purchase discounts, please contact CamberleyPress.com.

All facts, figures, and websites were verified as of March, 2011. If you find an error, please contact Camberley Press Ltd at CamberleyPress.com.

Cover Design, Title, Interior Design and Layout: Mininder Bath
Cover Photo: Shutterstock

10 9 8 7 6 5 4 3 2
Printed in the United States of America

℗ Camberley Press Ltd
   PO Box 74553
   Toronto, ON, Canada M9A 3T0
   CamberleyPress.com

Contents

About The Author   v

Acknowledgments   vii

Introduction 1

Chapter 1   Why Is Bullying Still A Problem? 17

Chapter 2   Focus On Prevention 35

Chapter 3   Kids' Bullying Is An Adult Problem 47

Chapter 4   Bullying 360°: Getting On The Same Page 81

Chapter 5   Cyberbullying: Bullying's Growth Industry 121

Chapter 6   How To Tell The Difference Between........... 151

Chapter 7   Bullying & Respect: The Key Connection...... 165

Chapter 8   Is It Bullying & What Should I Do? 203

Chapter 9   Bullying & The Law 233

Chapter 10   Tools We Can Use 275

Chapter 11   Stop Bullying Now! 10 Action Steps 299

Index 307

About The Author

Lorna Blumen is an educational consultant and bullying prevention specialist in Toronto. Her work is focused on children's and teen bullying prevention and the underlying skills needed to solve the problem: respect, conflict resolution, emotional intelligence, stress survival, and resilience.

Lorna runs training workshops for adults who work with children – teachers, parents, coaches, camp counselors, school councils, mental health professionals, and legal and medical personnel working for the protection of children. She also works with kids, in classrooms, after-school programs, and community workshops.

Lorna is a co-developer of the **Girls' Respect Groups** Program, an after-school program for middle school girls, led by high school girls. She is a co-author, along with Natalie Evans and Anne Rucchetto, of *Girls' Respect Groups: An Innovative Program To Empower Young Women & Build Self-Esteem!* [Camberley Press, 2009]. She mentors high school girls in the Girls' Respect Groups High School Leadership Training Program. Her favorite part of GRG is seeing kids step up to their potential. Natalie and Anne were high school students when they co-developed the GRG Program and co-wrote the book with Lorna.

Lorna was a contributing author to **When Something's Wrong: Ideas For Families**, the Canadian Psychiatric Research Foundation's best-selling handbook [Note: CPRF is now Healthy Minds Canada]. Her chapter "Bystanders To Children's Bullying" was published in the book **The Art of Followership: How Great Followers Create Great Leaders And Organizations** [Jossey-Bass, 2008].

Lorna has appeared on Canadian local and national TV and radio, spoken at international conferences, and contributed to national magazines for parents and teachers. She was on the Board of Directors of Parent Education Network from 1997 to 2006. Lorna received her BA from Wellesley College, her MS from Georgetown University, and her MBA from Stanford University. Email: Lorna@LornaBlumen.com. Blog: BullyingEpidemic.com

Acknowledgments

While a book may be written by one or several authors, there are many more people who play important roles in its creation and refinement. Some say *"Books are not written, they are rewritten."* Neither task could have been accomplished without the contributions of others to whom I am indebted and would like to mention here.

My thoughts and ideas about kids' bullying have come from my 15 years of experience working with adults and kids on bullying prevention and conflict resolution issues. Over time, I have come to understand that there are important skills that underlie and support successful bullying prevention – respect for self and others, effective stress handling, the skills of emotional intelligence, and clear communication – for adults and kids alike.

I have been privileged to run workshops and work with many adults, teens, and children, all of whom have taught me at least as much as I have shared with them. Thank you to the many parents, kids, teachers, principals, social workers, psychologists, psychiatrists, family doctors, lawyers, police, judges, preschool principals, teen volunteers, and camp counselors with whom I've consulted over the past decade and a half. They have come to me and I have gone to them for support, suggestions, intervention, and help. We have shared our knowledge and perspectives while working together to safeguard our kids, to extract kids from dangerous and damaging situations, and to give kids and adults the tools they need to develop strength, self-respect, resilience, and the skills for self-advocacy.

Some of the stories shared with me have found their way into this book, to illustrate the problems and challenges of identifying and rectifying bullying before it has gone too far. All names have been changed, all identities have been protected. Thank you for your contributions to the depth and texture of my knowledge and experience. I have deeply enjoyed my work with all of you and appreciate the ways you have pushed my brain and my heart to grow.

No one has pushed me to grow as a human being more than my daughter, Valerie. Children show you where you need to grow. They also allow you to see the whole world again through their brand new eyes and hearts. Through Valerie's eyes, I could see the need, 18 years ago, to start teaching kids conflict resolution skills – when the kids were little and the problems were small. Giving children knowledge and life skills to help them grow into their own strength has been its own wonderful reward – for me as a parent, and in the larger world. On the downside for Val, a few of the stories I've shared in this book are about her or about my role as a parent, so Val's identity has not been disguised as much as she might have preferred. Thanks, Val, for letting me share those stories – they are universal experiences of parents and teens. Love you.

On a very serious note, I would like to offer a prayer of apology to the many kids we did not save because we didn't recognize their plights until it was too late. It is Phoebe Prince, Tyler Clementi, Jamie Hubley, Dawn-Marie Wesley, Eric Harris, Dylan Klebold, Jesse Logan, and the far too many kids that we have truly let down, by not intervening on their behalf soon enough to stop the hurt from becoming unbearable. It is my hope that the deaths of Phoebe Prince and Tyler Clementi, which occurred in 2010 as I was writing this book, were heart-stopping enough to provoke a sea change in the way we treat kids' bullying, both face-to-face and online. I fervently hope that they will be the last children we lose to this bullying epidemic.

I couldn't have done my work without the work of others before me. I can never pay back those people who taught me. All I can do is "pay it forward." And if we heed the Dalai Lama, who speaks of the need to approach one another with "warm-heartedness," we can open the door to many solutions.

Thank you to Judge Janet Thorpe, family court judge from the Ninth Judicial Circuit in Orlando, FL, for her contribution to Chapter 9, Bullying & The Law. Florida has been quite forward-thinking about bullying, probing for preventive solutions. Janet's knowledge, experience, mother's heart, empathy, humor, and no-nonsense, commonsense approach are a foundational rock for all who know and work with her. Janet and I have been friends since we were 12. To have our professional paths meet as well has added a wonderful dimension to our long friendship.

My heartfelt love and respect go out to Girls' Respect Groups, our after-school program for middle school girls, led by high school girls. The young women who have been part of this program are spectacular examples of the amazing things that "ordinary" teens and preteens can do. It has been vitamins for my heart to work with all of you. My work with GRG and respect issues has widened and deepened my understanding of bullying. **Bullying Epidemic** is a better book for that reason.

I offer my deepest thanks to my key colleagues in Girls' Respect Groups. Mininder Bath has shared her seemingly endless supply of multidisciplinary talent with us and brings intelligence, creativity, and heart to our work together. Min designed the title, cover, interior design, and layout for this book. Min and I worked together on the **Girls' Respect Groups** book, where her illustrations gave life to our manuscript, making it fun, teen-friendly, and engaging. Min's elegant eye for design, her extensive knowledge of graphics and production, and her ability to grow into any new skill needed have been of invaluable help. I could not have entrusted this book to anyone who "gets it" more than Min. It's been my privilege to work with her.

I am also grateful to Rebecca Hessels, for her ever-growing list of capable talents, which she deploys daily in support of my work, including this book and our Girls' Respect Groups program. Rebecca has smoothly guided the update to the second edition of *Bullying Epidemic*. Thanks also to Lori Mignone from Girls' Respect Groups. Lori's keen eye for interesting ways to connect people over the issue of respect and the discipline of her business skills were enormous assets. I am fortunate to work with all these inspiring young adults.

My brain would like to thank my "dream team" of editors for rounding out ideas and fine-tuning the manuscript. Dale Blumen, an accomplished, thoughtful therapist, coach, and mother of four brought all those skills to bear as she pushed my ideas to clarity, elucidating relationships between thought, language, and action. Laurel Choat, an impassioned, creative children's art therapist, brought her skill, compassion, and mother's heart to this manuscript. Thank you for the many ways you've supported me and this work.

It was my pleasure to work again with Hannah Silverman who edited our *Girls' Respect Groups* book with heart, clarity, and precision. She has done the same for *Bullying Epidemic*. It was also wonderful to work with Janet Mowery, a superbly experienced editor with a gift for understanding nuanced connections.

Thank you to my husband Peter and other family members who have shown me the way on so many things. I am grateful for your love and guidance. Thank you especially to my dad, a retired surgeon who, at 85, calls me several times a week to make sure I've seen all the bullying-related news. We have frequent, in-depth conversations about the connections between bullying and many social problems. Thank you for still pushing me to grow and caring so much about me and my work.

Thank you to Marvin and Elaine Shedletzky, who generously offered a space of beauty and tranquility while I was writing the first draft of the manuscript. I am deeply grateful.

I use examples from real life because they are our best teachers. It does us no good to offer an anti-bullying curriculum as a classroom exercise while real bullying and exclusion are happening steps from our classrooms, playgrounds, and homes. These cases are always complex, and the "facts" may never fully be known, even by first-hand witnesses. Even in cases where I've been directly involved, it's impossible for me, or any of the participants, to have complete knowledge of the people and events. That's true for all human experience, where two people exposed to the exact same stimulus or situation may have significantly different views of "the facts" and their meaning.

As an outside consultant, I can't possibly know the school, the kids, or the adults anywhere near as well as the people who work, study, and bring their kids there every day. I'm a sounding board, contributing my ideas and experience. The school and the parents identify the needs of their specific situation. I push for action, and we work to refine, monitor, and shape. When we all work together, some small miracles happen. It's not magic – we each just do our job – but it can make a world of difference for a miserable kid and turn a whole school environment around.

I have tried to represent the cases in this book with empathy and insight, pushing myself and other adults to ask, *"What do we need to learn from this so we can do better next time?"* I do not mean to criticize any one school, school board, parent, teacher, or group of kids. The circumstances and dilemmas presented here are, unfortunately, increasingly universal experiences, from which we need to learn, so we are not condemned to repeat our mistakes and oversights. Once a problem has become big enough that the news media enter the fray and the story takes on a life of its own, despite our best efforts, it can be very difficult to represent issues fairly and equally. This should not stop us from trying to learn, grow, and change. We must always be open to revisiting an issue, as new information becomes available, often much later, with the emergence of new witnesses, new technology, or new knowledge.

I've selected the examples used in this book to highlight diverse aspects of bullying, common pitfalls, and risks that we need to be better aware of in the early stages to prevent their unforeseen combination into a "perfect storm." While I have researched and presented each story with as much accuracy as possible, knowing all the details of each specific case is neither possible nor required for us to learn from it. **What is crucial is that we use the information contained in these stories to improve our wide-angle understanding of the range of contributing factors that, left unattended, frequently combine in disastrous ways.** A tsunami in the open ocean may cause only a two-foot displacement of the sea surface, hardly enough to be noticed. But when it reaches the shore, the focusing influence of the shallow water can cause a 60-foot wave of destruction. So too with bullying. It may start small, but it can end big. And badly.

Reining in this epidemic of children's bullying requires early and consistent adult intervention. Adults must catch the small acts of low-grade bullying before serious damage occurs and before bullying behavior patterns become ingrained and reflexive. **All adults must pay attention and get involved. Adult leadership is critically important** – both for its own, intrinsic value as well as for the example we set for kids. With our own behavior, we must teach our kids to treat others with respect, to set boundaries on our own and others' behavior, and to protect those who are being bullied. **Working together, we can dramatically turn the tide to reduce children's bullying. If raising children is the work of a village, then it's time for all of us in the village to step up.**

With love and respect,

Lorna Blumen

Introduction

This world is what we have made of it. If it is ruthless today, it is because we have made it ruthless by our attitudes. We often don't acknowledge our violence because we are ignorant about it. We assume we are not violent because our vision of violence is one of fighting, killing, beating, and wars. If we change ourselves we can change the world, and changing ourselves begins with changing our language and methods of communication.

ARUN GANDHI
MK Gandhi Institute for Nonviolence

We have spent much of the past decade looking the other way, as the level of "acceptable" everyday aggression between human beings has grown exponentially. Our conflict resolution and problem solving skills have declined sharply. Our level of personal responsibility for mistakes has plummeted and our abilities to apologize, to accept an apology, and to release a grudge have virtually vanished. We have become a culture of adults who consider it entertainment to watch people be publicly bullied and humiliated on television and the Internet. Why, then, are we so surprised that children's bullying, in our schools and communities, continues to grow, often with deadly results?

We have nearly lost our fundamental respect for human beings and our anchoring boundaries of acceptable behavior towards others. We are obsessively occupied with drawing the dividing line between "Us" and "Them." We treat strangers and newcomers with derision and disrespect. We have little self-control and even less emotional maturity. The smallest mistake opens the floodgates to an emotional free-for-all tirade. *Animals* are treated with more respect for their emotional welfare than human beings these days.

As I started writing this book, we were roiling in the aftermath of the suicide of Phoebe Prince, a 15-year-old girl who in 2009 had moved, with her family, from Ireland to the small community of South Hadley, MA. Far from finding acceptance in her new home and school, it appears she entered teenage hell. Bullied and taunted by her peers, she was targeted for not knowing her place in the social hierarchy. Apparently, as a 9th grader, her relationship with a popular 12th grade athlete ruffled grade 12 girls' feathers and put a target on Phoebe's back. Verbal taunts, physical interference, and threats became her new reality.[1] Reportedly, some of the bullying took place in the direct line of sight of teachers and school officials, who did not intervene to stop or report it.[2] Five months after starting at South Hadley High School, Phoebe hung herself at home.

How could we have missed the physical evidence of Phoebe's abuse by her peers or the signs that Phoebe was suffering? Why

[1] K Cullen, "The Untouchable Mean Girls, *Boston Globe*, Boston.com, Jan 24, 2010
[2] P Schwor, "Patrick Slams School Officials In Bully Case," *Boston Globe*, Boston.com, Apr 10, 2010

did we fail to help her? Hindsight is always instructive, but **we've got to do a better job keeping kids off the path that ends in bullying revenge and "payback"** – with either an external target, like Columbine-style shootings, or an internal focus like Phoebe's **bullycide**, the suicide of a bullied target who feels there is no other solution. When kids are on that bad path, where tormenting another human being is seen as OK, it's too hard to tell *which exact day* will be the day when an agonized child [or adult] can no longer take it and will lash out in catastrophic ways.

Speaking of Columbine, an unhappy subtext of the Phoebe Prince suicide is that the Columbine High School shooting occurred 12 years ago. What have we learned – and put into action – since 1999? Not much, if measured by what happened to Phoebe, which seems shockingly predictable, viewed through Columbine glasses. Phoebe's experience duplicated many circumstances surrounding Columbine – a bullied kid, taunted by peers. Is there any difference between Phoebe being called an *"Irish slut"* and told *"Go kill yourself,"* with drink containers thrown at her head as she walked down the street, and Dylan Klebold and Eric Harris being called *"losers, dirt bags, homos, and fags,"* with food, ketchup, and even *feces* thrown at them,[3] with peers and frequently, teachers as witnesses?[4] How much humiliation are kids supposed to take before they snap?

Because we have failed to learn and change, we have been in a downward spiral of tragedies, connecting Columbine to Phoebe's

---

[3]Columbine: Understanding Why. Producer: J Hill, Kurtis Productions, Ltd and A&E Television Networks, 2002

[4]R Larkin, *Comprehending Columbine* (Philadelphia: Temple University Press, 2007)

death. A recent chapter: Tyler Clementi, an 18-year-old freshman at Rutgers University, committed suicide by jumping off the George Washington Bridge in September, 2010, in his first month of school. Why? Because his roommate and another classmate videotaped him having sex in the privacy of his own room and outed him by streaming the encounter online.[5] This is not "just" a gay issue. **This is about how we treat human beings, how we've allowed ourselves to lose our internal knowledge of the difference between right and wrong, and our failure to set and enforce our own internal behavior boundaries.** Reread Arun Gandhi's words at the beginning of this chapter.

A culture of "Us vs. Them," where one group of kids is labeled unacceptable, seemingly justifies inhumane treatment. It may be an *understandable* reaction to world events around us, including, but not limited to, the terrorist attacks on September 11, 2001. *Understandable, but with unanticipated, dangerous downstream consequences* that result from letting "fear of the other" rule our hearts and behavior.

Unable to stop the bullies on their own, with no help from peers or surrounding adults, bullied kids finally get the message that no help is coming from outside, so it's time to take matters into their own hands. Next scene: depression, alcoholism, cutting, drug abuse, and suicide for those "acting in," and shootings for those "acting out." How can we stand by and let these disastrous scenarios be repeated?

---

[5]Associated Press, "Rutgers Students Mourn Classmate," WashingtonPost.com, Oct 1, 2010

We have become hardened in the years since Columbine. School shootings no longer shock us, or if they do, the effect is momentary, muted, and not coupled with much further thought or action. The word "Columbine" has become part of the permanent lexicon, shorthand for what I described above. There is a shameful trail of destruction of young lives, from Dylan and Eric to Phoebe and Tyler. Several years ago, I met a woman who had written a book on bullycide with **five** other mothers who had all lost their kids to suicide in the aftermath of peer bullying.[6] After Tyler's death, we heard that one school in Mentor, OH, had experienced **four bullycides in the past two years!**[7]

We are getting the message that we are doing something profoundly wrong. How many young lives must be lost before we understand that looking the other way while kids are bullied is a big contributor to the hopelessness these kids feel? And what about the damage done to the *bystanders*, the kids who were "just" part of these environments? How much damage is done "even" when it's "not so bad" as to end in murder or suicide? We are just beginning to appreciate the enormous permanent damage inflicted on the surrounding players in environments where bullying is permitted to thrive.[8]

Without realizing it, well-intentioned adults are permitting, encouraging, and, frighteningly, teaching bullying to kids.

---

[6]B High (ed), *Bullycide in America: Moms Speak Out About The Bullying/Suicide Connection* (Phoenix: JBS Publishing, 2007)

[7]M Barr (Associated Press), "One School, Four Bullied Teens Dead By Their Own Hand," Yahoo.com, Oct 8, 2010

[8]S Proudfoot, "Bullying Doesn't Just Affect Victims, But Bystanders As Well," *Vancouver Sun*,VancouverSun.com, Dec 15, 2009

Adults tell kids not to bully, but our actions speak much louder than words. The level of societal bullying has skyrocketed and every day sets the standard lower. We have allowed so much bullying, particularly verbal bullying, to become woven into the fabric of daily life that we've had to desensitize our radar, screening out the vast majority. Something has to be **catastrophic** to get our attention today.

The building blocks, the everyday ingredients, are all around us. Adults bully one another at work and at home. Top-rated TV shows glorify belligerent bullies and bullying. Workplace bullying, road rage, and reality show emotional meltdowns and backstabbing are bad examples for our kids!

Adults bully kids frequently, often while trying to do something *good* – while trying to teach a child a skill or trait that's genuinely valuable. Hockey parents gone wild or a teacher trying to motivate a kid by "jokingly" calling him *"dumb as a box of rocks"* are examples of good intent wrapped up in the wrong package. And when kids bully each other, adults miss the warning signs until there's a major problem, typically intervening so late that the damage is beyond repair.

The most important message in this book is this: Kids' bullying is mostly an adult problem, about 80% [my estimate]. Part of the problem rests with our kids [about 20%], but they can only do their job when we do ours. Adults have been woefully inadequate in stepping up to our responsibility as moral leaders and boundary-setters in

kids' bullying. **Adults need to demonstrate much stronger leadership, so kids can become responsible for their own leadership roles.** Chapter 3 takes a long look at this problem.

Our focus has been much too narrow. We focus far too much on the bully, the "problem child." We don't spend nearly enough effort developing a wide-angle view of the factors in each environment that permit and foster bullying. **We must look at all components of the bullying system**, for it is a system – the bully, the target, and the bystanders, adults and kids alike. **Successful efforts to reduce bullying must focus on all components.**

And yet, restricting our focus to bullying is STILL too narrow. Bullying is just one manifestation of an interrelated set of problems, including the growing epidemic of dating violence, poor conflict resolution skills, lack of emotional self-control, lack of respect, and our difficulties welcoming and blending people into our increasingly multicultural communities. **There is a complexity to the interwoven nature of these issues that you miss if you only focus on one issue.** They're like a fishing net – you pick up one point of the net, but soon realize that the point you're holding is connected to every other part of the net. You can't talk about bullying without talking about respect, you can't talk about respect without talking about dating violence, dating violence leads us to the issues of emotional self-control and stress management, and so on.

Even though we think we know and understand what bullying is, our knowledge is often unclear and incomplete,

leading to inconsistent action or avoidant paralysis. We must look with fresh eyes and renewed determination to take action. We must be willing to re-examine the bullying and everyday rudeness we let slide beneath our radar. We must look at the tentacled connections that bullying puts forward into other social issues, and **we must be ready to step back into our leadership role as adult mentors and guides to children.**

Frankly, the solution to bullying is simple – "Just Stop It!" We don't have to love everyone or be everyone's best friend, but we must make a place for everyone and treat other human beings with dignity and respect, even and *especially* in conflict. We must be able to work and play with everyone.

Honestly, it's not that hard, if you start early and keep insisting on respectful treatment for all, by all. If you keep insisting on it, and act as if you really mean it, every day, kids will stop testing you to see if you *"really, really"* mean it. They will internalize those standards. That applies to workplace bullying, too!

In 2008, Dylan Beckham, a nine-year-old in Bowling Green, KY, stood by an autistic classmate and insisted that the bullying stop. Dylan's insistence on "No Bullying Here" spread to his class, his school, and throughout his hometown. Former bullies apologized to those they'd wronged and became their defenders. Two years later, Dylan, at the advanced age of 11, began fundraising with classmates and teammates in Bowling Green to help kids with autism. He has inspired the whole community. At this writing, they have raised over $10,000 toward a goal of $30,000 to help fund the University of Kentucky Autism Program.[9]

Dylan is inspiring. I didn't have that strong a voice when I was Dylan's age – I admire him for that. He was a true, everyday hero – at age nine. As adults, we know it's wrong to stand by and let bullying happen. What justification do we have for not stepping up to the plate and doing *at least* as much as Dylan?

Adults make a million excuses for our inaction – *"We don't have the right laws, the right program, the right books," "There isn't enough research," "The teachers are busy or weren't trained," "It wasn't my kid," "I didn't want to get involved," "The bully has as much right to be in this school as the kid she's targeting," "We didn't know that child* [with a documented list of multiple aggressive offenses against other classmates] *was going to target **that child he hadn't targeted before**."* The list of lame excuses is endless and disgraceful [keep reading, there's more]. Shame on us adults. We can do better and we must.

What's Unique About This Book?

This book is action-focused. It's full of tools and ideas you can use immediately. You don't need to buy a new program or a new set of binders or go for more training [although it's helpful to have everyone on the same page]. The real world gives us all the examples we'll ever need – if we just act on them.

---

[9]J Mink, "Autism Awareness: 6th Grader Working Towards Fundraising Goal," *Bowling Green News*, BGNews.com, Sep 3, 2010

This is a book for hands-on practitioners – people dealing with kids and their behavior every day. Bullying is not a one-size-fits-all problem. We must have a full range of ideas, tools, and solutions to bring to bear as we identify the nuances and work toward incremental improvements. We must apply our critical thinking skills. We must work together and be willing to step in and act quickly. If our intervention doesn't help, change the plan and keep trying. Again. And again. Until the problem is solved. And keep monitoring, at a lower level, after the solution.

It is the everyday, seemingly unimportant actions that adults take – the behaviors that we ignore or challenge – that either incubate the growing societal infection of bullying or strengthen our ability to hold the line and heal the wounds. Every time we look away, we allow the infection to spread. We need to act now.

Who's This Book For?

This book is for everyone who wants fresh insight into the cancerous problem of kids' bullying and its deep roots into everyday life:

- **Parents** who want to raise their children with resilient self-esteem and respect for themselves and others, even and especially in times of conflict.

- **Teachers And School Administrators** trying to build respectful school environments through their leadership.

- **Coaches** working to build teams of athletic strength and moral character.

- **Community Leaders** who champion the work of neighborhood repair, building communities safe for kids and adults.

- **Mental Health Professionals** who understand the importance of prevention, rather than lurching from crisis to crisis.

- **Physicians** who are alert to the physical symptoms and emotional distress that can be the warning signs of bullying.

- **Lawmakers** who foster the legislative connection between prevention and enforcement, while protecting every child's right to attend school and community activities in peace and without fear.

- **Media Organizations** working to build consensus and community commitment, by sharing deeper knowledge and understanding.

- **Everyone** who wants to reduce the levels of interpersonal aggression and rudeness in today's society.

- **Everyone** who would like to be able to make a mistake without the other party going ballistic.

- **Everyone** who is willing to say *"Oops, I'm sorry"* when they make a mistake and hurt someone else and commit to not doing it again.

- **Everyone** who is willing to forgive a first mistake and not carry a grudge.

- **Everyone** who is interested in paving the way for a return to civility.

How To Get The Most From This Book

Make this book work for you. I'm not the only one with good ideas. More than anything, I hope that the ideas I present here will provide the inspiration for you to develop and fine tune your own ideas and action items, customized for your unique community with its specific personality, strengths, and weaknesses.

Woven throughout the book, and particularly in Chapter 10, Tools We Can Use, are ideas for turning understanding into action. Making notes or highlighting can be an easy way to identify new ideas to try or ways to fine tune existing actions for better results. Separating the notes into "Try This Now" and "Ideas For Later" can help you prioritize where to start.

Tap into the spirit – and expertise – of like-minded adults. Share your ideas, your successes, and your questions on our BullyingEpidemic.com blog or our GirlsRespectGroups.com website and we'll post them for all to use. Use this book as the sand to **your** oyster – the little bit of friction that makes you think, refine, focus and see things in a new way. We need everyone's help, shared pearls of wisdom, as we confront and hold the line against bullying.

Who Will Benefit If We Make Changes?

Everyone will benefit from a more respectful world. Our kids will be the obvious and biggest beneficiaries, when we adults change our behavior and stop teaching and enabling bullying in children's environments. Beyond that, our adult lives will improve too, as we use our retuned eyes and ears to change long-standing toxic habits in our adult workplaces and living spaces. We must look fearlessly at our current practices of ignoring, enabling, and [yes] rewarding bullying leadership and bully bosses, both real ones and made-for-TV dictators.

It is possible to change things for the better. It is possible to pull ourselves back from the edge. It is surprisingly simple, requires little training, and mostly involves the skill of "ordinary adults," you and me, although experts and specialists can guide and shape our efforts. **We must be willing to pay attention at an earlier stage, to step in and act the first time we see bullying by kids or adults, to correct behavior while it is still a simple mistake, before it becomes pathological or diseased**.

We can do this. We have many powerful examples of societal change, even in the recent past, to use as road maps to improvement. We used to think it was OK to punish kids by hitting them. We used to think it was OK to drink and drive. We have come a long way in our thinking on these topics. We've come a long way towards changing our behavior too, but as we can see, it takes time to close the gap between what we *know* is the right thing to do and *doing it consistently*. Israel Knox, professor of philosophy, once said: *"Wrongdoing is the gap between the standards we profess and the actions we perform."*[10] We must each work daily to close that gap.

---

[10] I Knox, "An Ethical Humanist View Of Rosh Hashanah" in P Goodman (ed), *The Rosh Hashanah Anthology* (Philadelphia: The Jewish Publication Society, 1992)

We must be willing to reclaim our role of adult leadership and be ready to act on it. Yes, we will make mistakes as we become stronger leaders and more capable guides for kids, as we stand up against bullying by adults or kids. We may each have to say *"Oops, sorry, I thought that sounded like bullying, but I'm glad to say I was wrong. I may have overreacted."* I would much rather make the occasional kind-hearted, well-intentioned mistake than let another Phoebe Prince suffer in silence and hang herself in a stairwell. Wouldn't you?

How do we respond to those who say *"Bullying's not such a big problem. We're just hearing about those suicides because news travels fast on the Internet."*? We say: *"If we even know of **one child** who feels like killing herself because of bullying, how can we look away? We are lucky to have the Internet as an early warning system."* We just need to do better on the "early" part, to intervene long before the suicide or homicide.

As we clean up our kids' environment, we can improve the adult world too. If we don't stop bullying at its earliest, easiest stages, with kids, what do we think will happen to the little bullies [and targets and bystanders]? They will become BIG bullies, targets, and bystanders and take those bad behavior patterns into their adult lives and workplaces. A 2009 study by the Workplace Bullying Institute and Zogby International called bullying "a silent epidemic," with 37% of study respondents reporting being bullied at some point in their work lives, and another 12% reporting they witnessed someone else being bullied at work.[11] Frequently the bullying is done by the boss, *the person selected to lead others!* **Bully bosses and leaders dot the political and professional landscape. Why? Because we have been willing to overlook bullying behavior. Maybe we think it's an all-or-nothing package. This must change.**

We must insist on better behavior from ourselves, our elected officials, and our public figures, including sports figures and celebrities. We can work to keep our best characteristics while smoothing out the rough edges of our weaknesses. People must understand that in order to keep their jobs and earn the big paycheck, they have a **responsibility** to score points AND to behave with kindness, respect, and dignity toward others.

If we keep insisting on it, we can create a societal shift. But we must stand up for our values. A professional basketball team cannot expel, then reinstate a player who chokes his coach and threatens to kill him and wonder why kids and adults keep bullying.[12] Everyone makes mistakes, and everyone should get a second chance, but there is a limit, a point beyond which we must say *"Sorry, you've gone too far."* Basketball talent and All-Star status should not exempt *anyone* from the rules of human decency and self-control. **When it comes to bullying, everyone is accountable.**

---

[11]"Tired of Work? Bullying Might Be To Blame," Oprah.com, Oct 1, 2009
[12]M Puma, "The 'Choke' Artist," ESPN.com/Sprewell, Dec 1, 1997

Bullying is both very simple and very complex. If we handle it early, it's very simple. If we look the other way, allowing bullying to infect our homes, schools, and communities, it's impossibly complex to know when and where the next crisis will occur, and there's virtually no way to "repair" it. There is no rewind button.

Is this approach *always* easy? Not always, and not at first. It's like being a Zen master. It looks simple, but it takes some work to reach the "effortless" stage. And while it's not too difficult, there are no shortcuts. Mistakes must be caught, damage repaired, responsibility shared, genuine apologies offered, and changes made of heart, spirit, and behavior.

Bullying prevention is much more about the small things that we do every day than it is about organizing high profile events like Bullying Prevention Day or Week or Month [although these activities can get people energized and focused]. Small, everyday, consistent actions send the loudest message that we will no longer tolerate bullying in our homes, schools, workplaces or communities, and that we will work together to make that happen. Our willingness to step in encourages others to join us in this work. **It is my hope that this book will push you to rethink and reintegrate your understanding of bullying and will light a fire of determination in you to stand up, united with others in steadfast determination to halt this corrosive, deadly epidemic. For our kids and for ourselves.**

1

Why Is Bullying Still A Problem?

Despite at least a decade filled with thousands of programs for bullying prevention, conflict resolution, self-esteem, empathy, and social skills, not to mention corporate team-building and Outward Bound–style "week-in-the-wilderness-with-my-team" high ropes activities, why is bullying still such a problem, for both adults and kids? What are we doing wrong, and why are adults so ineffective at controlling bullying?

There are many contributing factors to the stubborn persistence of this issue. Let's look at a few.

1. **What Is Bullying, Anyway?** We don't even agree on what bullying is – and isn't – or where to intervene. How could we be so confused and inconsistent after all this time? There are several obstacles in our path. **First, no two bullying situations are exactly alike**, making it hard to have a precise rulebook. The complexity requires us to look for the nuances, to dig deeper, to resist the urge to slap a solution on the most obvious – or loudest – symptom. It requires extra time and attention, adult resources that are in short supply.

Second, different people react differently to the same stimuli, and everyone's individual response depends on their current mood, fatigue, stress level, and other factors. What hurts Stacy's feelings might not bother Monique, and what bothers Stacy today, with her mother sick in the hospital, might have rolled off her back last month.

2. **Adults Are Often Inflexible Or Too Limited In Their View Of What Constitutes Bullying.** As parents, teachers, and other adults working with kids, we must upgrade and expand our views and our definitions of bullying behavior to clarify and understand the situations we encounter. We must investigate beneath the surface, beyond the most obvious symptoms. **We must let the *intent of the behavior* and the *effect on the target* guide us in our assessment of whether we're dealing with bullying.** Even when it's not bullying, adults often have a "behavioral guidance opportunity" or the chance to set an example with our own behaviour.

   Our first objective is to bring more clarity and consistency to our views of bullying, so that we may apply adult guidance in an appropriate and effective manner, with better results at an earlier stage of the problem. **Our second objective is to be able to look, with a wider-angle lens, at the *many* ways adults *could be* intervening more effectively in kids' behavioral issues,** whether or not the problem is bullying. Let's keep those ideas in mind as we move forward.

There is a risk of getting tangled up in semantics and nit-picking as we update and deepen our understanding of bullying. The manifestations of bullying keep changing too, making the task more complex. We can vacillate between not recognizing bullying or its building blocks clearly enough and, at the other end of the spectrum, labelling *everything* as bullying. Situations don't always fit neatly into categories, and complex behaviors *often* fit into multiple categories simultaneously. Chapter 4 will help us develop reasonably consistent but flexible definitions of bullying as we refine our framework and guidelines.

Let's reach beyond semantics to learn how to recognize when someone is hurt, intentionally or accidentally, and our supervision or guidance is needed to resolve the problem. As parents, educators, and coaches, we will have many such "behavioral guidance opportunities" along the path to adulthood.

3. **Our Focus Is Too Narrow**. I alluded to this obstacle earlier, but let me be more specific here. We focus too closely on several aspects of bullying, and in doing so we can miss the bigger and more accurate picture. Specifically:

   - **We focus too much on the bully and the target**. We need more focus on bystanders' responsibility to intervene when someone or something crosses the line. **Bystanders must be empowered – and expected – to help create safe school and community environments.**

- **We focus too much on the "endpoint,"** the occurrence of severe harm or extreme violence. We ignore the clues, the "breadcrumb trail," on the road we've travelled to get there.

- **We focus too much on how to punish** and "repair" after bullying has caused harm. We need to be proactive and put much more effort into prevention. Stay tuned for Chapter 2.

- **We focus entirely too much on the kids' role in kids' bullying. Instead, we need to look closely at the adults' role** – causing, teaching, or enabling kids' bullying. Adults must commit to clean up bullying in our adult lives so we can be credible guides and mentors, "walking our talk."

4. **We Accept Bullying As A Normal Part Of Growing Up, Of School And Adult Life.** *"Boys will be boys," "Girls will be girls," "Everyone goes through it," "Your kid should toughen up," "Why should I teach my daughter to be nice at school? Wait till she grows up and sees the work world."* If adults feel that bullying is an accepted [or acceptable] part of life, and relinquish their responsibility to guide and set limits on acceptable behavior, then kids will continue pushing the limits, driving them incrementally lower. Kids have always tested and pushed the limits. That's part of their job. But it's **our** job, as adults, to set and enforce reasonably consistent limits. When kids know that you mean it, they stop testing and accept and internalize the limits.

We think we invented bullying recently. We didn't, although we're getting pretty close to perfecting it. My grandmother, born in 1900, was an elementary school teacher. She told stories about being bullied when she was five, and later dealing with bullies in her classroom as a young teacher. Some of the bullies were taller than she was. But she was firm and didn't back down. She was a bit of a daredevil – she was known as "Motorcycle Annie" when she was a kid! She had a great sense of humor. Maybe those traits helped her establish rapport with her students – that's important, too.

5. **Adults Set A Bad Example**. Our own adult behavior leaves a lot to be desired. Road rage, workplace bullying, and explosive emotional meltdowns are everyday occurrences. Reality shows might seem like entertainment to us, but to an inexperienced young mind they're a road map to "grown-up" attitudes of intolerance and behavior devoid of self-discipline, caring for others, or community contribution. Chapter 3 holds a mirror up to all of us. We can do better.

6. **We Can't Eliminate All Bullying**. There's a certain amount of aggression hard-wired into human chromosomes. No anti-bullying policy is going to change that. Nor would we want it to. There is a very positive side to human aggression. Our natural competitive instincts also bring out the best in us, pushing us to strive to improve, to invent, to create, to grow, and to learn. We are sharpened by working with and learning from others who are more knowledgeable, more experienced, or more talented.

It would be much easier if bullying were a binary condition – either it's there or it's not. Like computers, a 0 or a 1. Unfortunately, it's not that clean. With bullying, we need to hover around a balance point – somewhere near .3! We can go a little beyond that, but we need to pay attention and intercede when we've reached the limit. We need to keep monitoring, guided by our rules and our instincts, making mid-course adjustments. You don't fly a plane from Los Angeles to New York on a single, fixed heading. It's a constant process of checking and applying small mid-course corrections that keeps planes flying on target. Same for humans.

7. **Kids' Bullying Can Be Genuinely Hard To Identify**. Adults aren't *supposed* to see kids bullying one another. It's their mistake if we actually see it. Kids do most of their bullying in the places where adults *aren't* – on the edges of the playground, at recess, at lunch, on the bus, in the bathroom, in the locker room, or on the computer after school. Even the most experienced, kind-hearted, and empathic teachers *looking* for bullying in response to a parent's request often can't find it. I've experienced that as a parent.

Bullying and insults can be very subtle, especially as delivered by preteen girls. A small change in inflection or facial expression shifts the same words from enthusiastic support to sarcastic put-down [*"Those jeans are so cool"*]. Sometimes saying *nothing* is an act of bullying; for example, when a girl waits for support from her friends and they fall dead silent.

While there are certain words or actions that are clearly unacceptable ["Loser," "He's so gay," slamming a kid into a locker, pinching a girl's breast or butt or licking your lips at her as she walks in the hall between classes], we have to be smarter and more flexible, evaluating events in context, looking at the intent, the background of the friendship, and the perhaps unintended effect of an action on the target.

Let's return to the example of "girlfriends" being deadly silent and freezing out one of their friends or schoolmates by not giving support [nodding, "uh-huh"] when expected or desired. A parent or teacher could be standing right in the middle of that interaction and, without knowing the immediate background of the friendships, she would not realize that she's watching girls' exclusion in action. As we know, the landscape of girls' friendships can change so rapidly that you need a play-by-play announcer to keep up. We can help change that, too. See Chapter 7 about the work Girls' Respect Groups is doing with teens and middle school girls.

8. **Our Uncertainty Leads To Inaction**. All those shades of grey can make it hard to know for certain when we're too close to the line. Our uncertainty leads to inaction, but doing nothing is not neutral. When we're right at the edge, the next small misstep can have serious, sometimes deadly consequences. We need a much bigger safety margin.

9. **Adults Look Away From Adult And Kids' Bullying**. Even when we're reasonably sure it's bullying, we're slow to step

in. Sometimes we're unsure of the whole story and don't want to accuse people unfairly or overreact. Sometimes it's just too much work to get involved. It's not until there's a real crisis that adults get involved.

10. **Adults Say** *"Stop Bullying"* **With Our Words, But Our Actions Say** *"Bullying's OK."* We fail to intervene; we let bullying situations drag on and on. We convince ourselves we're doing something when we pass the problem to someone else's office or purchase another bullying prevention curriculum. We can confuse paperwork with *action* as the clock ticks. I worked with one school, kindergarten to grade 8, which had 18 different programs for bullying prevention, conflict resolution, social skill building, and encouraging empathy! Having the programs is one thing. Creating a safe, bully-free environment can be quite different.

We make lame excuses for not intervening – *"The bully has as much right to be here as the kid who's being picked on,"* or *"The bus driver could have gotten in trouble for touching a child"* who was being beaten up by other kids on the bus. It's not enough to tell kids in September *"No bullying"* and then fail to act as if we really mean it. This applies both to home and school.

11. **Adults Enforce Boundaries And Rules Inconsistently**. On Monday, a kid gets detention for knocking the lunch tray out of another kid's hands, or he's punished at home for an equivalent infraction against a sibling. By Friday, adults are

worn out, distracted, or can't be bothered, so we let it slide. Nobody's perfectly consistent, but letting too much slide encourages kids to keep pressing the limits.

Adults can't be everywhere; nor should they be. When adults are the only ones responsible for setting limits, a culture develops in which kids press the limits of bad behavior *until* an adult catches them. **We want kids to internalize those limits, to know better, and to feel disappointed, with *themselves and with each other,* when they behave inhumanely toward another human being. That's peer pressure at its best.**

12. **Adults Tell Kids To Take Responsibility For Their Actions, But Adults Have Become Masters Of Responsibility Evasion**. We make excuses for and pathologize our bad behavior, then slap a diagnostic label on it. *"Not my fault. Need rehab for it."* Alcoholism, drug addiction, and sex addiction are just the tip of the iceberg. Were you aware that road rage has become an officially recognized psychological problem? It's now considered part of Intermittent Explosive Disorder, an impulse control disorder, according to DSM-4, the ***Diagnostic and Statistical Manual of Mental Disorders***, published by the American Psychiatric Association.[1]

The vast majority of impulse control problems result from or are made much worse by our own failure to set, practice, and

---

[1] *Encyclopedia Of Mental Disorders*, MindDisorders.com

enforce consistent boundaries and self-discipline for ourselves and our kids. With no limits, and every bad behavior blamed on someone or something else, we keep ratcheting downwards to new lows.

Speaking of ratcheting downwards, a Toronto woman sued a Canadian cell phone provider, blaming it for her marriage breakup.[2] Apparently, she was having an affair, revealed through her cell phone bills, which had previously been mailed to her separately, under her maiden name. When her husband called the provider to arrange home phone and Internet service at the couple's home, the provider mistakenly "bundled" the woman's personal cell phone bill into the package, mailing the bills for all services to her husband. Marriage breaks up. Surprising? No. Wife apologizes and takes responsibility? No. Wife blames cell phone company. Surprising? No. Shocking, but not surprising. [OK, I was a little surprised, too.] Good examples for the kids – both having an affair and blaming someone else? No.

Self-control and self-discipline are learned skills that require practice and refinement. Like muscles, they work better the more we use them, gaining more consistency as our brain matures, especially the prefrontal cortex, the area responsible for executive functions, impulse control, and delayed gratification. Even people with damage to this area of the brain can learn discipline and self-control. And

---

[2]B Powell, "Toronto Woman Sues Rogers After Her Affair Is Exposed," *Toronto Star*, TheStar.com, May 17, 2010

fortunately, all the exciting new research about neural plasticity supports the idea that we can indeed grow more complex neural networks, with intention, practice, and time. As with a muscle, if you rarely use self-control, don't expect it to work when you really need it.

13. **Parents And Teachers View Each Other As Adversaries.** This is a **BIG** problem. We point fingers, shaking our heads at how *"those parents"* or *"that school"* or *"those teachers"* aren't doing enough to create a bully-free environment or to solve a bullying situation already in progress. **We have to stop this – now!** Teachers and parents have different, unique roles in kids' lives. We combine our efforts, as a team, for the benefit of our kids. We have to do a better job offering help and support to each other. It would be great if everyone were on the same page, but that's unrealistic. **We need to stop using perceived inaction on somebody else's part as justification for our own insufficient action in our own sphere of influence.**

We have to stop looking at each other as "The Obstacle." Parents or schools sometimes ask me to run a bullying prevention workshop that is clearly being offered as a remedial effort to pacify one constituency, either vocal parents or teachers. I insist that parents, teachers, and all school personnel be present for this activity. **It is politically important that we see one another's eyes around the room and recognize that we are united as a team, with unique roles, abilities, and responsibilities.**

The potential power and results from this team approach are amazing. One afternoon, I walked into my daughter's high school office. I was there as a parent, for a meeting about my daughter. A woman behind the counter looked at me and said *"You're Lorna Blumen. You saved my daughter's life!"* I didn't even *know* her daughter; I had never laid eyes on her. This woman had been to a bullying prevention workshop that I'd run at her daughter's school. At one point, something I said caught her attention. The mother looked instinctively around the room, met her daughter's teacher's eyes, and in that instant they both had an *"Aha!"* moment about what was bothering her daughter at school. Working together, they turned a bad situation around for a little girl who had been desperately unhappy at school.

This story illustrates three important points:

(1) **Parents and teachers *must* work together on this.** We each play unique roles. We handicap ourselves when we limit our view of the situation or the tools for changing it, by focusing on only one set of adults in a kids' world. Not only do we work better and more effectively together, but there are many things we cannot see or do without each other's help.

(2) My role in this situation was an extension of the last point. I did not, nor could I, help this girl on my own. I just did my part, which made it possible for the next person to pick up on what I had done and do *her* [or his] part.

Had any one of the three of us [parent, teacher, or I] not been there, this problem might never have

become clear. It certainly would have taken longer and cost that young girl more anguish at school.

(3) **The depth of that mom's emotional reaction is a perfect example of the extreme caring that we all, parents and teachers, put into our work with kids –** extreme caring, extreme concern, and extreme relief when we nip a dangerous situation in the bud or extract a child from a hurtful environment where they're miserable and filled with dread.

14. **When We Finally Step In To Help, We Often Use The Wrong Tools.** A common mistake in trying to solve bullying problems is using conflict resolution skills. A fundamental difference between bullying and conflict is that conflict is between equals – the roles can reverse – while bullying is *never* between equals. How can you tell that conflict resolution skills are being tried? When you hear, *"We let the kids work it out by themselves,"* that's a big hint. And while I'm a big fan of teaching kids skills so they **can** work out many of life's problems, that approach (1) only works for conflict resolution, (2) takes many repetitions [50-100] of adults actively guiding the kids through solutions until they are internalized, and (3) should **never** be used for bullying or any situation with a big, one-way power differential between the parties. We'll look at this problem in depth in Chapter 6. I won't be spoiling the ending to say now that, by trying to use conflict resolution skills to solve bullying, once again we're giving kids the message that adults don't get it, that adults won't protect the target, and that kids are on their own to solve it.

That's actually how I got into bullying prevention 15 years ago. When my daughter was young, I sat on the Board of Directors of Parent Education Network, a Toronto-area community services agency that has done a wonderful job, since 1968, offering parenting skills workshops. In my dual roles as parent and Board member, I saw the need to teach kids conflict resolution skills when the kids are young and the problems are small. It seems self-evident now, although we're still not doing a good job of it, but back then, in North America, there were few resources focused on teaching conflict resolution skills to young kids, especially in a preventive mode.

I developed a curriculum "disguised" as a drama class. Conflict is the basis for all drama, after all; like human aggression, there's much that's *good* about conflict. I started teaching conflict resolution skills for elementary school kids, initially in classrooms, directly to the kids. The longer I worked in conflict resolution, the more bullying kept coming up, so I added a piece about bullying to my conflict curriculum. By then I was teaching the teachers and other adults who worked with kids – coaches, camp counselors, etc. I had begun to understand that I could reach more kids by teaching their teachers [and parents and coaches]. I also realized that no matter what work I did with the kids and their teachers, what was *really* important was what they did when I *wasn't* there. **The whole environment has to change.**

15. **We'd Like A Quick Solution Or We'd Like To Make It Someone Else's Problem**. Wouldn't it be great if the bullying problem that appeared in the principal's office at 1 pm was solved by 3 pm, preferably with a magic wand? Love that. Unfortunately, real life rarely works that way, but we behave as if it does. We pay attention to that 1 pm bullying problem just long and hard enough to make it go underground, possibly keeping it on our radar till the end of the week. Then, because it's not screaming at us anymore, we put it on the back burner and pay little attention to it, waiting for another bad, above-the-radar occurrence to cycle it back up to the top of the pile. We don't think of it that way, but that's what happens.

Adult attention on a kids' bullying issue will drive the problem underground for a while, while the searchlights are still on, but it will come back. With virtually all bullying problems, by the time it lands in the principal's office, it's been going on long enough that there's no quick fix. It's not that hard, but it will take three to six months to solve it, requiring that adults pay moderate-level attention to the problem, monitoring for recurrence. Heard of "attention deficit?" This is one place where the adult version shows up. In today's overdrive world, it's truly a challenge to keep paying attention to something that isn't right in your face, even if you know it's important. Kids know when adults stop paying attention, or even worse, when we've only paid lip service to the problem. Like jungle cats creeping back after the safari jeep lights are out, the problem will continue.

Another way to make it look as if we've done the quick fix is to pass the problem off to someone else. Parents and teachers pass the problem back and forth, often blaming each other for not doing enough. Eventually, the problem may get passed to the principal, to the school board, sometimes to the teachers' association, but it usually lands back in the kids' laps [more accurately the **kid's** lap – typically the target]. Now the problem's been all over the school district and comes back unresolved, weeks or months later. What's the take-away message for the target? Adults won't help, and you're on your own to solve it. That's a recipe for trouble, possibly disaster.

16. **Along With Evading Responsibility, Adults Have Become Deficient In The Skills Of Apology, Forgiveness, Accountability, And Repair, And Have Largely Stopped Teaching These Skills To Kids**. Mistakes are part of learning. Some mistakes harm others, usually unintentionally. An apology should be offered quickly and easily, also as part of the learning experience. **Apology should be a small thing, not a big thing**. It should happen so often, so naturally, that we don't think twice about it, and we don't view it as capitulating or losing face. And the apology that you make your four-year-old give, head down, when he doesn't mean it? That doesn't count – you gotta mean it. Sometimes we have to wait till the child is ready to apologize, which is hard to keep sight of on our multi-tasking agendas. Use a sticky note to make sure it gets done by the end of the day, and tell the child that your expectation is that he prepare

himself to be ready by then. Our failure to insist on real apology and repair, for ourselves and our kids, damages us and our relationships. If you have never learned to apologize or release a grudge, it's exceedingly hard to learn at age 40 [but not impossible, so keep trying!].

After apologizing, we must be accountable for and repair the hurt or damage caused by our mistakes. That includes the commitment to learn what we need to learn, change our behavior, and not make that mistake again. That requires intent, attention, and practice.

Distressingly, when we add up all the factors that contribute to bullying still being a problem, we're forced to the inescapable conclusion that, not only do we not have the problem solved, we're actually just *beginning* to work on it!

2

Focus On Prevention

Prevention is the only real solution to bullying and many social problems. Anton Chekhov, the Russian playwright known for his stories about complicated Russian families, famously said, *"If there is a gun hanging on the wall in Act I, then it must be fired."*[1] Instead, why don't we choose *not* to hang the gun on the wall? This is what I mean by putting ourselves and our kids on a different path. Once you're on a bad path, every day you end up asking, *"Is **today** the day the gun's going to come off the wall?"* And once the gun is off the wall, it's a crisis, and our backs are to the wall to solve it. Prevention gives us more and better options and the luxury of time to observe and fine-tune our approach.

There is too much focus on after-the-fact punishment and attempts to "repair" the damage. Punishment can never make up for what was done to Phoebe Prince, nor bring her back to her family. Two months after Phoebe died, the school had a "special tribute luncheon" in Phoebe's honor. Where was that special luncheon when she enrolled at South Hadley High School in September, welcoming her as a new student,

---

[1] A Chekhov, Letter To A Gruzinsky, Search.com/reference, Nov 1, 1889

introducing her to the community, and identifying her as someone who should be extended extra help, courtesy, and the opportunity to make new friends? Where were the adults watching closely to make sure she was extended a hand in friendship, paired up with kids to show her the ropes in her new school, and invited to kids' homes and social events after school? This is not a problem unique to South Hadley High. Our failure to welcome and embed newcomers into their new communities creates serious downstream problems. More on this later, especially in Chapter 10.

I've several times been on speaking agendas with kids who survived the Columbine shootings. Many of them are motivational speakers, some for charitable foundations bearing the names of students who died in the shootings. These surviving kids, now young adults, are amazing examples of resilience, of strength and commitment to salvage something valuable from an unfathomably horrible experience. Yet there is no road back, no rewind button. Their lives have been permanently marked, their paths, their bodies, and their psyches permanently altered by being at the epicenter of the destruction, as were ours to a lesser extent, from the shock waves that propagated outward from Columbine.

Yes, some of that damage resulted in the survivors experiencing intense personal growth, and I'm sure all the survivors are wise beyond their years and have much to teach us. But I submit that 16-year-old kids don't need to get shoved into adulthood that traumatically and that Columbine was largely a preventable disaster.

There is a big cost if we miss the early chances to intervene in kids' bullying and set things back on the right track. The early chances are the easy and cheap options. Clean-up, damage control, and punishment are never as good as prevention.

There will never be enough metal detectors, school suspensions, and lawsuits to stop bullying. You have to catch the kid *before* he [or she] takes the gun to school. And by "catch," I don't mean just finding the gun before it gets to school. I mean connect that kid to his caring community, early on, so the thought of needing to bring a gun to school never enters his or her mind.

Why are we so bad at prevention? Adults and kids miss or fail to act on hundreds of clues that were in plain sight. Watch some of the forensic look-back tapes on Columbine or similar tragedies [Columbine is the most extensively studied in North America]. We make a million excuses for everyday bullying and harassment: *"It's just kids," "They'll grow out of it," "What did you do to deserve it?," "Your child is just too sensitive," "We've done everything we can to solve this problem," "Not my child," "There's no bullying problem in this school/team/group of friends," "Why bother? The real world is full of exclusion."* Adults don't get involved until there's serious emotional or physical injury or a tragedy. Sometimes, a lawsuit motivates action; again, too late. Then we have a memorial luncheon or a candlelight vigil at the George Washington Bridge. And set up a Facebook memorial page. Useless.

The clues are there. We just have to see them and act. We need to retune our radar, to put on what I call our "detective hat and glasses." Spend two to four weeks acting like a detective in your own home, school, and community, looking again, with fresh eyes and ears, at the way kids and adults interact with and treat one another. You'll be shocked to realize how much we've all been tuning out.

Underneath these sobering facts, we have an exciting and energizing opportunity. We can change and begin to correct some of the neglectful practices that have permitted so much damage and destruction of young lives. We have an opportunity to make our kids' lives better, right now, and to prepare them for the next chapter of their lives, lives with much less interpersonal aggression, anger, and bullying.

I ran a workshop where a dad said, *"Why should I teach my daughter to be fair or kind? Wait till she gets to the workplace."* Several parents literally leaped to their feet and said, *"If we start to change things now, by the time our kids get to the work world, it will be a **different place!"*** I believe that whole-heartedly. We can't sit around doing the same old thing and expect a different result. That's the definition of insanity. Our challenge is to engage adults and kids in our communities **before** the next big problem or tragedy occurs.

Bullying In Schools: Problem And Great Opportunity

Before we go further, I'd like to talk about the problem of kids' bullying in schools. This is where we see most of kids' bullying, and even when the bullying is cyberbullying and technically occurs on computers or cell phones that are not on school property, the damage and dread created off-campus certainly are also felt at school. We have been wrong to compartmentalize these as separate issues. Fortunately, we are learning and changing our approach. More on cyberbullying in Chapter 5.

There is, however, far too much blame placed on schools for kids' bullying. It would be easy to conclude that the school environment is problematic, but we would be wrong or vastly oversimplifying. Just because kids' bullying occurs at school doesn't mean that the school caused it, or that the school should be solely responsible for tackling the problem. Simply put, **bullying is a problem of social groups, for both kids and adults.** Any place people come together in groups, there is a natural competitive tendency which, left unguided and unchecked, can easily escalate into full-scale bullying. **We see most kids' bullying at school because that's where kids spend most of their time in social groups.** Important, but that knowledge doesn't solve the problem – yet.

Because of this, however, school communities have a special, almost unique ability to begin to solve the problem of bullying in our communities. Several natural features give schools the wonderful opportunity to lead the way. Schools can be the nucleus of change.

Let me elaborate on my definition of **school community**. It's more than just teachers and kids. A school community starts with all the kids that go to one school. Surrounding them is the circle of *all* the caring and altruistic adults who function as kids' guides and mentors. It's a pretty long list:

- **Parents** – a crucial component of the school community

- **Teachers**

- **Principals And Vice-Principals**

- **School Staff** – Guidance Counselors, Coaches, Classroom Assistants, Recess and Playground Supervisors [teachers, volunteers, or paid assistants], Lunchroom Supervisors [all categories], Custodians [custodians see lots of bullying], Bus Assistants, and After-School Program Supervisors.

- **Summer Program Coordinators** – Camp Counselors and Supervisors running programs for this same group of kids. These programs can be run at the same school, elsewhere in the local community, or even at remote locations. Wherever this population of kids hangs out in the summer, the adults guiding them are a de facto part of the caring adult community around them.

Every single adult in the school community has an ethical [and sometimes legal] responsibility to safeguard the kids, and that includes stopping and preventing bullying, wherever it occurs.

Why are schools uniquely qualified to be in the forefront? Here are the ingredients that make school communities so ideal for combating bullying:

- **Schools Are A Focal Point For Caring Adults United In The Desire To Help Kids Grow Up**. We are tremendously lucky to have all the resources listed above, and even more important, all these warm-hearted individuals, as the Dalai Lama would call them, who care about and who care for our kids, surrounding them in the "it takes a modern village" concept of raising and educating children. No, these people are not saints. Yes, we all have bad days, but these are people who were specifically motivated to seek out careers in the care, shaping, and education of young people. And our kids are *enormous beneficiaries* of the love and attention that is lavished on them in pursuit of preparing them for adulthood. It helps to keep that in mind, even when mistakes occur.

- **Kids Are Long-Term Members Of The School Community**. Kids typically belong to the same school for several years – three to eight years, even occasionally 12 years. Teachers are long-term members too. This creates consistency in the composition and values of the environment. Kids are under the consistent guidance and watchful eyes of caring adults and peers as they grow and their brains mature. In this consistent, nurturing environment, they can make loving, supportive connections and learn to adopt and conform to positive societal values. They learn compassion, empathy, sharing, problem solving, and compromise – along with geometry, biochemistry, and social studies.

- **Schools Are Big Enough To Have Social Complexity**. Kids have the chance to make many friends and to experience many [small] social problems and dilemmas. Kids learn that they don't love everybody, nor do they have to, yet they can craft perfectly pleasant working relationships with a wide variety of adults and peers. This builds the skills of social competence and confidence.

- **This Positive, Supportive Environment Offers The Opportunity For Real Change, For Both Adults And Kids**. When there *is* a problem, those watchful, caring eyes and their long-term membership in the community will provide the support kids and adults need to change their behavior and guarantee that there is good follow-through. Adults and kids have the opportunity to learn new and better social skills, cooperation, and how to contribute to their community, with lots of time to practice and correct mistakes. Kind-hearted adults need to be vigilant and keep encouraging and insisting on hard work and improvement. Adults and kids can make huge changes supported by a caring community with high standards.

Put it all together and there is no better place than school for kids to grow and mature, under the consistent eyes of watchful, caring adults, in a real-life laboratory for learning the real-world skills of emotional intelligence. The progress kids make at school should be reinforced and furthered by reasonably consistent standards at home and in the community.

And while the upside is huge, the downside is, too. The damage caused by kids' bullying can last a lifetime, for children *and* for all the adults around them. We will focus in detail in Chapter 4 on the short- and long-term damage resulting from playing *any* of the roles in the bullying drama –

bully, target, or bystanders. But first let me highlight a few additional, big picture problems.

Bullying comes, in large part, from an underlying lack of respect, for oneself and for others. It shows up in all the components of the bullying system. Kids who are overt, active bullies, as well as bullying *followers*, the kids who come under bullies' influence as toxic supporters, are often trying to make or cement friendships, albeit in an inappropriate, toxic manner. For whatever reason – damaged attachments to their primary adults or poor decisions about the social skills needed to thrive in their environment – these kids are looking for the approval of others. They are not sufficiently secure in their own sense of self-respect to resist the allure of building friendships and alliances at the expense of another child, and certainly not strong enough to stand up and object when they witness bullying or exclusionary behavior.

These kids, pathologically needing others' approval, require a remedial course in self-respect in order to move forward in life. **We want kids to grow up to be adults who have internalized a healthy set of parameters for self-knowledge, self-discipline, and self-respect**. That's our ultimate goal, as adult guides to kids.

We're on shaky ground if we always need someone else's approval, or don't have a well-grounded sense of our value as a human being. We can become limited by our fear of stepping out of our very small comfort zones, *especially* as we come face-to-face with our own mistakes and imperfections.

We can do a better job grounding kids in self-respect. We cannot *eliminate* the destabilizing influence on self-respect of the preteen years, but adults can help kids enter those years from a more secure and grounded position. We can also provide more support for self-respect along the way, in a preventive mode, rather than by punishing bad behaviors that are really the *symptoms* and *results* of shaky self-respect. Like Sleeping Beauty's fairy godmothers, we cannot remove the "curse" of the harsh parts of the preteen and teen years entirely, nor would we want to, for from that struggle emerges a wonderfully complex adult human being. But we can soften the blow. Prevention puts us on a better road. We'll pick up the discussion of self-respect and self-esteem in Chapter 7.

In case you're wondering, I'm *not* advocating that we become rule-bound and try to legislate all bullying away [impossible]; nor do I think we should require all kids to remain an arm's length away in all directions from their nearest neighbors at school. Quite the contrary.

We *need* to cultivate the ability to tease and laugh with one another and the ability to laugh at ourselves. In fact, our brains develop better when we are exposed to close physical contact with others, including in organized competitive and aggressive games.[2] It's *good* for our brains to spar with others, physically, verbally, and mentally – on organized or informal sports teams,

---

[2] M Gurian and P Henley, *Boys And Girls Learn Differently!* (San Francisco: Jossey-Bass, 2001)

on debating teams, in "pro & con" presentations, and with competitive word and math games.

These controlled, competitive activities [notice the word *controlled*] help both the emotive and rational brain functions develop and help us learn how to regulate and manage the strong emotions that come as a chemical cascade when we're engaged in intense physical activity. It's all about balance, and teaching balance and boundaries takes time and lots of practice, along with some mistakes.

But don't we need a program? Nope. Real life provides all the examples we'll ever need, if we immediately spend the five extra minutes [often fewer] it takes to work through the problem while it's fresh in people's minds and still small. I can't tell you how many elementary school teachers have told me variations on this story: *"I had just finished teaching today's unit on bullying prevention and sent the kids out to recess, and by the time I got out there I had to pull them off a learning-disabled classmate they were taunting."*

Why does that happen? It's not that we have pathologically bad kids; it's an issue of brain maturity. It's the ability to pull your abstract and concrete brains together, which doesn't happen till kids get older. In the meantime, though, we are modeling important lessons in kindness, respect, empathy, helping one another, accepting differences, and problem solving, so when the kids' brains are finally mature enough to really understand empathy, perspective, point of view, and reciprocity, they already have good behavior patterns built in. The immediacy of the problem on the playground [or elsewhere] brings life to our lesson plans. Use it.

There's no such job as Director of Bullying Prevention either. It's everyone's job, every day. In fact, having one person "responsible" for preventing bullying is almost a sure indicator the program will fail, because everyone else in the community will think it's not their job.

You're the experts on your kids. You know better than anyone else what's going on in your homes, schools, and communities. You know what your strengths are, and what things are going well. You also know where to start to fix the problems. [Hint: start with some small ones!]

That said, it is really helpful to have the adults [parents, teachers, coaches, etc] mostly on the same page, to view problems with similar eyes, and to be consistent guides for the kids. An easy way to do that is for everyone in the community to read a book like this or Barbara Coloroso's book on bullying, *The Bully, The Bullied, And The Bystander* [I'll refer to it in Chapter 4], or download info from one of the many bullying prevention websites. Then get together and discuss it.

The rest of this book is about recognizing where we can improve, as adults and kids, having the courage and commitment to step up to our responsibilities, and leading the way.

3

Kids' Bullying
Is An Adult Problem

If you only remember one idea from this book, it should be this: **kids' bullying is an *adult* problem**. Without realizing, adults are teaching kids how to bully with our own adult bullying behavior. Further, we allow and apparently condone bullying when we don't prevent or stop it. Without intending to, we are creating environments that protect and encourage bullies and bullying. *It's the exact opposite of what we mean to do!*

Adults model rude talk and bullying behavior in front of kids daily. Adults bully other adults, and adults bully kids, often without conscious intent. As a result, the "acceptable" level of societal rudeness and disrespect keeps increasing.[1] When I was a kid [my daughter's sure that was when dinosaurs roamed the earth], it was easy to tell the difference between "normal" [acceptable] and "rude" speech. Today, there's a razor-thin line separating the two. F-bombs, sarcasm, and mean-spirited putdowns are commonplace. It's very hard to tell where "acceptable" ends, which makes it much too easy to shift into "rude," even unintentionally.

---

[1]O Libaw, "We're Ruder Than Ever, Poll Finds," ABCNews.go.com, Apr 3, 2010

Because the level of "normal" verbal aggression is now so high, we've gotten used to it. We now set our radar screens even higher [or lower], to permit more, and ruder, exchanges without reaction. It's easy to see how this has caused the quality of our daily interactions to spiral incrementally downward, without noticing, until one day we suddenly wake up and say, *"Whoa! That's too much! How did things get so bad?"* **Rude does not need to be the new normal**. We need to reclaim and reestablish civility and respect, in which there's a big, discernible difference between rudeness and normal conversation.

Listen to the everyday rudeness our teens and preteens encounter in school hallways:

- *"Shut up"*

- *"Byotch," "Bitch"*

- *"Slut," "Ho"*

- *"You're so gay," "That's so gay"* [a shirt, an activity, a mis-spoken phrase, listening to the "wrong" music; almost any misstep will do]

- *"Brainer!"* [if you think this still means someone who's smart, look it up]

When I was a kid [I promise that's the last time I say that], *"Shut up"* was the rudest thing you could say to someone. You certainly would never have said it to any adult. In today's language, we use *"Shut up"* so often, it's become a synonym for *"You're kidding!"* As in *"I got an 80 on my algebra test."* "No *way! Shut up!"* The problem is, *"Shut up"* is still rude. We have just allowed ourselves to become desensitized to the rudeness. And each level of desensitization seeds the next level down.

In this context, it's easy to see how we're permitting and even encouraging our kids to bully and exclude one another. What we're also encouraging is *intolerance to diversity.* The *"That's so gay"* putdown fosters intolerance in two ways simultaneously: (1) It's a dismissive criticism of the person on the receiving end of the putdown, often for something trivial. It puts a constricting straitjacket on kids, who dare not step out of line in their thoughts or actions, lest they be leveled with a withering eye roll and a gay label for wearing the wrong shirt [I'll talk about Pink Shirt Day in Chapter 10]; and (2) It's also a putdown of gays. As Ellen DeGeneres said in the aftermath of the Tyler Clementi suicide, *"If the inflection went **up** at the end of the sentence ['That's so gay!'], maybe we could see that as a compliment."* Bullying is all about differences, real or fabricated, negative ways to set kids apart from the group. More on this in Chapter 4.

Kids' bullying is an adult problem, which we've taught to our kids and allowed to grow. It's about:

- How adults speak to and act toward kids
- How adults speak to and act toward other adults
- How we let kids speak to and act toward one another
- Everyday behavior that we accept or ignore

With that in mind, let's focus on some adult behaviors that need an upgrade.

Adults As Bullies: Teaching It To Our Kids

There are several ways that adults show up as bullies or as the teachers of bullying in kids' lives. Sometimes we bully kids directly, often while trying to teach them some important life lesson or skill. More often, though, we just set bad examples for our kids. Adults tolerate bullying far too often and for far too long, in our workplaces and from our leaders. When we play the roles of [unwilling but accepting] targets or bystanders in our own adult lives, we silently teach kids the lesson that they can expect to be bullied at the hands of others when they grow up, and that they are expected to bear silent acceptance of the bullying of other adults and kids right in front of them.

Sometimes, adults bully other adults in front of kids – road rage, parents or ex-spouses fighting unfairly with each other, parents bullying teachers at school, and teachers and principals yelling at each other [yes, schools have typical workplace drama too]. This real life theater is often played out with kids in the front row seats, learning lessons we don't realize we're teaching. Kids observe and think: *"Hmm, this is what it's like to be an adult. When I get bigger, I can rage at anyone. I can do that. I'll start practicing now, so I look adult and mature"* [said in teen or child internal language, of course].

Taking a clear look at and becoming aware of our inadvertent roles as professors of bullying goes a long way towards identifying the problem. The next steps are committing to change, keeping our ears tuned for mistakes, and being willing to apologize and try again, with our mistakes serving as our guides to growth. Let's look further.

Adults Bully Kids

Like the US, Canada has its own bullying problems. In 2004, Hockey Canada, the governing body for amateur hockey, was so concerned about the level of *adult* bullying in *kids'* hockey that it introduced a public service campaign, *"Relax, It's Just A Game."* Over several years, it aired many attention-getting TV and radio public service announcements, in which adults and kids reversed roles, with the kids playing the bullying "coaches" to the parents. Their "Golf" video featured an adult golfing foursome on a putting green.[2] As one adult bent over his putter, lining up his shot, his kid coached, while the dad's adult friends looked on:

Son: *Come on, Dad, focus. Widen your stance. Don't slouch! And don't screw up. This is the big leagues. What are you doing? Keep your eye on the ball!*

Son [as the dad misses his putt]: *That was pathetic!*

Dad [in a small voice]: *Sorry.*

Son: *Yeah, well "sorry" doesn't cut it.*

---

[2]Hockey Canada, Golf Video, "Relax, It's Just A Game" Public Service Ad Campaign, 2004

Hockey Canada's "Police" video showed a kid in the back seat of his dad's car, while the dad's getting a ticket from a police officer:[3]

> Police Officer [to dad]: *License and registration. Did you know you made an illegal left turn back there?*
>
> Dad: *No, I didn't know that.*
>
> Son [from back seat]: *Oh, you've got to be kidding. That call stinks! You stink! Right, Dad? Tell him. You're not just gonna sit there and take this, are you? Stand up to this moron [punches the back of the dad's seat]! Tell him that call was crap. Don't hold back. Let him have it!*
>
> Son [to the police officer]: *What are you looking at, loser?*

Can't you just imagine the look on the dad's face as the son is saying this to the police officer? Can you feel that sinking feeling inside, as you connect empathically with how you would feel were you in the dad's place? Now can you imagine how a kid on the receiving end of those criticisms from an older, bigger, more powerful adult might feel? How about the Golf video? How do you think your kid might feel being "instructed" that way, especially in front of his peers?

When I show these spots in my lectures and workshops, the adults in the audience laugh, cringe, and grin sheepishly as they recognize words they've heard coming out of their own

---

[3]Hockey Canada, Police Video, "Relax, It's Just A Game" Public Service Ad Campaign, 2004

mouths or the mouths of other adults, directed at kids – their own kids or kids they teach or coach. When you hear the same words coming out of a kid's mouth, aimed at an adult, it grabs your attention and makes you think.

Here's the irony. **We're actually trying to teach our kids something good – maybe even great.** Persistence, better skills, tenacity, strength, focus, sticking with goals – these are all wonderful life skills for kids to learn, in and out of sports, **but the package these lessons come wrapped in is just as important as the lessons themselves.** At the very least, adults diminish the efficacy of the lesson by cloaking it in a demeaning delivery. Over time, when kids know that this is the humiliating format in which these lessons are taught, they shut down, further weakening our connection and our influence with young people – tragically, at a time when they need our guidance the most.

Hockey parents have been known to harass and physically interfere with other child hockey players. Mario Lemieux, a hockey icon, experienced adult bullying in kids' hockey firsthand. Even as a kid, playing Pee Wee league hockey [ages 11-12], Mario's ability was extraordinary. He earned a lot of adult attention, some of it very negative and totally inappropriate. His Pee Wee coaches described how adults booed, spat, swore, and threw coffee at young Mario.[4] They often had to escort him safely in and out of the arena. Fortunately, the coaches were both police officers in their day jobs.

---

[4]M Christopher and G Stout, *On The Ice With … Mario Lemieux* (New York: Little, Brown & Co, 2002)

Wayne Gretzky's dad tells much the same story. I am almost without words to explain this infantile, irrational, and dangerous behavior on the part of supposed adults, let alone the horrible example they taught their own kids. Fortunately, these hockey greats were strong enough, even as kids, and had enough positive support around them, to overcome those obstacles. There is, however, no excuse for this kind of behavior – in adults or children. **Compete, yes. But the people on the other team are human beings, not just obstacles in your way.** One of the things I love about hockey is that the same teams can meet two games in a row with a different winner each time, even if one of the teams is appreciably bigger and stronger and has a better record. It's a great life lesson: You might denigrate and humiliate the people you best this week, but next week they can easily best you, and you'd better hope they're not as small-minded.

Adults Bully Adults: The Workplace

Kids get additional bad training from adults in the work world. Long-standing bully managers are promoted and elected to positions of authority and power, and long-standing adult workplace targets and bystanders go along, look the other way, and make rationalizing excuses for the recurrent outbursts and their lack of intervention.

Gordon Brown, recent British Prime Minister, was revealed in 2010 to be a petulant workplace bully, reported to yell at, swear at, and shove his staff, stab his car seat upholstery, smash office equipment, and throw office supplies.[5] Job applicants were routinely apprised that they would be taking a job in an environment of "extreme physical abuse and violence done to objects." Staff members were concerned enough to have called a national bullying helpline several times.

Here are some of the excuses made for his behavior:

- *"It happened in the heat of the moment"* [Just how many moments?]

- *"He's very strong-willed"* [Great, but strong-willed doesn't mean uncontrollable, nor should it excuse vomiting emotional and physical abuse on those close to you]

- *"The country wants a leader who'll push things forward"* [How far are you willing to let him push? Aren't there limits and boundaries?]

These are lame, self-serving excuses, from targets and bystanders, justifying our own inaction and failure to step up to protect others and to change an abusive work environment. Although these people were the targets and victims of Brown's abuse, and Brown's actions completely unacceptable, adult victims do bear some responsibility for complicity, for allowing environments like this to be created, one week at a time, by continuing to work there and looking the other way when others are targeted. We hope it won't be too harsh when it's our inevitable turn on the hot seat.

---

[5]S Lyall, "British Premier Struggles To Repaint Blotched Image," *New York Times*, Feb 22, 2010

A shocking story came to light in the Toronto suburb of Mississauga. The City of Mississauga Transportation Department was revealed to have a boss who was physically binding and beating his employees.[6] Duct tape and paddles. Caught on video. Over a period of five years! Sound unbelievable? Unbelievable to me, too. But it built day by day, and the conspiracy of silence, by the perpetrator, victims, and bystanders, enabled it to get worse.

Certainly there are employees who leave the employ of bully bosses or resign from work environments where there is a bullying "survival of the fittest" approach. Usually these employees leave quietly, often without filing reports or complaints. In addition to the personal and emotional cost to the targeted individual, the dollar cost to workplace productivity is huge. There's a big cost of worker inefficiency in environments where you always have to keep one eye and part of your brain scanning the environment for danger. Even bigger is the cost and inefficiency of having to train and retrain a revolving door of employees to replace the ones who quit in fear and discouragement. And finally, there's the cost to heal and repair the emotional damage and post-traumatic stress of targeted workers,[7] who account for a disproportionate use of sick and disability time and resources.[8]

---

[6] J McLean and D Rider, "Police Probe Duct-Tape Hazing At Mississauga Workplace," *Toronto Star*, Jun 03, 2010

[7] T Query and G Hanley, "Recognizing And Managing Risks Associated With Workplace Bullying," Chartered Property Casualty Underwriters eJournal, 63(7), Jul, 2010

[8] C Mattice, "The Cost Of Workplace Bullying: How Much Is Your Corporate Bully Costing You?," NoWorkplaceBullies.com, Jul, 2009

Back to Gordon Brown. Even worse, after the story broke, instead of taking responsibility, apologizing, admitting to a problem [even admitting to 10% of the accusations would have been plenty], and saying *"Oops, busted. Time to make some changes,"* the spin doctors and image consultants stepped in, trying to spin Mr. Brown as a "softer and more emotional character." Oh, puh-lease! These behaviors, excuses, and ex post facto rationalizations are not OK, and are not a substitute for taking responsibility for mistakes and working to get back on the right track. **Mistakes happen daily, but the way the mistake is handled reveals the character of the individual and their chosen advisors. As Maya Angelou said, *"When someone shows you who they are, believe them."*[9]**

Something to think about: Would you want your child working for Gordon Brown? Would you tell your child *"Suck it up, he's famous and powerful and it goes with the territory"*? Would you tell her to file a human rights complaint? Does working for Brown or someone like him look so good on a résumé that it's worth risking your physical and emotional safety? Is it worth risking your character and your self-respect for not stepping in to help another employee in your office being bullied by him?

Unfortunately, by the time it gets to this stage, there's no real way to fix it. It is, frankly, too late to rehabilitate someone who's been promoted and rewarded for bullying behavior for more than 30 years. But despite the grim prognosis, we shouldn't ignore it. The

[9]Goodreads.com

bully should be encouraged, politely, but firmly, to make some changes to his surface behavior and be required to apologize for and repair the damages, to the extent possible. We need to set boundaries on bullies' behavior, even if it's hard or too late for them to change dramatically or permanently.

Once again, the only road through this problem is – on a different road. We must catch these incidents, these people, early in their careers as bullies, and set them firmly on another path. We cannot expect a 60-year-old, 30-year-career bully to turn on a dime, hit himself on the forehead and say, *"Just kidding. No problem. I'll change right now."* Implicit in this prevention program is the responsibility of bystanders and targets to speak up and insist on behavior change. More on how to do that later.

There are many reasons why we are attracted to, seek out, and tolerate toxic leaders in our adult professional and political arenas.[10] That's beyond the scope of our immediate work with kids in this book, but it's imperative that adults search out and eliminate bullying in all walks of adult life too. Otherwise, we will continue to operate in the same toxic behavior patterns – bully, target, and bystander – and we'll continue to teach those toxic behaviors and our acceptance of bullying behavior to our kids. **If we do not walk our talk, we can never be credible to our kids as mentors and guides. Yes, mistakes will be made, but honest mistakes in the face of observable,**

---

[10] J Lipman-Blumen, *The Allure Of Toxic Leaders: Why We Follow Destructive Bosses And Corrupt Politicians – And How We Can Survive Them* (New York: Oxford University Press, 2005)

continued efforts to change are much less damaging than continuing to look the other way.

Update: No sooner did I write the section on Gordon Brown, then he was back in the news, this time for referring to a constituent as a *"bigoted woman,"* while wired for sound.[11] While I am completely sympathetic to the risk of unfortunate over-exposure with your mic still turned on, the real problem is that once you're used to thinking of and speaking of people in pejorative put-downs, they *will* pop out sometime. Time for brain retraining. Once again the real world gives us all the interesting lessons we'll ever require. No need for extra bullying prevention lesson plans!

Adults Bully Adults: In Schools

In addition to the kids' bullying that goes on in schools, there are often layers of adult bullying. Unfortunately, this teaches kids two things: (1) It must be OK for kids to bully if adults are doing it; and (2) Kids can get some great pointers on how to bully, for immediate use or to file away for when they're older.

Here are some ways that adults act as bullies in schools:

Parents Bully Teachers. Sometimes teachers bring parents bad news about their child – their academic performance or behavior needs an upgrade. It happens to almost all of us, as kids and as parents. What's important is what happens next. In today's

---

[11]S Lyall, "British PM Gordon Brown Caught In Gaffe Over 'Bigoted Woman' Remark," *Toronto Star*, TheStar.com, Apr 29, 2010

contentious and litigious environment, where nobody's responsible for their own behavior and it's always someone else's fault [a slight exaggeration, but I stand by the main points], parents' first responses are often both defensive and evasive. *"My kid didn't do it," "My kid's not the bully," "My kid didn't deserve that grade," "I want my kid on the team"* – often delivered in a menacing and aggressive manner. Recent estimates from the Ontario English Catholic Teachers Association [Canada] say 55% of teachers and education workers feel they've been bullied by parents or guardians, students, colleagues, or someone in a superior position.[12] US statistics are similar.[13] Even worse, this interaction between parent and teacher often takes place directly in front of or within earshot of the child. Think what we're teaching them.

While it's undeniably uncomfortable to receive bad feedback about your child, it's even worse to put the teacher on the defensive and close the door to investigation and collaboration. Partly this comes from the recent development that parents and teachers now view each other as adversaries, even before any specific incident has occurred [more to come on that topic].

Even if your child's teacher said, *"Your kid's horrendous. She's the worst kid I've ever seen in my 25 years of teaching"* and you said, *"My Kendall??? Why she's an absolute angel. She has wing marks on her back and has never misbehaved since the*

[12]E Noble, G Lewis, D Kennedy, and G Pollock, "Addressing Workplace Bullying In Ontario," OECTA.on.ca, Jan, 2006

[13]J Williams, "Hovering Parents Bully Teachers: Educators Report Harassment From 'Helicopter' Caretakers," *Baltimore Sun,* Mar 4, 2010

day she was born," you know that neither statement is true; nor could you prove either statement true. No two people share the same reality, even when viewing the same event. Much more useful than finger-pointing is to open the door to investigation, to ask more questions, to try to find the middle ground, and to ask what you can do to help.

There's no point in going down the road of *"Oh, no she didn't,"* *"Oh, yes she did."* It's what Michele Weiner-Davis calls a "cheeseless tunnel."[14] There's nothing positive, no reward at the end of that tunnel, so why go there? Even mice learn, after a few attempts, to recognize cheeseless tunnels and stay out of them. Instead of being triggered into an emotionally defensive and offensive response, it's much more resourceful to stop for a minute and think to yourself, before responding, *"I'm being emotionally triggered by hearing this unexpected bad report. It's probably not as bad as I'm hearing it, so let me calm myself down and take it as a message that I need to hear more and investigate further. Let's see if we can find some middle ground here."* This is a very difficult skill to master, especially when we're under stress, but we all improve with practice. I struggle with this one frequently. When we handle our own stress better, we have much better responses and, as a result, more options open to us. We'll look at stress handling later too. [Note: Recognizing and avoiding cheeseless tunnels is a valuable part of stress control in all areas of life. Back away from the tunnel!]

---

[14]M Weiner-Davis and B O'Hanlon, *In Search Of Solutions: A New Direction In Psychotherapy* (New York, WW Norton & Co, 2003)

I also encourage teachers to think carefully about how to present difficult information to parents in a way that invites cooperation and support. It's in everyone's best interest – parent, teacher, and child – to be on a supportive team, especially in times of crisis or difficulty. We understand that message intellectually, but we don't always act that way.

Teachers Bully One Another. School, for all its lovely qualities, is just like every other workplace, and therefore has its share of workplace bullying. Principals yell at, blame, or don't support teachers; teachers yell at one another; people get left out of important emails, announcements, meetings, or parties; people sit quietly at staff meetings while someone behaves like a belligerent bully; teachers go on sick leave for stress-induced mental health issues. Same old thing. Search it out and stop it.

Stopping bully bosses and peer workplace bullies can be politically difficult and dangerous to your job, not to mention your mental health. It can be dangerous to be the lone complainant, the single whistleblower, especially when there's a positional power differential between you and the bully [eg, the bully is your boss]. It's even difficult when you and the bully are at the same level [eg, you're both teachers]. It's much less dangerous to tackle these problems in a group or coalition. We'll talk about this more from the kids' perspective when we discuss the role of bystanders. The principles are the same in both the adult and child situations, though the specific implementation will differ.

Adults Bully Kids: In Schools

Teachers Bully Kids: Occasional Mistakes. Everyone occasionally makes a bad decision in the heat of the moment or makes a joke or blurts something out that misses the mark or has unintended consequences. Or we say the right thing but our body language tells a different story. Badly chosen jokes, putdowns, labels, sarcasm, eye-rolling [adults do it too], and mean-looking faces all take only a moment to do, but can have a disproportionately long-term effect. Parents make these mistakes too.

For these smaller problems, some awareness of our personal delivery style and the willingness to apologize go a long way. If we don't clean up our mistakes, they can become stepping stones to permanent bullying, often not by us, but by others who step into the opening created by our thoughtless [truly, without thought] words or actions.

A parent told me the following story: Her daughter had just started grade 7. One of her teachers, a nice guy with a good sense of humor, called on her in class towards the end of the first week, but couldn't remember her name [I can sympathize with that!]. In a moment of awkwardness, he said, *"I'll just call you Shorty."* He was just trying to cover his awkwardness with a joke. No problem.

What he didn't realize at the time was that he had just opened the door for all of her friends and frenemies to call her Shorty – with or without humor. For the next two days, she was Shorty, not just to kids in the class, but out on the schoolyard and rippling out to kids who hadn't even been in that class.

To this teacher's good credit, he came back a few days later and made a public apology in class. The message: *"Oops, I goofed. In a moment of awkwardness, I tried to make a joke, and it didn't come out so well. I didn't think about the problems it could create. I'm sorry."* That was huge. Not only did he apologize to and set things right with the girl, but he did it in front of the entire class. What a wonderful example to kids that adults make mistakes too [by grade 8 they already know that, but you get the point], and [here's the important part] **when they do, they take responsibility and apologize**. The ripple effect on that one was enormous too. A small action with a huge impact. That's leadership.

Teachers are human and make mistakes. The challenge is to catch the mistake quickly and correct it. If we fail to see our own mistake, perhaps someone else might spot it and bring it to our attention, kindly. It's much easier to take responsibility, apologize if needed and, importantly, change the behavior, before it becomes ingrained or there's too much water under the bridge.

Teachers Bully Kids: Long-Term Bullies. There are different kinds of teachers and coaches – some are quiet, gentle, and positively encouraging, like your favorite 1st grade teacher; some are louder and try to motivate you by pointing out your weak areas, often at high volume and with related hand gestures and props. Different kids respond to coaching differently; some prefer one style over another. No matter which style you or your kid prefers, there are some common guidelines:

- All team members should be treated as valuable, even those with less-developed skills.

- Everyone on the team and all supporting personnel should be treated with dignity and respect at all times, regardless of how important their job is to the team. Criticism and feedback should be delivered within this framework.

- Be careful not to cross the line from enthusiastic criticism to bullying.

The key is matching up the right kid with the right coach or teacher. That said, you don't always have a choice of coaches – if a kid wants to be on a specific team, it usually already comes with a coach, who already has a coaching style. The responsibility really falls to the coach[es], to be able to read a player well enough to know which style works best for that player and to be flexible and skilled enough to coach each player a bit differently, according to *their* needs, even if it isn't the coach's most natural or comfortable coaching style. Kids will notice, and appreciate, the coach who makes the effort to deliver the message in the way that works best for each kid.

Kids have to be resilient too. In life, we are not always matched up with our best coach, or teacher, or parent, or boss, or work colleagues. We have to be flexible and resilient enough to roll with it, and learn what we need to know or do, to be able to be our best, even and especially in less-than-ideal circumstances. See more about resilience in Chapter 10.

Bobby Knight, "the winningest college basketball coach of all time," seemed frequently to cross the line to bullying.[15] His fists sometimes made contact with his players, and his "props" sometimes flew [eg, a chair tossed in anger during a game]. He was known for verbally berating his players at loud volume, and was caught on tape choking a player on his Indiana University team.[16] Penalties? Few. A one-game suspension for the chair incident. Slamming his fist on the scorer's table cost Knight a reprimand [it cost IU $10,000]. The tally of aggressive incidents is too long to list here, but go look it up, so you can see the price we're willing to pay and how much we're willing to look the other way to win basketball games. For all his detractors, he had a lot of unquestioning supporters too. When Knight was fired from IU in 2000, after an altercation with a student, thousands demonstrated in protest.

Part of the problem? Knight's complete unwillingness to change: *"I have no apologies to make whatsoever for anything that I have done in an attempt to motivate kids."*[17] Another problem: Our willingness to tolerate that approach. It doesn't have to be all or nothing, black or white, 0 or 1, take me or leave me. There are shades of grey available. We have to insist on appropriate behavior limits and keep working towards them.

---

[15]S Delsohn and M Heisler, *Bob Knight: The Unauthorized Biography* (New York: Simon & Schuster, 2006)

[16]R Abbott, The Knight Tape, CNNSI.com, Sep 09, 2000

[17]R Abbott, The Knight Tape, CNNSI.com, Sep 09, 2000

Bobby Knight had many fine characteristics that inspired many kids to great achievements, but success under his coaching regime came with too many costs. Had he been stopped years earlier, urged and encouraged to soften a few [not all] of his sharp edges, we might have had another ending to the story: an amazing coach, who knew when to be tough and when to be kind, who inspired his kids to greatness, brought out the best in them, and taught them self-control, discipline, emotional maturity – and basketball.

Bobby Knight is, unfortunately, not an isolated example of bully coaches. Manchester United football manager Alex Ferguson is known for: (1) getting winning results from his team, (2) being one of the longest-serving managers [the longest of those currently managing], and (3) his long-standing reputation as a bully – of his own players, of other teams' coaches, and of referees. He was, nonetheless, knighted in 1999 for his service to the game.[18]

These pervasive examples of adult bullying, in addition to the obvious problems they cause, are contributing to a growing wave of unprincipled and undisciplined kids' behavior. **We are, by our adult misbehavior and our failure to take responsibility and apologize, teaching our kids to behave rudely and not to accept responsibility.** As Jane Nelsen said, *"Misteaks r wunderfull opportuniteez 2 lern."*[19] So set an example. Remember, kids are listening!

---

[18]L Taylor, "Jeff Winter Says Sir Alex Ferguson Is A 'Bully' After Attack On Alan Wiley," Guardian.co.uk, Oct 05, 2009

[19]J Nelsen, *Positive Discipline* (New York: Random House, 2006)

Coaches We Admire: Win-Win

Tony Dungy, retired National Football League coach of the Tampa Bay Buccaneers and the Indianapolis Colts, is a great example of the kind of coach that we can admire and should emulate. A Super Bowl-winning coach who set an NFL record for consecutive playoff appearances by a head coach, he viewed his coaching role as that of a teacher. He valued faith and family ahead of coaching, he didn't yell at, demean, or attack his players, and he remained calm under intense pressure. He was named one of *Time Magazine*'s "100 Most Influential People in the World" in the "Heroes and Pioneers" category in 2007.

Lovie Smith, head coach of the Chicago Bears, was an assistant coach to Tony Dungy in Tampa Bay in the late '90s. Smith said of his former boss: *"I got a chance to be around him in some pretty tough situations. Most people think football coaches have to scream and intimidate. Tony has taken the opposite approach. He has a teacher's mentality – if there's a problem, show your guys how to solve it. Today's players are looking for coaches with a strong faith in what they're doing. Tony taught me this lesson, and I think all leaders – politicians, teachers, and business managers – can learn from his example."* [20]

Tony's best-selling book, **Quiet Strength: The Principles, Practices, and Priorities of a Winning Life**, spent 25 weeks in the top 10 on the *New York Times* best-seller list, an all-time record for a book about sports. Clearly, we are hungry for news

---

[20]L Smith, "Heroes & Pioneers: Tony Dungy," *Time Magazine*, May 03, 2007

of leaders who can inspire us to achievement, both on the sporting field and in life. Perhaps his greatest achievement is that, while aspiring to greatness, he remained in touch with his humanity and his core values and taught that lesson, by his everyday example, to young athletes.

Bullying And Humiliation As Entertainment

Adults have made a huge negative contribution to both kids' and adult bullying with the creation of reality shows. Most of these shows feature a weekly competition, where people or teams are voted off the show, the team, or the island, until there is one person or team left standing. So far, no problem. Here's where things get ugly:

- Scheming and conniving to hurt others is glorified and rewarded.

- Interactions between participants are often cruel and humiliating. The show is made more "interesting" by participants' lack of self-discipline and self-control, so anything that provokes or adds fuel to a fight is highly encouraged.

- Each week gets worse. There seem to be no lower limits. We get sucked in. It's like watching a car accident. It's horrible, and you know it, but you can't look away.

Exhibit A: "American Idol." There are two types of singers who are contestants on "American Idol": (1) Young adults who cannot sing. They are specifically brought on the show to be humiliated.

This is cruel and wrong. Stop this now. (2) Young adults who *can* sing. Are they all rock-star quality? No. But they can sing, and they have worked hard to become good enough to earn a chance on "American Idol." Here's some of the feedback Simon Cowell gave them on their performances [Simon has left the show, but his imprint lives on, as a template for reality shows]:[21]

- *"That was terrible, just terrible."*

- *"If you want to pursue a music career, don't."*

- *"I'm not trying to be rude, but you suck."*

- *"You weren't as good as you thought."*

- *"Someone should shoot your music teacher."*

These kids are talented and, more important, they love music and they've worked hard to get to this skill level. As the mother of a teen, I've been deeply happy and grateful when my child has had a passionate interest in something healthy and productive. It's what parents hope for, to have a child so dedicated to a goal that she wants to take lessons, practice, improve, study with her peers, study with experts, and continually push herself to grow. **How dare we, in the name of cheap "junk food for our brain" entertainment, demean and discourage kids who are so focused and such hard workers?**

Exhibit B: "The Apprentice." Donald Trump as my kid's boss? I certainly hope not. Here's how he treats his workers:[22]

---

[21]AngrySimon.com
[22]ThinkExist.com

- ***"YOU'RE FIRED!"*** [bellowed at the employee, in front of 15 peers]

- *"Everyone hates you. Everyone."*

- *"I don't know why you think you're such a great salesman. Your performance was terrible."*

I hope my daughter works for a boss who encourages her, teaches her, and gives her a chance to try new ideas and skills. And when something doesn't work out, I hope her boss says, *"Hmm, that didn't work well. Let's see what we need to learn from this so we don't end up here again."*

As adults, we have enough life and work experience to laugh at a Donald Trump and to know that we really would not enjoy working for him or anybody who treats us as a disposable target for verbal abuse. Here's the problem: **Our kids do not have the depth of life or work experience to discount this belligerent bullying as "just TV."** They look at a Donald Trump or a Simon Cowell and they learn the following not-so-hidden lessons, which they then incorporate into their real lives:

- This is how adults behave.

- Learning and effort are not valued.

- I can only win if someone else loses.

- The way to succeed is to undermine and denigrate the people around me.

- It's OK to have poor problem solving and poor people skills.

- It's normal and expected to receive feedback on my performance in a humiliating, insulting, aggressive manner. This will continue into adulthood.

- When I become the boss, I will be expected to deliver feedback on my employees' and associates' performances in the humiliating, insulting, aggressive manner in which I have been schooled. If I am really good at my job, I will be even more humiliating, insulting, etc, than the generation that preceded me.

We are setting our kids up to be bullies and bullied targets in every arena of their life, in every personal and professional relationship, for the rest of their lives.

If that's not bad enough, we are also turning respect for the education system on its head. I don't just mean schools. All learning is based on the premise that new, young, uneducated students train with and learn from seasoned, experienced, [usually] older teachers, guides, coaches, and mentors. How much longer will that system last when we are training kids in the art of ripping people apart for being inexperienced or only moderately talented? What if we had approached our kids in that way, as parents or teachers? What if our parents and teachers had approached our education in this way?

- *"Wow, you're so small. You can't even stand up or walk. Forget it."*

- *"Gee, are you stupid! You don't even know the alphabet. You'll never learn to read. I'm not even going to try to teach you."*

- *"You're a hopeless hockey player. Who cares if you're three?"*

- *"Drive a car? Are you kidding?"*

- *"Business school? Don't bother."*

Without realizing, we're creating a culture that demeans learning and that trains, rewards, and protects bullies. It's the exact opposite of what we want to do!

For those of you saying, *"But wait, it's just entertainment,"* yes, it is entertainment, BUT:

- That TV "entertainment" style of interacting with people [rude, in-your-face, devastating putdowns] has become the new norm in our schools, homes, and offices.

- Adults have to do a much better job drawing a sharp line of distinction between TV and reality – what's on TV and what comes out of our mouths in real life. As Ron Morrish, a Toronto-area parent educator, said, *"I use the 'Vegas Approach' with my kids – what happens on TV stays on TV. I tell my kids, 'They may talk that way on TV, but that's not how we speak to each other in our house, at school, or in our community'."*[23]

- We have to talk with our kids about these shows, helping them develop critical thinking skills.

---

[23]R Morrish, *Secrets Of Discipline* (Fonthill, ON, Canada: Woodstream Publishing, 1999)

- We can do much better for entertainment. We can choose to foster entertainment that brings out the best in us, not the worst. Then we won't need to do so much explaining.

- We can exercise our power by setting limits and watching fewer shows that demean people, effort, and learning. We can write complaint letters to TV networks and production companies when entertainment crosses the line.

Red Line Films proposed a reality show called "Office Fight."[24] They would find two office colleagues who've been unable to solve a problem between them, and set up a boxing ring in the office so the coworkers with the conflict could "box out" the solution to the problem, winner take all. Good idea? Teaching our kids good workplace skills? Think not. Talk about it in class and over dinner with your kids. I talked about it in my parent, coach, and teacher training workshops at the time. Many of us [and our kids] emailed Red Line and told them what we thought. The show never went forward; I hope the community action had something to do with it. This was a great real life opportunity to teach critical thinking and community action to our kids.

I am NOT saying we should throw out our TVs or that TV, the Internet, or popular culture should never offer light-hearted, humorous entertainment. I am, however, strongly suggesting that adults take a more purposeful leadership role in shaping the

---

[24]C McCarthy, "New Reality Show Lets You Beat Up Your Co-Workers," news.CNET.com, Aug 28, 2007

content and output and draw the line where the "humor" is mean-spirited or at someone else's expense.

Here's an example where community support creates the opportunity for real change, but we're still missing the boat. In the immediate aftermath of Tyler Clementi's suicide, several gay and straight entertainers made TV and radio public service announcements offering "support" and "encouragement" to bullied gay teens. *"Just hang on,"* they all said. *"It'll get better."* *"Call 1-800-Don't-Kill-Yourself."* The **only** part of this that's even partially helpful is the offering of a last-ditch desperation handhold in the form of a 1-800 number. Pathetic.

Why am I so dismissive of these "efforts to help"? Despite their well-meaning intent, what they offer doesn't help at all – in fact, just the opposite. *"Just hang on"* says, again, that adults aren't going to do anything about it – kids just have to tough it out. Wrong. *"It'll get better."* Wrong again. And when you're really, really hanging by your fingernails at the edge – don't call me, call that 1-800 number. Wrong, wrong, wrong – to leave kids to face that desperation. Alone. You've just reinforced the message that this WILL happen again. And again.

Try this instead, if you're serious about helping:

"Tyler's death has shocked us into realizing that we tolerated too much abuse when we were your age, and we still tolerate too much abuse of human beings. Nobody helped us. We did just have to hang in there. We're not going to let that happen to you."

"We're going to make some changes. From now on, all actors will no longer take acting roles that demean other human beings. We will not participate in entertainment projects, including reality TV, that ask us to demean ourselves or others and perpetuate a culture that accepts and applauds bullying as entertainment. Bullying is wrong. Against gays. Against everyone." Better.

Unfortunately, that story is not unique. In Ottawa, Canada, Jamie Hubley, a gay 15-year-old Grade 10 student, committed suicide after four years of relentless bullying by peers. On four different antidepressants, in a therapist's care, Jamie's blog frequently expressed his hurt and growing emotional fatigue. His last post: *"I'm tired of life. It's so hard, I'm sorry, I can't take it anymore. I don't want to wait three more years, this hurts too much."*

Jamie's Dad was an Ottawa City Councillor, so the story got a lot of notice. Predictably, the response was similar to Tyler Clementi's suicide a year earlier. *"Need more money for teen mental health", "Need stronger anti-gay bullying laws".* Wrong.

Jamie had no mental health issues until Grade 7, when kids on the school bus held him down to *stuff batteries down his throat.* Four years of bullying ensued, in and out of school, face-to-face and online, known to a wide circle of peers and adults around Jamie.

Once again, this is about much more than gay kids or adults. This is about how we treat *all* human beings, setting boundaries on our own and others' behavior, and stopping it early before it spirals out of control to an unrecoverable consequence.[25]

Adults Can Help: Teach Critical Thinking Skills

Adults can help kids become critical thinkers. It's important that kids learn not to accept everything they see and hear unquestioningly. They must learn to think complexly, to sort out, within any situation, good from bad, right from wrong, admirable from dishonorable.

Start young. Elementary school kids as young as grade 3 are now aware of celebrities. We are an overly celebrity-focused society, but use this great opportunity to teach your young kids that celebrities are people too, with some admirable and some not-so-admirable characteristics. We must help kids learn to discern and think critically, whether or not the topic is bullying.

A non-bullying example: Britney Spears, for all the trouble she's experienced in her adult life, was a tenacious, focused, disciplined kid. Watch her early video footage, performing and competing, and you'll see a kid who worked very hard to learn to refine and focus the natural talent she'd been given.[26] We can admire and emulate *some* characteristics of our celebrities and heroes, without having to think that everything they do is great.

We can channel our critical thinking skills to create change in our communities. Our efforts can make a big difference – whether it's

---

[25] A Burke, "Gay Ottawa Teen Who Killed Himself Was Bullied,"cbc.ca, Oct 18, 2011
[26] J Bryant, "Biography For Britney Spears," IMDB.com, Dec, 2005

working for a political candidate or changing the content of our media. Of course we should pick our battles and spend our time and energy as effectively as possible. But when we choose to get involved and collect other like-minded, energetic people around us, each willing to do a small part, we can do some small things that make a BIG difference. Along the way we can teach our kids valuable critical thinking skills and some lessons in community collaboration that they'll need for the future.

- **Educate Kids About Product Placements**. Those cars, computers, clothes, and sunglasses on TV – virtually all the manufacturers paid a lot of money to get their products placed in highly visible "non-advertising advertising." Teens are paid by makers of teen products to wear, talk, and blog about their products [look up "haul videos"], creating an aura of "cool" to boost sales. Watch TV with your kids to see how many product placements you can spot. The more you look, the more you will see.

- **Speak Up And Ask For Change**. In 2008, Scholastic Canada came out with "edgier" Valentines for school kids.[27] Some of the greetings: *"It worries me that you are so stupid"* and *"We'll be the kind of friends who throw up a little every time we see each other."* Concerned parents and teachers contacted Scholastic, which discontinued the cards. Mistakes get made, bad judgment exercised. The problem is letting it go uncorrected.

- **Speak Up And Ask Questions**. The November 2006 issue of *Shape Magazine* described research at the University of Oklahoma which found that gossiping about

---

[27]C Weeks, "Parents, Teachers Shocked At R-Rated Valentine's Cards For Kids," *Globe And Mail*, Jan 31, 2008

a third party builds stronger friendship bonds between the gossipers. The article was titled "Why You *Should* Gossip."[28] Not surprising – uniting against a "common enemy" brings people closer together. That doesn't make it right.

I emailed *Shape Magazine* and the lead researcher at U of O. Just because you *can* build a stronger friendship at someone else's expense doesn't mean you *should*. Resist the temptation and take the slower road to friendship, over shared interests, goals, and activities. I think the study is interesting precisely *because* it highlights the attractive allure of such "junk food for the brain," and makes us aware that we should be on guard against creating "friendships" in that manner.

I use this *Shape* article in teacher training workshops and in the Girls' Respect Groups programs, encouraging teachers and parents to discuss these kinds of articles and ideas with their children, at home and in class. Make it a classroom or family activity to write an email back to the magazine, explaining why you agree or disagree with the article. Even if you don't send the email, you're encouraging kids to think for themselves, which is the main point of the exercise.

- **Promote Articles, TV Shows, And Other Media That Support Positive Values And Bring Out The Best In Us**. In February 2010, *Shape Magazine* headlined an article "Nice Girls *Do* Win At Work," featuring research done at UC Berkeley showing that the more generous you are at work, the more influence you have.[29] Another great article for discussion, at school or at home, helping our

---

[28]"Why You *Should* Gossip," *Shape Magazine*, Nov, 2006
[29]"Nice Girls *Do* Win At Work," *Shape Magazine*, Feb, 2010

kids to develop critical thinking skills and an orientation to action. We adults can peel back some of our jaded layers along the way too!

"Extreme Home Makeover," on ABC TV, is a rare TV show that spotlights our best values. Each week the show finds a deserving family in desperate need and, with huge, hands-on community participation from local construction trades and a virtual army of local volunteers, demolishes and rebuilds the family's home in a week. The families chosen for the home makeover are often community leaders and heroes in their own right, who have helped many others before needing help themselves. While an undeniable tear-jerker, "Extreme Home Makeover" demonstrates human values that are precious:

- People who need help should get it.
- When you can give help, you should give it.
- We are all responsible for helping one another.
- Giving benefits the givers, at least as much as the receivers. Episode after episode shows the transformative power of the simple act of uniting to help others. Construction crews are moved to tears, describing their week working on the house as the most amazing thing that's ever happened to them and thanking the family for the opportunity to participate.

While there's clearly a lot that adults have done, or not done, that has seeded the growth of bullying, there is also much power for change resting in our individual and combined hands. We need to do a better job using that power for community good, and to teach our kids how to think for themselves, how to think complexly, how to step in and help others, and how to stand up and say *"No"* when needed.

4

Bullying 360°:
Getting On The Same Page

Why is it important that we approach bullying issues with a consistent viewpoint? Consistency lets kids know the boundaries and helps adults know where to step in. When adults disagree about what constitutes bullying and whether and where adults and kids should step in to help out, the confusion results in paralysis. Unfortunately, our inaction sends the unintended message that bullying is permissible. Kids need to know, consistently, what we expect from them, and ultimately what they should expect of themselves, as they internalize appropriate standards for behavior.[1]

It would be simple and convenient if the solution to bullying problems only involved the bully. Send that bully out for bully remediation classes [that someone *else* teaches], and the bully will come back to our home or classroom "all fixed." Sorry, it doesn't work that way. **Bullying only occurs within a system that permits it**. If there's bullying in your kids' environment, it's

---

[1]Part of this chapter builds on work previously published by the author in L Blumen, "Bystanders To Children's Bullying: The Importance Of Leadership By 'Innocent Bystanders'" in R Riggio, I Chaleff, And J Lipman-Blumen (eds), *The Art Of Followership: How Great Followers Create Great Leaders And Organizations*, (San Francisco: Jossey-Bass, 2008)

being supported or enabled, even if you don't yet recognize the structures and behaviors that permit and encourage it. Inconveniently, **the entire system must change – parents, teachers, school staff, bullies, targets, and bystanders.** This is also true for adult workplaces. We must search out and become consciously aware of the behaviors and systems that allow bullying to occur, that provide active or passive support. We must identify our enabling contributions and commit to change, all around the bully, to no longer support or enable bullying.

A frequently voiced excuse for inaction is that we lack a uniform definition of bullying. Don't hold your breath waiting for one. **We can *never* fully enumerate on paper or in law all the details and nuances, the myriad ways in which bullying gets manifested**. By the time the list was made, it would be out of date. Unfortunately, bullying is an evolving "discipline." That, however, is no excuse for allowing it to continue. Every bullying situation *is* somewhat unique in the details, and as we discussed earlier, we must be a bit flexible as we identify it and evaluate our options. Generally speaking, however, we know when an action was mean-spirited or a genuine mistake. Respond accordingly.

That said, a common platform will help us solidify our understanding of the general characteristics of bullying and will enable us to view and assess each situation with knowledge, insight, and increasing accuracy. With that goal, this chapter is devoted to describing and defining various aspects of bullying.

Let's not reinvent the wheel – we can use and benefit from the earlier work of others, standing on their shoulders, rethinking, revising, and refining as our knowledge and understanding have grown with time and experience. Dan Olweus from the University of Bergen in Norway and Barbara Coloroso in Littleton, CO, are two of the many people who have contributed so much to our understanding of bullying.[2] I frequently recommend Coloroso's important book, **The Bully, The Bullied, And The Bystander**.[3] It's a wonderful, easy-to-read discussion of the components and complexities of kids' bullying. In my workshops, I recommend that entire school communities read the book – all the adults in the school community, as we defined "school community" in Chapter 2, and any children who are old enough to understand it. When a whole community reads the same book, they're 80% of the way to being on the same page, to viewing the problem with the same eyes. Get together, book club style, to discuss the book – do it over dinner and it's a community-building event. It's a great forum in which to discuss opinion differences and practice adult critical thinking skills!

Bullying: A Working Definition

Building on Coloroso's definition, bullying is characterized by:[4]

- A persistent one-way power imbalance in which the bully has all the power and the target has none.

---

[2] Olweus Bullying Prevention Program, Olweus.org (Olweus virtually invented the field of bullying prevention; His program is widely considered to be effective and well researched)
[3] B Coloroso, *The Bully, The Bullied, And The Bystander* (Toronto: Harper Collins, 2002)
[4] B Coloroso, *The Bully, The Bullied, And The Bystander* (Toronto: Harper Collins, 2002)

- The deliberate use of power and aggression by the bully towards the target.

- The intent to hurt the target – physically, socially, or emotionally [often a combination].

- The intent to cause fear, both in today's attack and the threat that attacks will recur in the future.

- Repeated attacks, but don't ignore the single occurrence.

- Escalating intensity with recurrence.

- An underlying lack of respect for self and others.

- The bully's underlying sense of contempt, entitlement, and lack of empathy for others.

When we work with younger children, we use a simplified definition of bullying, adapted from Allan Beane's work:[5]

Bullying is when:

- a stronger or more powerful person

- hurts or frightens

- a smaller or weaker person

- on purpose

- one time or more

- with unkind words, unfriendly touching

- or by keeping them from having friends

---

[5]A Beane, *The Bully Free Classroom* (Minneapolis: Free Spirit Publishing, 1999)

Three Types Of Bullying

There are three main types of bullying: verbal, physical, and relational. Cyberbullying is primarily relational, but its complexity gives it its own category. A brief description of each follows.

1. **Verbal Bullying.** This is by far the most common type of bullying. Verbal bullying is everywhere. We've allowed it to become woven into our culture. Low-level, everyday insults, criticisms, rudeness, swearing, and putdowns are so ubiquitous that we tune most of it out. Adults rarely intervene here. The problem with ignoring it is that we're providing a scaffold for further bullying – even harsher verbal aggression or escalating to physical or relational bullying.

   Verbal bullying doesn't have to be complicated – one word will do. *"Loser," "Whatever," "Idiot," "Slut."* Dismissive and cold, it clearly sends the message *"You're not one of us."* Verbal bullying can even be silent – eye rolling or the "L is for loser" sign, held up silently to the foreheads of your frenemies, like ratings by a group of Olympic judges.

2. **Physical Bullying**. This is the best-recognized form of bullying. We have long-standing mental images of physical bullying: a group of boys beating up another boy behind the school; a boy being pushed hard against, or completely into, or being blocked access to a school locker; a boy's backpack ripped from his shoulder and the contents strewn on the floor or held up for display.

Today's physical bullying goes far beyond those iconic images. Food and drink thrown on you in the cafeteria or on the street like Phoebe Prince; pantsing; sexual touching, groping, and pinching in the hallways – this is just the beginning of an endless list of creative acts of physical and emotional terrorism. I'll leave you to decide whether making faces and sounds miming oral sex at someone is an example of verbal or physical bullying.

Physical bullying is where adults tend to intervene. That's good, but it's often really late. These situations – physical bullying and even non-bullying fights – develop over time. Adults monitoring the playground from a fixed viewing point at the school wall often miss the building blocks. Then we're confronted, late in the game, with solving the *"He hit me"* problem. We can do a better job averting these problems and catching them earlier, when we wander around the playground, all through recess, watching and listening for incipient problems.

We tend to think of physical bullying as boys' domain, and it's true that boys do more of it than girls. Girls, unfortunately, have been catching up and there are some sickening examples of girl-led and girl-instigated physical bullying, including the shocking case of Reena Virk, a 14-year-old beaten and left to drown by a mostly girl gang of her peers in Victoria, BC, in 1997.

As they did after Columbine, eddies of destruction spun out from the Virk murder, filling court dockets and therapists' couches for a decade. And not much has changed since either tragedy. Girl gang beatings and one-on-one fights in response to real or imagined slights, often well-publicized in advance to ensure a crowd with cameras, don't shock us anymore. A grade 7 gang of girl bullies beat up a girl classmate at a Whitby, ON [Canada] school, steps from the principal's office, moments after leaving a mediation session with the principal about their bullying behavior.[6]

3. **Relational Bullying**. Relational aggression is the real or threatened social exclusion and isolation from former or current friends, or insurmountable barriers placed to prevent the establishment of new friendships. If boys are the primary physical aggressors, girls specialize in relational bullying.

What hurts so much about girls' relational bullying is the loss of friendships. Girls' friendships, all-important through the middle and high school years, are based on close emotional connections. Teen girls typically view themselves through the mirror of their friendships [more on self-esteem issues later]. Emotional closeness is usually more important to girls than to boys, whose relationships tend to be more activity-based. Denying a girl access to a close, connected relationship with her peers is devastating. Being obviously or covertly excluded from after-school and weekend social events, from everyday or special occasions, is really hurtful.

---

[6]M Mandel, "Bullies Torment Ontario Girl," cnews.canoe.ca, Feb 26, 2010

Relational bullying can take many forms, behind your back or in your face. *"You can't be our friend if you sit with Shawna,"* *"This table is just for 'The Populars'"* [I'm not making this up!], *"Do my math homework or I'll tell Jessie you said she's fat"* [whether or not she ever said that], *"You can't sit with us if you don't wear a skirt on Friday."* Girls have completely lost friendships over these issues. And it can happen in an instant: *"I went home from school on Friday. I came back on Monday and I had no friends."*[7]

Grudge-holding magnifies these girls' relationship problems. Real or imagined slights take on a life of their own, continuing for years, growing to larger circles of peers, and following a girl from middle to high school.

If you think relational bullying is only a middle school problem, read this email sent to me by the mother of a 1st grade girl:

"My daughter Jenna is drawn to a girl in her class, Kendra, who is very strong-willed and spirited. Kendra can sometimes be very mean to Jenna, saying things like 'I won't be your friend if you play with Marla.' [Kendra doesn't like Marla.] *I told Jenna that when Kendra is mean to her and hurts her feelings, she should tell her that she can't be her friend that day because she's not being nice. When she decides to be nice, then they can be friends. This advice worked wonderfully for my older daughter when she was in grade 1,*

---

[7]Oprah.com, Jan, 2005

but Jenna is adamant that she desperately needs to be Kendra's friend. She even gave Kendra one of her sweaters so that they would stay friends.

I just got an email from another mom saying that Jenna and Kendra have been teasing her daughter, even though the daughter asked them more than once to stop. The mother also said that Jenna is okay when she's not with Kendra. That leads me to believe that Jenna goes along because she feels that if she doesn't, Kendra will say they're not friends anymore.

I told Kendra's mom that Kendra keeps threatening to end the friendship if Jenna doesn't do what she wants, and she has spoken with Kendra. Kendra has apologized to Jenna, but obviously it's still going on."

Doesn't that sound just like middle school? Actually, 1st grade can be an especially rough year. Kids are just realizing they're not exactly the same as their friends and that everybody doesn't always love everybody else. Kids start jockeying for friendships, sometimes using hurtful techniques they've learned from their peers or older siblings.

4. **Cyberbullying.** We'll discuss cyberbullying in its own chapter later, but it needs a brief mention now. Cyberbullying is the high-tech product line extension to relational bullying, but its ease of use and the enticement of apparent anonymity make it a common accompaniment to all the other kinds of bullying. What begins in school as "old fashioned" girls' exclusion

continues and escalates relentlessly, online and via cell phones, long after school has ended. Morgan Jones, the Whitby, ON, 7th grader mentioned previously, received text messages and Facebook threats that she would become "Morgan 'Rest In Peace' Jones" if she went to an upcoming dance. Morgan was new to Whitby from Nova Scotia; the torment started a few months later. Sound familiar?

Bullying tends to peak in middle school. Things typically calm down in high school, as kids begin to settle into their sense of self, feel more secure and less vulnerable, and therefore feel less driven to do mean things to other kids to ensure their own social standing.

This is not always the case – Reena Virk and Phoebe Prince were high school students new to their schools. In those cases, bullying structures built in middle school found tolerant, even nurturing, environments at the high school level, where bullies continued to sharpen their skills, this time under the less-watchful eyes of adults.

"Payback" in the form of Columbine-style shootings usually happens in high school. High school kids who've been taunted and victimized since elementary school or middle school have much more free time in high school, with much less adult supervision. The Columbine rampage was meticulously planned, on a website, a year before the shootings. Teens also have more mobility and more money to turn their plans into reality. It's the perfect availability of resources for revenge fantasy design and execution, for kids who've waited *years* to get back at their tormentors. **The best time to stop these high school plans is** *in elementary school, before they happen*.

Key Players In Bullying

There are three components to the bullying system:

1. Bully
2. Target
3. Bystanders

We have all played all three roles – bully, target, and most frequently, bystander. All efforts to reduce bullying must involve all three components, with short- and long-term strategies. Let's look at each in turn.

The Bully

As we realize from our discussion of physical bullying, we need to update our picture of bullies. Bullies come in all shapes and sizes – and clearly in both genders. **The defining characteristic of bullies is that they seek power and use it to hurt others.** Bullies lack empathy and usually have poor relationship skills. In some cases, the bully is actually trying to build a relationship and does it by collaborating with one child to bully another child. Remember the "Why You *Should* Gossip" premise? A shared enemy can build a friendship. Gabor Maté suggests that bullying may result from earlier attachment disorders that lead kids to seek attachment in indirect, emotionally closed, toxic ways.[8] A recent Dutch study by René Veenstra[9] supports this, suggesting that bullies strategically target kids who've been rejected by the peers the bullies want as friends.[10] It's a socially manipulative way of making friends. While not adept at forming *healthy* relationships, bullies can be skilled relationship manipulators, especially girls. Tracy Vaillancourt's work shows this.[11]

Bullies can have low self-esteem or they can have too-high self-esteem, which leads to their sense of entitlement that it's OK to treat people poorly. Sometimes, low self-esteem can be masked by behavior that looks like over-inflated high self-esteem.

Bullies often feel powerless or disenfranchised in some other area of their lives, at home or at school. Becoming a bully in a different environment or with a different cast of characters is often the child's attempt to restore his sense of self-respect and power. Being willing to dig further, for understanding and compassion, can help us select the tools that work best for each situation.

Bullies are often surprisingly popular in middle school – powerful, because of their strong, pathological, and manipulative social skills, although their popularity declines in high school if they

---

[8]G Maté, "The Bully Syndrome: A New Look At A Contemporary Malaise" (presented at the 17th Annual Idaho Prevention Conference, Apr 15-16, 2010)

[9]R Veenstra, et al, "The Complex Relation Between Bullying, Victimization, Acceptance, And Rejection: Giving Special Attention To Status, Affection, And Sex Differences," *Child Development*, 81(2), 480-486, Mar 24, 2010

[10]P Paul, "Maybe Bullies Just Want to Be Loved," *New York Times*, NYTimes.com, May 21, 2010

[11]T Vaillancourt, lecture presented at LAMP Community Health Centre, Toronto, Oct 27, 2008

haven't mended their ways. Many popular kids, however, are so uncertain of their friendships that they willingly bully other kids that they perceive to be of lower social rank, to increase or preserve their own social standing.

Here's the tragedy: **many childhood bullies actually have strong personalities with great leadership potential**. Maybe Gordon Brown was one of these kids. They're just using their personal power in inappropriate ways. **Our job, as the adults and peers around them, is to guide them, firmly but politely, onto the right path** – *without excluding or bullying the bully* along the way.

I've seen amazing examples of change. A 6th grade girl was an egregious bully – *"This table is for my friends," "You can't be our friend if you're her friend."* She played the game of Trust with a boy classmate, where one kid stands behind another kid, to catch him as he falls, trustingly, back into her arms. She let him fall to the ground and then laughed. Ouch!

This girl received some serious "Time To Change" messages from her teacher, her peers, and her parents, AND they all remained friends. Her friends did not bully or excommunicate her. Three years later, this girl was *elected* head of student council! I just love this story – I still get goose bumps every time I tell it. These situations present **powerful opportunities for redemption and change**, not to mention opportunities to find tomorrow's leaders, if we just pay attention and do our job providing a little guidance.

Childhood bullying patterns, left unchallenged, persist into adulthood. Where do we think those little bullies go? They show up in our workplaces, in our homes, and in our communities. We recognize them as adults, but we don't recognize our own complicity in creating adult bullies by failing to intervene, when it's cheap and easy, to get these kids back on the right path.

Adult bullies have their own issues as they reap the consequences of their long-standing bullying behavior patterns. They have more problems holding onto jobs, more problems in their personal relationships, more issues with drugs and alcohol, and they are more likely to have police records.[12]

The Target

Targets can become targets for almost any reason – real or fabricated. Kids look for differences, any characteristic that they can use to "carve you out" from the crowd, to establish an "Us vs. Them" framework, which seems to justify the exclusion. If a child is notably different, he's an easier target. Here are some examples:

- **New To The School, Community, Or Country**. Kids who are new tend to have fewer friends and be less embedded in the school community. Sometimes there's a language barrier, too. We do a pretty bad job of welcoming and integrating new kids into the social structure [Hint: it takes longer than a week. See Chapter 10].

- **Physical Differences**

[12]A Sourander, et al, "Childhood Bullies And Victims And Their Risk Of Criminality In Late Adolescence," *Archives Of Pediatrics And Adolescent Medicine*, 161(6), Jun, 2007

- **Age**: Old or young for your grade.

- **Size**: Big or small, thin or overweight [overweight kids are disproportionately picked on].[13]

- **Disabilities**: Especially physically observable disabilities.

- **Intellectual Differences**: Learning disabled [especially once labeled by the school]; Gifted [ditto]; Gifted + LD [these characteristics often co-exist, making a child doubly vulnerable to bullying].

- **Personality Factors**

  - **Sensitive**: Kids know how to bait and get a rise out of these kids.

  - **Submissive**: Bullies won't find much resistance here.

  - **Aggressive**: These kids are often hyper-reactive. Like sensitive kids, they can be easily baited and upset, which is endlessly "entertaining."

  - **Annoying**: Interesting case; some kids seem to "bring it on themselves." These **provocative targets** get little sympathy or empathy from their peers *or* from teachers and school officials. These kids do not deserve to be bullied. They *do* need protection, help, and practice learning better social skills to soften their rough edges.

  - **Introverted.** These shy kids often have few friends and keep to themselves. Not well-embedded in the social structure, they make easy targets, especially walking by themselves between classes or after school. These kids often need help learning social skills [see below]. Speaking for myself, as a grown-up introvert who loves people, introverts need the social skills to develop "shades of grey," a variety of levels of introversion or extroversion, which they can choose

---

[13]S Gordon, "Bullies Target Obese Kids," Yahoo.com, May 3, 2010

[yes, choose], as appropriate for the situation. Same goes for extroverts.

- **Cultural Differences**. Sorry to say, taunting because of cultural differences is still going on and has come back even more strongly in our xenophobic reaction after the September 11, 2001, terrorist attacks. Sometimes overt, more likely covert. *"Your lunch smells funny," "What's in your hair?"* [said with a sneer, not curiosity].

- **Family Income Differences**. This often shows up as kids being taunted and excluded for not having the "right" jeans, clothes, backpacks, accessories, or the ability to attend [pay for] additional after-school and weekend activities. Membership in a group of friends shouldn't have to be bought with a $200 pair of sneakers. That said, kids need to have *some* of the symbols of commonality with their peer group, without going too far – again, find a balance.

- **Social Skills.** Kids acquire smooth social skills at different ages. Some kids are quite astute at amazingly young ages, others not so smooth even by high school. Many adults have not fully acquired smooth social skills either!

  For kids lacking social finesse, adults [parents and teachers] can step in and help teach these kids some useful skills: how to make friends, how to maintain friendships, how to "break the ice" when entering an established group, how to tell a joke, etc.[14] Adults can contribute many small things to help a kid feel more socially confident and secure.

---

[14]The American Girl "Smart Girl" series has great books devoted to girls' social skills for the 9-14 age group: *A Smart Girl's Guide To Friendship Troubles, Guide To Boys, Guide To Parties, Guide To Style, Guide To Starting Middle School, Guide To Sticky Situations.* AmericanGirl.com.

Kids with some disabilities, like Autism Spectrum Disorder, are uniquely vulnerable because of their lack of social skills. Unable to read social cues from faces, and often very slow to learn these cues, even with adult support, these kids are easily subjected to the same "joke" again and again. Time for adults to step in and insist that kids help others who don't have their same skill package. Then we must monitor and follow up, to make sure classmates are providing positive support *as well as* not making these kids targets. This kind of adult and peer support also applies to the earlier discussion of kids with other LDs.

Although it can take a long time to train facial recognition skills and social cues in kids with ASD or other mirror neuron defects, it's worth the effort. Many kids can really improve their perceptions or develop an internal flowchart to help protect themselves from harm or humiliation: *"If I see this expression* <a sneer>, *then it might mean this* <they're taunting me>, *I should try to do this* <walk away or go to another friend>." Rotating buddy systems will help protect these children too.

- **Harsh Parenting Styles**. Recent research indicates that growing up with inflexible, brick wall-style parents teaches kids to fight back when under attack, rather than to problem solve. These kids often end up as targets or bully-targets [they bully some kids and are bullied by other kids].[15]

- **Sex**. As kids get older, they are more likely to be on the receiving end of sexual taunts, miming, "casual" groping, pinching, and slapping, both in school hallways and out of school.

---

[15]F Joelving, "Spanking Your Kid Could Hatch A Bully," Reuters Health, Reuters.com, Apr 12, 2010

- **Sexual Orientation.** In high school, kids' burgeoning sexuality and their uncertain first steps into the world of dating and romance can be truly damaged by taunts questioning and denigrating their sexual orientation. The aimless *"He's so gay"* of 6th grade becomes a menacing indictment in high school, not only hurtful in its own right, but damaging to the target's ability to connect romantically.

Dylan Theno of Tonganoxie, KS, was subjected to vicious sexual innuendo starting in middle school. Taunts of *"faggot," "homo," and "banana boy"* were just the beginning. Following him to high school, his tormentors told every potential girlfriend that he was gay and had been seen masturbating in the boys' room.[16] After five years, including Dylan's dropping out of school and a lawsuit, the school district was ordered to pay Dylan $250,000. As Dylan said *"That's five years of my life that I had to live – just depressed, angry, scared. I can never get that back."*

His mother described the moment when she knew it was time for her to listen to Dylan and let him leave school, after years of "working with" the school district: *"Here he was, a teenage boy, curled in fetal position and sobbing. It wasn't right. He was done. I had to listen to him, despite all my efforts, and my encouraging him to stick it out, be hopeful, expect change. Taking my kid out of school was the best thing I ever did. I saved him."*

For a child who truly *is* questioning their sexuality at this stage [more than the typical amount], the effects can be even more damaging.

---

[16]"School Ordered To Pay $250,000 To Bullied Teen," ABCNews.go.com, Aug 12, 2005

The target can be mistakenly identified as a bully. Kids left on their own to defend themselves can finally "snap." Taking matters into their own hands, and before reaching a Columbine-style retaliation, desperate targets punch back, beat up, or cyberstalk the bully, in an effort to level the playing field and exact some justice. Parents of targets sometimes *encourage* fighting back, at a loss for other ways to stop the problem, frequently after repeat encounters with a school or school board that insists that they've "handled" the problem or there is no problem.

When the bullied reactor finally hits back, often in a fury, he or she is typically taken to the office, with phone calls home to parents, detentions, and/or suspensions. Beating someone up isn't right, no matter the provocation, but adults have to give kids more options. We can't leave kids alone to defend themselves and then be surprised by what happens.

The target can be mistakenly identified as a behavior problem. A parent came to me with the following problem: She had been told that her grade 3 daughter had an anger management problem and should be taken to a therapist for counseling. The daughter, Norah, made one mistake on her math test and completely flipped out, screaming and crying, inconsolable for half an hour. Norah's mother took her daughter to a therapist, who interviewed each of them separately, then together.

Bringing them together again at the end, the therapist said, *"Norah doesn't have an anger management problem. She has a bullying problem. She's being taunted by two kids, mostly on the playground."* Her mother was aware of this, had reported it to the school at least twice, and had spoken to me previously about it. *"Norah has been unable to stop the problem herself, her peers haven't helped, and the teachers either don't see it or don't understand what's going on."*

Sound like the Columbine building blocks?

"Norah is taking it, taking it, taking it on the playground, doing her best to hang on and not show how much this is hurting her. Then she comes back into the classroom and gets her math test back, with one mistake. The math test isn't the problem; it's the final straw that breaks the camel's back. Norah can't hold it in any more. All her emotions come rushing out, like a broken dam."

A big obstacle to effective handling of bullying incidents is that adults often rush to make on-the-spot diagnoses of the loud, very noticeable problems that are right in our faces, without taking time to observe the child or group of kids long enough to understand the context, nuances, and contributing factors to the problem. More on that in Chapter 8.

The target is often made responsible for the solution. When a child finally screws up the courage to come tell an adult that he needs help because he's a target, we often jump to the wrong "solution." *"Just stay out of their way," "Why don't you use the stairs at the end of the hall and avoid the bully," "You didn't want to go with them anyway," "You can go help with the younger kids at lunchtime instead of going out on the playground."* It's well-meaning advice, designed to take the target out of the bully's path, but the problem is that there's no requirement for the bully to confront or change his own behavior. It clearly conveys the message that the bully's behavior is accepted, if not acceptable, and we just have to work our way around it. Some of these "remove the target from the bully's sight" ideas can be used for a few days, as short-term tactics, until everybody figures out a better long-term plan, but they are *not* a long-term solution on their own.

Adults often don't appreciate how difficult it is for a kid in middle or high school to ask an adult for help with a bullying problem. There is *nothing* worse for most preteens or teens than to feel forced to admit (1) that they can't handle it on their own [how juvenile is that?] and (2) that they need *an adult's help* [which means they've also been unable to get their peers to help them]. So when our kids come to us in this state of extreme distress and vulnerability and we tell them, *"Too bad. You're on your own. You probably caused it. And by the way, it'll probably get worse,"* how likely do you think they'll be willing to come tell us when it *does* get worse?

Being a bullied target causes long-term damage. In addition to the immediate damage to heart and body, there are real incentives for adults to intervene early, to help get a target off the target path. Like bullying behavior patterns, target behavior patterns persist. There's a certain amount of truth to the saying *"Once a target, always a target."* We need to get kids out of the impact zone before those expectations and bad behavior patterns are ingrained. We can work on it and change it early!

It's more than just behavior patterns. Tracy Vaillancourt's continuing research shows that being a bullied target can cause brain damage.[17] Brain changes seen in bullied kids are similar to those seen in neglected and abused children. The prefrontal cortex and hippocampus are altered – areas that affect attention, focus, impulse control, and memory. Bullied kids score lower on cognitive tests and show evidence of chronic high stress, which kills brain cells. Cortisol and testosterone levels are affected, which can damage physiological development through puberty. Full height is not achieved, muscle mass is impaired, memory declines, depression increases. Dreading every day as a stress marathon, silently praying that nothing bad happens today, kids are driven to feel that suicide is acceptable – in fact, *the only* way out. It's chilling to hear a child say *"If I killed myself, at least I'd be done with the problem."* Parents, teachers, and school boards need to take this problem seriously. It's not just *"Boys will be boys" [or GWBG].*

It's no surprise, then, that targets carry their target issues with them into adulthood too. Kids who are used to having their boundaries routinely transgressed don't know where healthy boundaries should be set, how to articulate when someone crosses their boundary, or how to step back. This sets targets up to continue being taken advantage of – at work, in adult dating

---

[17]A McIlroy, "Beyond The Blow To Self-Esteem, Bullying Can Hurt The Brain, Too," *Globe And Mail*, GlobeandMail.com, Mar 11, 2010

relationships, in other personal and family relationships. Adult targets also have more problems with depression, body image, and self-esteem.

The Bystanders

Now that we've looked at the bully's role and the target's, let's investigate the biggest part of the bullying problem – bystanders. **Remember this: There are NO innocent bystanders**. Bystanders are implicit colluders with bullies, enabling them to continue, whether the collaboration is conscious or unintentional. Bystanders to children's bullying can be children or adults, usually both. Let's look at kids first.

Kids As Bystanders

Bystanders can be active or passive. Active bystanders may cheer the bullying on, or organize a ring of spectators with cell phone cameras as paparazzi at a public beating. Active bystanders speak the language of acceptance. *"Everyone talks that way," "She's a loser," "Nobody invites her"* – these are the words and attitudes of collusion to exclude.

Passive bystanders allow bullying by looking the other way, without intervening or reporting. *"We weren't doing anything."* Sometimes it's hard to tell – was it actively passive bystanding or passively active bystanding? Let's not split hairs – let's just stop it!

A word about the common *"We were just kidding"* or *"It was just a joke"* defense. Not wanting to accuse anyone unfairly, uncertain of the next step, well-meaning adults are frequently stopped dead in their tracks by this excuse. Unfortunately, doing nothing allows the bullying to continue and kids learn that this is an effective way to side-step punishment or consequences. Instead, **we must sensitize kids and adults to the** *effect* **they've had on another human being,** *whatever* **the stated intent of their action or inaction**. If it truly was unintentional, a genuine apology swiftly follows. More denials and you can be pretty sure you've caught some bullies red-handed.

Why don't kids intervene? Let's look at a few reasons, most of which apply to adults too:

- **Bystanders fear retaliation** or that they'll be the next target, in or out of school. This is a legitimate fear in today's schools and communities.

- **Because of this fear, bystanders try to protect themselves** by aligning with the bully and her peers, or at least not misaligning.

- **There is peer pressure, real or perceived, to conform**. Middle school is practically *defined* as a time when no kid wants to stand out.

- **It takes major guts for one kid to stand up** and go against a bullying incident already in progress.

- **There is virtually no pressure or expectation for bystanders to act**, and there are no consequences when they fail to intervene to protect.

- **Kids have learned that intervening doesn't help**. Bullying has become a long-standing, accepted part of many schools [or teams, camps, or groups of friends]. Even when bullying is brought to adults' attention, follow-through and consistency are poor and bullying swiftly returns, making the intervener vulnerable to "no tattling" code reprisals.

- **Bystanders, especially kids, don't know how to solve the problem**, especially when it`s a problem other than physical bullying. They don't know how to confront the bully effectively.

- **Bystanders don't know how to move a group to intervene** and are thus unable to tap into the power of the group.

- **Bystanders misjudge the seriousness of the incident**. Unless it's physical bullying, there are no bruises, and the target typically tries to make it look as if it doesn't really bother him. All the hurt is on the inside.

Adults As Bystanders

On to the adults. Adults are commonly passive bystanders to kids' bullying. Adult bystanders can be parents, teachers, school officials, or any adults in a child's orbit – the lunchroom assistant, the school custodian, or the teacher who witnesses a middle school girls' "freeze-out."

Bullying is often hard to detect. It's *purposely* hidden from adults. Even experienced adults have trouble finding it. We're often unaware that the single incident we're seeing is part of a larger pattern. We must learn to check further and keep track of these "one-off" incidents, so we don't have 15 teachers or camp counselors each seeing a single incident, thinking there's nothing more going on.

We dismiss our kids' concerns. *"What did you do to cause the bullying?"* or *"You didn't really want to go with them."* Adult attitudes can be rigid and change-resistant: *"What difference would it make?," "Bullying's been going on for a million years – just tough it out," "Call 1-800-Someone Else, Not Me"* [Note: 800 help lines provide much useful information to kids and adults, but we must not rely on them as the sole or main means to lend support to or extract a kid from physically or emotionally dangerous bullying situations].

Adults Make Excuses For Not Helping Bullied Kids

We make lame excuses for our non-intervention, often hiding behind twisted versions of policies and rules meant for a different purpose. *"The bully has just as much right to be here* [in school] *as the target."* Uh uh. Only when she's not causing harm to others.

Si'Mone Small was in 7th grade when he was beaten up on a Jacksonville, FL, bus by a group of bigger boys who had previously bullied him in school.[18] The adult bus driver did nothing to intervene. **Big time bystanding,** by both the bus driver and the other kids on the bus. I mentioned the bus driver earlier, who said he *"could have gotten in trouble for touching a kid,"* as a defense for why he hadn't stepped in to protect Si'Mone. This wasn't a case of sexual touching or corporal punishment. The bus driver would have been *saving a kid who was in trouble and needed help.* Interestingly, the person who stopped the attack was a **smaller girl**! She stepped right up between Si'Mone and the much bigger male instigator, stood her ground, and demanded that the beating stop! All caught on video! Kudos to her! We'll have more to say about this story in Chapter 9.

I was disheartened to see a story titled "Why It's Not Always Bad To Be Bullied."[19] The story cited a UCLA study which suggested that there are *benefits* to being bullied: kids learn (1) how to stand up for themselves, (2) how to solve conflicts, and (3) that not everyone is going to like them. Moreover, children who responded to peer aggression with their own peer aggression were more admired and respected, and judged to be more mature and socially competent by both peers and teachers.

I think (1), (2), and (3) are all important life lessons that kids *must* learn, but leaving them to be bullied, unprotected by adults, is an abusive, harrowing way to accomplish this. Are adults trying to make themselves feel better for looking the other way while kids get victimized?

---

[18]G Tuckman, "Caught On Tape," *Anderson Cooper 360*, *CNN*, May 20, 2005

[19]D Derbyshire, "Why It's Not Always Bad To Be Bullied: Learning To Fight Back Helps Children Mature, Says Study," DailyMail.co.uk, May 24, 2010

At best, responding to a bully by punching him or her is a case of kids making the best out of the bad situation they've been left in by adults. Google "Casey The Bully Punisher." If we fail to teach kids how to prevent or solve bullying problems, or we take away their backup tools, *especially* adult support and intervention, we can't be surprised when kids respond with the tool of last resort – a punch in the face. It *is* a way for a desperate kid to set a boundary and preserve self-respect by standing up for himself when nobody else will. Kids need to learn to set limits and boundaries, but not that way. And how can adults admire that behavior? Is that the best we can do?

Desperate parents often coach their kid to respond with physical violence, sometimes as a last option, sometimes by not taking the time to think through and reach for better options. Either way, relying on peer violence to suppress kids' bullying is a huge admission of defeat – by adults and kids alike.

Let's not justify lack of adult help by looking for a silver lining in a childhood traumatized by bullying. Bullying is not OK. Period.

Update: The UCLA study results may have been misrepresented in the press, although several media sources reported the findings. The study design has also been criticized. While careful study design and reporting accuracy are both important, and whether or not the study was designed or interpreted correctly, we have all heard similar erroneous thinking about bullying. *"Let the kids sort it out," "Kids need to toughen up for the real world,"* or *"Can't like everyone."* While there may be an element of truth in those statements, they are misapplied when we use them as self-serving rationalizations to excuse the failure of adults to extract kids from damaging situations.

Adults Are Usually Ineffective When They *Do* Step In

Adults usually get involved very late or too late. Sometimes kids don't tell us anything until they're at or near the breaking point. But more often, we know something's going on. We've seen enough, and even though we don't have the whole story, our gut tells us our oblique observations could be the breadcrumb trail to something bigger. Unfortunately, we usually do nothing at this time, waiting for more evidence to come to us. Instead, this is when we need to take a more active, less passive stance. This is *exactly* the time to search it out – waiting until it comes to us can have unanticipated, irrevocable consequences. **Doing nothing is NOT neutral.**

When we do intervene, we often use the wrong tools. Conflict resolution skills are often applied, incorrectly, to bullying problems. Conflict resolution solutions *do not work* for bullying, and in fact can make the problem much worse. More on this in Chapter 6.

Bystanders Pay A Price, Too

We might be tempted to think that bystanders, if they keep their heads down, can slide through some pretty hostile, bully-encrusted environments with minimal damage. But we know from our experience with adult workplace bullying that it doesn't work that way. Kids are even more damaged than adults by being left on their own, or feeling as if they've been left on their own, to defend against bullies.

> *They came first for the Communists, and I didn't speak up because I wasn't a Communist*
>
> *Then they came for the Jews, and I didn't speak up because I wasn't a Jew*
>
> *Then they came for the trade unionists, and I didn't speak up because I wasn't a trade unionist*
>
> *Then they came for me, and by that time, no one was left to speak up*
>
> PASTOR MARTIN NIEMÖLLER
>
> January 6, 1946
>
> Explaining the inaction of Germans during World War II

Bystanders feel unsafe, powerless, and unprotected in environments that support bullying. You might think that your child or student is concentrating on math in math class. Far more likely, he's worried about needing to go to the bathroom before the next class and trying to decide which boys' bathroom presents the least risk of getting his head swirled in the toilet by a group of bigger kids. One of my friends' kids *never* used the bathroom at his elementary school because he knew that's where bullying occurred. Even though he was never targeted personally, his radar was on "high," with a keen awareness of possible trouble spots.

Even if you were *"only"* given a "swirly" once, or even if it never happened to you, *all kids are affected* by the threat of bullying. Like the girl whose gym clothes have been thrown in a toilet and urinated on by gym class peers several times [not making up any of these incidents], just *thinking* about the possibility of it happening again or *entering school* in the morning is enough to prime a kid's blood pressure and cortisol levels – markers of Post Traumatic Stress Disorder.[20] School avoidance can often be a symptom of bullying – of your kid or others.

Adults who think *"At least it's not my kid being targeted,"* and therefore don't get involved, are not seeing the whole picture. In an environment that permits the bullying of one kid, your kid can easily be the next one. Who will protect your child if you and your child look the other way when others are being bullied?

Bystander guilt follows kids and adults for years. Dawn-Marie Wesley, a 14-year-old girl who hanged herself in Mission, BC, in 2000, was tormented by girls at her school. The day she died, she received a text message saying *"You are so dead tomorrow"* [probably *"u r so dead 2moro"*]. After months of torment, she believed them and killed herself that evening, rather than let them do the job. Interviews of her surviving friends reveal their heartbroken guilt, years after her death, even though Dawn-Marie *specifically asked them not to do anything*, not to get an adult's help.[21]

There are secrets we should not keep. It's hard for *adults* to tell when we've crossed the line from secret to impending crisis.

---

[20]T Vaillancourt, Lecture presented at LAMP Community Health Centre, Toronto, Oct 27, 2008

[21]*It's A Girl's World,* Director: L Glazier, National Film Board of Canada, 2004

How can we expect 14-year-olds to know? We need to teach and insist that adults protect kids and kids protect one another, not letting anyone get pushed so close to the edge.

Without Realizing It, We're Enabling Bullies

A problem at a Toronto elementary school sharply demonstrates the damage done by halfhearted adult intervention.[22] For three years [you can tell we're already in trouble here], a 6th grade girl had been the target of verbal and physical bullying by a female classmate. The targeted child had recurrent nightmares and had needed medical care for bruised ribs. The child's mother had asked for help, from both the school and the school board. Eventually, the school's solution was to assign a full-time adult bodyguard to shadow and "protect" the targeted student at school. In addition, the child was asked to spend lunch recess with the younger kids at school, "helping out," in an effort to remove her from the danger zone of recess with kids her own age, including the bully.

It's clear that these efforts to solve the problem were, at best, ineffective. Eventually, the mother brought the story to the media to publicize her daughter's situation and push for more effective action.

While this is, unfortunately, a story that can happen anywhere, and indeed has, it provides a good opportunity for us to look clearly at the responsibility adults can and should exercise, in

---

[22]M McAllister, *Global TV News*, *Global TV*, Toronto, Jun 8, 2005

their varying roles, in a 360° circle around kids. Some things to think about:

- Should a child require a bodyguard to attend school safely? I hope not. And if a bodyguard is the best solution we can think of, isn't it the *bully* who should be guarded, to keep other children safe?

- Assigning the girl a bodyguard or creating a special program to keep her busy and away from the bully during school hours can actually make the problem *worse*, isolating her from her friends and, ironically, making her *more* vulnerable to bullying outside of school, either in person or on the Internet.

Even more troubling were the excuses given by the adults involved in this situation. School board officials were interviewed, some on camera, offering the following excuses:

- *"The bully has as much right to be here as the target."*

- *"We have a Safe Schools Action Team and programs coming out."*

Adults tend to over-rely on bullying prevention lesson plans and programs. We also have a tendency to react to crises by developing even more programs and enacting more rules and laws. None of these are substitutes for dealing, hands-on, with the real problems that present themselves every day.

We misuse the few rules and laws we have and hide behind their partial truths. A bully should have *"as much right to be in school" only* if she's not hurting others. But then she wouldn't be a bully.

Other problems with this approach:

- This "solution" makes the *target*, not the bully, responsible for the solution. There is no effort to make the bully confront her own behavior and change. The restrictions are all on the target, in an effort to keep the target from the bully's path.

- This was a long-standing problem – three years – and was not confined to the girl targeted in this story. Other children had left the school over this issue.

- The environment operated in fear of the bully. Parents and students declined to speak on camera *"for fear that their children would be targeted next."*

With these actions, or, more accurately, inactions, adults enable the bully. We've turned the whole environment inside out to accommodate the bully, resulting in the systematic, long-standing, and pervasive disregard of the right of a 6th grade girl [and all our kids] to attend school in physical and emotional safety. We've put no pressure on the bully to change, and possibly made the target even more vulnerable outside of school.

It's no wonder that kids take away the accurate message that adults don't get it and are woefully ineffective at trying to help kids or protect them in these situations. What behavior can we expect from our kids if this is the best the adults can do?

The short-term solution to this problem was clear: Remove the child. If your child or a child in your school has been in a situation like this for three years [or even one year], despite repeated attempts to solve the problem, including escalation, the school and school system have clearly demonstrated their inability to do so at that time. Remove the child. **This is not the correct solution, but in the short term, there is no other option. Parents and school officials need to be strong enough to take this step, in the short term, while we resolve to do better in the future.**

Real damage occurs to kids while adults waffle. Adults must exercise better leadership and work with serious, unrelenting effort to solve bullying problems. The burden of responsibility rests with adults, not kids – at least for right now. Here's why.

What Bystanders Can't Do – Yet

In today's school and community environments, there can be real danger for a child bystander who intervenes, without genuine, sustained support from peers or adults. It would take a real act of courage for a single child to face down a group of bullies in the midst of a bullying attack – verbal, physical, or relational [that's why we should be so amazed and proud of that girl in Jacksonville who faced down Si'Mone Small's bullies]. The bullies are frequently older and bigger, usually with more social power, too. And that courageous bystander is rarely recognized or rewarded for her moral and physical strength and bravery. Just the opposite.

As a result, I don't recommend that a single child stand up and thrust himself into the middle of an incident. Not today. Ironically, though, that is *exactly* what we are working towards, our ultimate goal. Perhaps surprisingly, our goal is NOT to prevent all bullying and to teach everyone to always be polite and kind to one another [OK, it is our goal, but it's not realistic]. Instead, **we need safe environments,** where one kid can say, *"Oops, you crossed the line. That's bullying. We don't treat people like that here."* And the other kid will say, *"Hey, I didn't realize. Thanks for letting me know. Sorry."* It would be said in appropriate kid language, of course, more like: *"Quit it!" "K. Sorry" "np."* And that's the end of it. No problem, no taking your life in your hands to intervene, no risk of retaliation, just a mistake, a correction, an apology, and life goes on.

We must keep that goal of reclaiming and creating safe, bully-free environments foremost, and work towards it as a top priority, starting now. Adults and kids should live and work in environments where mistakes are caught early, anyone can point them out at no personal risk, the offender takes responsibility and apologizes, and the target accepts the apology and releases the [small] hurt.

What Bystanders *Can* Do – Now

Adults must lead the way, showing no tolerance for bullying, consistently and relentlessly searching it out and removing the oxygen that allows it to thrive. No more adult bullying, inconsistent adult words and actions, looking the other way

until there's an unavoidable crisis, half-hearted attempts to intervene, etc. It's only through this unwavering, *"Yes, We Mean It"* demonstration of adult leadership, guidance, and determination that adults and kids will learn, with certainty, where the line is and that each and every one of us is expected to do our part to create and maintain safe, accepting environments for all.

While adults must shoulder this responsibility, there is an important duty for kids too. In the transition, while adults work to create safe environments, where mistakes are caught early and can be brought to a group's attention by any group member, kids also have a responsibility. Until it's safe for individual kids to stand up to stop bullying, **we can teach kids to stand up *as a group* to object to the bad treatment of others.** We can give them the language of positive peer pressure to use: *"We don't treat people like that," "Hey, he's having a bad day. Come play/work with us until he's over his bad mood." And* to the bully: *"You can come play with us too, when you've got it back together. Take a few minutes and calm down"* [Note: this works for adults too].

This approach teaches several key lessons:

- **Bullying won't be tolerated** and will be stopped at its earliest stages.

- **Anyone can be and everyone is responsible for creating and maintaining safe, pleasant, civil work and play environments.** As a member of the class [school, team, workplace, camp], everyone is expected to contribute to that goal.

- **Mistakes happen, it's no big deal.** When you make a mistake, take a positive time out to calm yourself down and, when you're ready, come back to your friends, who still like you. Make amends as appropriate. We are helping kids learn the skills of emotional self-control and self-management. They might teach us something along the way!

It's important that we teach this to kids, and the adults around them, starting when kids are young. If we wait until they're teens, it will be a tough sell to undo those years of hardened, unpunished bullying. Additionally, empathy plummets during the teen years.[23] It will rebound, and most of us who were toughened teens, myself included, mellowed into acceptably empathic adults, but why try to teach someone those skills during the *least receptive period of his life*?

Bystander Intervention Works!

Interestingly, **the single most effective tool for stopping a bullying attack is intervention by bystanders** [like Si'Mone Small's defender]. **When bystanders intervene,[24] bullying stops in half the time.[25]** In 1998, Debra Pepler wired a group of Toronto elementary school girls for sound and put video cameras on the playground. This was the first close-in observation of girls'

---

[23]S. Goudarzi, "Teenage Brain Lacks Empathy," MSNBC.com, Sep 8, 2006

[24]T Crawford, "Prey Grounds," TheStar.com, Apr 6, 2007

[25]D Pepler, W Craig, and W Roberts, "Observations Of Aggressive And Non-Aggressive Children On The School Playground," *Merrill-Palmer Quarterly*, 44, 55-76, 1998

playground bullying, and the results were shocking. Here was incontrovertible evidence of the emotional cruelty that girls can casually inflict on one another. The news wasn't all bad, though. The study clearly demonstrated the strongly persuasive and deflective influence of intervening bystanders. The bullying was stopped dead in its tracks when even one girl objected, stood up for the target, or deflected the barrage.

There are many small, yet effective strategies we can use, as adults and kids. All we really have to do is open our eyes, see problems earlier, and be willing to step in. Stepping in earlier gives us a much smaller problem to deal with, many more options, and a much better outcome.

5

Cyberbullying: Bullying's Growth Industry

Now that we've got the basic toolbox for looking at bullying issues, let's take a more detailed look at cyberbullying, bullying's newest, fastest-growing, high-tech product.

Cyberbullying is the use of electronic media to bully or threaten. In the time it took me to write that sentence, someone has developed a new twist on how to use an existing technology to cyberbully or has invented an entirely new tech platform from which the cyberbullying product line can be extended! The rapid pace of innovation makes it impossible to construct an all-encompassing definition of either cyberbullying activities or the means and equipment by which they are propagated. It also makes it dangerous to wait for evidence-based best practices to evolve from research. Before the report is written, it's out of date. Adults need to refine and upgrade our knowledge, actions, and guidance continuously, as new information becomes available – every day, in our schools and communities, as well as from big picture research.

We do not need to be IT experts to be effective guardians in this area. We just need to keep learning, asking questions, and most importantly, showing up in our kids' lives to provide guidance and boundaries.

Cyberbullying has become the "flavor of the month," the hot topic in bullying prevention – and with good reason. The rapidity of evolution, the growing sophistication, the subtlety of kids' cyberbullying, and its hidden nature until it reaches adult awareness as a full-blown crisis on the verge of disaster, make us understandably nervous and anxious to get our arms and brains around this problem.

There is a risk, however, to focusing too narrowly on cyberbullying alone. It's the same problem of narrow focus that we discussed in Chapter 1. When we focus too sharply on cyberbullying, we miss the larger context in which cyberbullying is set.

Here's the take-away point: Cyberbullying never happens by itself. Cyberbullying *always* exists in environments where in-person, face-to-face bullying already exists. Cyberbullying thrives in cultures that permit interpersonal aggression. Cyberbullying, with its apparent ease, anonymity, and near-immediate gratification, is a simple, logical extension of bad behavior patterns already ingrained and tacitly approved. If kids have failed to internalize appropriate standards of behavior for face-to-face conduct, they will *not* behave better online. Obviously, the same is true for adults, and my workshops on kids' cyberbullying use many examples of *adult* cyberbullying that set and teach abysmally low standards for kids to adopt. So if you're seeing cyberbullying, start looking for and identifying the other types of systemic bullying that already exist in your environment.

Without understanding the larger context in which cyberbullying thrives, it is impossible to control it by focusing merely on technology containment strategies and punitive consequences for egregious and surreptitious online behavior. It's like melting the tip of the iceberg – the rest of the iceberg is still there, waiting to trip us up.

Cyberbullying can include, but is not limited to, the following activities:

- Spreading gossip, lies, or rumors.

- Colluding to harm or exclude someone.

- Impersonating someone else, often by gaining access to the target's passwords, PINs, and profiles.

- Revealing personal or embarrassing information about the target or getting the target to reveal it himself or herself, often in supposed confidence. The cyberbully then reveals that info to a third party or an entire mailing list.

- Posting or sending embarrassing or private pictures or videos.

These activities can be done with the target's awareness or behind the target's back.

Cyberbullying Tech Tools

Cyberbullying delivery methods are expanding exponentially, keeping pace with the enlarging scope of the Internet and the proliferation and increasing sophistication of hardware and software. The 24/7 nature of cyberbullying, and its apparent anonymity, is what makes it so frightening to be cyberstalked. Old style, face-to-face bullying ends when you go home. There's no relief from cyberbullying. Online social networks like MSN, Facebook, Skype, and Twitter broadcast to all your "friends" when you get online, giving the bullies a heads-up that their quarry is nearby. Of course, a target doesn't even have to be online to be cyberbullied. And with social networks, cell phones, and email, a bully can post or send messages, photos, or videos to dozens of bystanders with the click of a mouse.

Dozens of contacts? More like hundreds! Have you ever seen how many contacts teens have in their cell phones? Even before smart phones made transferring contact info a snap, teens were the only people I knew willing to spend the time to key hundreds of contacts into their old-fashioned cell phones using a-b-c keystrokes! Kids' Facebook "friends" can number in the thousands. Don't underestimate the size and scope of the teen network or the strength of focus and hard work that a teen can bring to a project – for good or bad.

There's an extra dimension to the fear and dread created by online bullying. Face-to-face bullying lets you see the identities of your tormentors. Online, it's easy for a tech-savvy child to cover her tracks by impersonating someone else in the social group or school. It's often unclear to the targeted child who the real perpetrators are, keeping them unbalanced and frightened, not knowing friends from enemies, both in and after school.

Here's an incomplete list of cyberbullying's popular delivery vehicles:

- Email

- Instant Messaging [Services like MSN, AOL, BBM]

- Text Messages

- Voice Mail

- Websites [A teen's own website or teen community websites]

- Online Bulletin Boards

- Blogs [Your own or someone else's]

- Cameras [Still and video; can be used to film prearranged fights or beatings, which are then posted to the Internet]

- Cell Phones [Contain combined technology; most have cameras, some have video; virtually all can text, some can email and browse the Internet; smart phones do it all]

- Social Networking Sites [Facebook, Twitter, MySpace, Formspring, LiveJournal, LavaLife, dating sites intended for older teens or young adults, but easily accessed by preteens and teens faking older identities]

- Video Gaming Sites [Games where you earn points for carjacking, raping, or killing breed intolerance and desensitize kids to violence. The games are often interactive with other online players, and some sites have chat areas or bulletin boards for player communication during or after games. While they can be a place where game developers and players swap playing strategies and software hints, they can also be a breeding ground for swaggering racism, misogyny, and homophobia.]

While many adults need to hire an IT consultant to set up a website, blog or Facebook page, most children, teens, and young adults can do it in a heartbeat [OK, an hour], and if they don't know how, they each have 10 friends who do. The availability of cheap laptops, tablets, wireless networks, and wireless data plans puts a lot of unsupervised computing power in kids' hands [and ours], 24/7. It's a power we all need to use with self-control.

Cyberbullying's Key Issues

Let's take a quick look around the cyberbullying landscape:

1. **Profile Of A Cyberbully**. Who are the cyberbullies? Boys, girls, face-to-face bullies, face-to-face targets, students bullying other students, students bullying teachers – it's an interesting mix.[1] Recent studies have shown that boys cyberbully more, in keeping with their generally higher rates of bullying, but most studies indicate that girls, with their

---

[1] G MacDonald, "Cyber Bullying Defies Traditional Stereotype," FairfaxTimes.com, Sep 1, 2010

generally earlier-maturing and more advanced verbal and writing skills, are the "leaders" here.[2]

And while face-to-face playground bullies go home and continue their handiwork online, many online bullies are actually face-to-face *targets*, looking to level the playing field and exact a little revenge. Kids who feel weak and impotent as schoolyard victims feel powerful turning the tables on their tormentors and [falsely] protected by the aura of anonymity.

Cyberbullying is primarily kid-on-kid, or more accurately, kids-on-kid, but students have also harassed teachers online, through Facebook and "Rate My Teacher" websites. Developed first at the college and university level, then high school, there are now rating sites for middle and elementary level teachers. There have been some shocking examples of kids directing sexually crude and offensive material to principals and teachers through their Facebook pages.

2. **The Apparent Anonymity Of Sitting In Your Room, Writing On A Computer, Removes Most Of The Barriers To Bad Behavior.** Kids and adults say things online that they would never say if they were eyeball-to-eyeball with the target. In the words of an 8th grade girl, *"It's easier to fight online, because you feel more brave and in control. On Facebook, you can be as mean as you want."*[3]

---

[2]N Willard, "An Educator's Guide to Cyberbullying and Cyberthreats," Center For Safe And Responsible Internet Use, csriu.org, 2006
[3]J Hoffman, "Online Bullies Pull Schools Into The Fray," NYTimes.com, Jun 27, 2010

Kids still think that cyberbullying is anonymous, that it's private, like a conversation between two kids in someone's playroom. It may start off in the playroom, but posting malicious misinformation online takes it to a whole new level. Most ISPs and cell phone companies are now required, by law, to retain conversation records that can be tracked directly to a specific computer or the IMEI of a specific cell phone.

3. **Emotional Immaturity And Lack Of Emotional Self-Control Can Spiral Out Of Control**. Justin Bieber, 16, a Canadian singer and preteen heartthrob, was the target of sarcastic put-downs on shavedbieber.com.[4] That's bad enough. His loyal fans sprang to his defense, but they went way too far, issuing death threats: *"Someday I'll be behind you with a gun."* We need to be responsible for our own Internet behavior. Just because it's easy to send this type of message does not make it right. Emotional self-control, please! Adults, our guidance and supervision are really needed here. Help kids learn how to stand up for others without violating someone else's rights.

4. **Whose Problem Is It – Home Or School?** Until recently, this was another area of finger-pointing. The school position was that the majority of cyberbullying wasn't occurring on their property or during school hours, so it wasn't their problem. But the fight or beating filmed and posted online today and the girls' gossip on MSN tonight come back to school

---

[4]"Bieber-Blocking App Triggers Threats Against Creator," CTV.ca, Jun 2, 2010

tomorrow, poisoning friendships and creating isolation and menace for kids in the school community. As our understanding has grown, we realize home and school must share oversight responsibility for this issue. Schools are starting to craft cyberbullying addenda to their "no bullying" and safe schools policies. Parents are starting to include "no cyberbullying" in their discussions about online conduct and safety with their children. We're still in the formative stage in both arenas, though, so there's much room for improvement.

"**No cyberbullying**" policies, stronger reporting requirements for cyberbullying episodes, and a menu of punitive consequences indicate that we are *starting* to pay attention to the problem. They are not, however, a substitute for, nor are they as effective as, small-scale, everyday preventive attention and action. These efforts are the *beginning* of the work, not the end of it.

5. **Whose Problem Is It, Part B – Prevention or Enforcement?**
   Until recently, cyberbullying was the only kind of bullying that had significant legal consequences. Because cyberbullying leaves a retrievable trail, it has been prosecutable as harassment, threats, libel, or occasionally as hate crime. The police have been the primary line of defense and frequently, they were the only adults talking to kids about online bullying. Their approach is, understandably, enforcement-driven rather than preventive, and their consequences are punitive. *"If you cyberbully, we will take away your computer."*

There should definitely be consequences for misbehavior, but the emphasis should be on prevention. While we are starting to focus on cyberbullying, we are once again over-emphasizing enforcement and punishment. Efforts to criminalize online misbehavior may have the unintended consequence of driving it further underground, as kids become reluctant to get themselves or peers in legal trouble which could result in a permanent police record as an online sex or hate crime offender. As a result, online problems may not appear until even *later* in the timeline.

Relying on the law will not provide the "magic wand" solution [much more on this in Chapter 9, Bullying & The Law]. The law has been, by its mandate, both slow to address cyberbullying [and bullying, in general] and myopically narrow in its focus.

JC, an 8th grade California girl, videotaped friends at a café making mean-spirited remarks about a classmate named CC, with JC's encouragement and direction.[5] JC then posted the video to YouTube. Her school gave her a two-day suspension. Her father, a lawyer, sued, saying the school had no right to discipline his daughter for an incident that took place outside of school.

Maddeningly, the judge felt the relevant legal issue was whether the school had experienced "significant disruption" as a result of the video. Ironically, because the school intervened

---

[5] J Hoffman, "Online Bullies Pull Schools Into The Fray," NYTimes.com, Jun 27, 2010

promptly, it experienced minimal disruption. The judge ruled in favor of JC, requiring the school to pay JC's legal fees. Where, in all of this, are the rights of the individual, the rights of CC, and every child, to attend school feeling safe, unhumiliated, and unafraid?? **Jails are required to protect prisoners from one another – why not schools?** JC's father reportedly admonished JC for her behavior – *"That wasn't a nice thing to do."* Glad that was handled.

6. **We're Focused On The Wrong Risk.** Adults typically think of online safety as protecting kids from sexual predators. Unfortunately, the predators are predominantly *us*. The incidence of peer-on-peer cyberbullying significantly outnumbers predator cyberstalking.[6] Kids expose themselves to risk by joining online activities without exercising sufficient judgment, by not utilizing the security features that *are* available, and by posting too much personal information that's accessible to their *frenemies*. Isolated kids, with no friends because of bullying or for other reasons, are much more vulnerable to "looking for love in all the wrong places," often online.

7. **Adults Don't Know What Kids Do On Computers**. We assume that our home and school computers are safe. We slap on some filters or "net nanny" software to block some sites and we think our job is finished. As long as we don't hear any yelling or see any blood, our kids are OK, aren't

---

[6]N Willard, *Cyberbullying and Cyberthreats: Responding To The Online Challenge Of Social Aggression, Threats, and Distress* (Champaign, IL: Research Publishers Press, 2007)

they? Who wants to disturb a quiet kid? Unfortunately, quiet is not always safe.

We're kidding ourselves if we don't realize that kids can defeat those filters and lockout codes faster than we can set them up. At my assistant's college, it was a point of pride and a standing competition to see how early in the day the random lockout codes could be defeated. A slow day took till 10 am. Just Google "bypass Internet filters" and you'll see what I mean.

That's another example of teen creativity and persistence. Now we just need to focus it on the *right* activities! There has always been and there will always be *some* anarchy on the teen menu, but adults can do a better job of guiding, setting limits, and providing lots of positive alternatives for kids to sharpen their creative teeth.

Once again, what's needed is *not* stronger lockout software or an adult to stand guard, 24/7, at your computer. Even if your house or your school has state-of-the-art lockout software, your kids are going to go somewhere – someone else's house, someone else's school, the library, an Internet café – where the restrictions are set more loosely, or not at all. That's when our kids need to know – *inside themselves* – how far is "far enough."

8. **Social Media And Networking Are Our Kids' Social Lifeline.** Kids' social lives are very different than ours were. Ours were all face-to-face and on the telephone. Kids today can hardly

breathe without access to social networking sites. Many teens are happy – even happier – to stay home on a Saturday night, as long as they're connected to their friends on the Internet. An all-or-nothing approach, *"No, you can't use Facebook at all,"* is unrealistic on a long-term basis. Kids will access those networks *somewhere*, even if it isn't in their own home. And I guarantee you that if your kids are accessing the Internet outside your home, they are doing so with less guidance than you would like. A more useful approach is for parents and other adults to help kids grow into the "shades of grey" skills that they need to know in order to have fun using the Internet with reasonable safety.

Kids' intense desire to stay connected online makes them (1) more likely to divulge personal info, (2) more likely to lie about their age to gain online entry to popular sites, (3) less likely to use available Internet safety and privacy tools, and (4) less likely to enlist adult help in the early stages of a cyber problem. They fear that adults will remove or limit their online privileges and access, especially if the kids have contributed to their own problem by not using the safety tools adults recommend. This is yet another reason to keep an open communication channel between adults and kids when things are going well, and especially when they aren't.

9. **Private Behaviors, Mistakes, And Humiliations Go Global**. Remember Tyler Clementi. Just because you *can* videotape someone having sex and post it online, *does not mean it's OK to do it*. Learn how to think about doing something wrong

and then *not do it*. Your next thought has to be, *"But I wouldn't do that. It would be the wrong thing to do."* **Control yourself. Adults, we must relearn self-control and we must start teaching it to our kids again.** Add it to that list of "Behaviors To Practice 100 Times Before We Get It Right."

Less catastrophically, kids [and adults] sometimes do dumb or embarrassing things – that's not new. What *is* new is the ability to post these cringe-worthy moments online, broadcasting a kid's momentary clumsiness, mental or physical, to an audience of millions.

In 2002, a Canadian high school student videotaped himself imitating *Star Wars* movie combat, using a golf ball retriever as a double-bladed light saber. Found by his high school classmates and posted to the Internet, his *Star Wars Kid* video went viral, with 900 million estimated viewings.[7] It's still online today. What was once the fuel for private or highly localized embarrassment now has the potential to cause real trauma, from both the magnitude of the exposure and by its endless availability years after the original incident. **We need to let people have their embarrassing moments with a little more privacy. We need to protect one another, so the same courtesy and sheltering are extended to *us* in *our* own moments of stupidity.**

---

[7]"Star Wars Kid Is Top Viral Video," news.bbc.co.uk, Nov 27, 2006

Cyberbashing, briefly mentioned earlier, is a shocking but not surprising example of the intersection of bullying and technology. Cyberbashing is an intentional, premeditated, prearranged beating or fight, where only the target doesn't know about the plan in advance. It's organized with the specific intent of posting the video footage to the Internet. Kids show up to these planned arena-style beatings carrying HD video cameras to ensure the best quality video. The final footage is sometimes edited to near-professional quality, including the addition of music and subtitles. Nice touch.

10. **Cyberbullying Can Remain Underground, Or At Least Out Of Adult Sight, For A Long Time**. By the time adults are aware of a problem, sometimes because of a threatened school shooting or a kid feeling suicidal, a lot of damage has been done and it's often an emergency. We have more resources and get better results when we can handle these issues *before* the crisis stage.

Adults need to guide kids to set boundaries and limits, helping kids internalize these standards. Kids can then make their own appropriate decisions, not always needing to rely on adults as external enforcers and arbiters of acceptable behavior. The sooner we can help kids download and internalize these guidelines and learn how to apply them flexibly, the sooner we can be out of the enforcement business. [Just kidding – a parent's or teacher's work is never done.]

In order to be credible, we adults need to clean up *our* act. Egregious examples of adult cyberbullying abound. When adults show so little self-control, it's impossible for kids not to follow – and go one better. Here are a few examples of *adult* online bullying:

- In an email sent to a co-worker, in the subject line: *"You are worthless."*[8] Part of the email read: *"I hope someday the rest of the office sees you for the small, pathetic IT loser you are and beats you within an inch of your life in the parking lot."* Even worse, the email was sent anonymously, through a website which forwards these messages to their intended targets.

- Want to break up with your boyfriend or girlfriend, but don't have the guts to do it face-to-face? IDUMP4U will call your soon-to-be-ex-beloved and break up with her on the phone for you, recording the call and posting it online for future public listening.[9] The site's creator says he's *"providing a public service."*

  I cannot imagine *anyone* whose life would be improved by hearing the audio file of an unknown person sobbing, crushed to find out the person she loves has just dumped her in this callous and cruel-hearted manner. Interestingly, the site developer was on the receiving end of some not-so-kind breakups when he was younger. Bullied target taking online revenge? If you can't break up in person, or at least on the phone, you're not emotionally mature enough to be in a relationship.

  Even if someone provides this kind of website, *we don't have to use it*. Admittedly, it's much easier not to use it

[8]D Andreatta, "Taking Office Rage Into The Ring," *Globe And Mail*, Sep 3, 2007
[9]IDUMP4U.com

when it isn't right in front of us. It's very hard to *not* look at an accident or resist a piece of chocolate cake sitting in front of us.

That's where self-discipline comes in. Self-discipline is like a muscle. You have to practice and train it, so when it's put to the test, it works. Don't expect to never practice self-discipline or boundaries, then be able to resist a huge temptation, one mouse click away. This applies to adults and kids equally.

Part of the process of training our kids and letting them make some of their own decisions will be the interesting and creative mistakes that *will* occur on the way to adulthood. No matter how fully you've covered the topic of Internet safety and appropriate online behavior with your kids, there will *always* be something you didn't think of that will show up in this weekend's or next month's mistakes. Then it's time to adopt the *"I'm glad this happened now"* approach, viewing the mistakes as opportunities to close that knowledge gap the next time.

Teen Sex And Cyberbullying: A Dangerous Mix

The sexting suicide of Jesse Logan, age 18, is an example of the perfect storm of trouble that can brew up from inappropriate technology use when adults and peers are looking the other way.[10] Jesse, a decent kid in her first serious dating relationship, sent naked pictures of herself to her boyfriend [that's "sexting"]. Those are Problems #1 and #2. When they broke up, the

---

[10]M Celizic, "Her Teen Committed Suicide Over 'Sexting'," Today.MSNBC.MSN.com, Mar 6, 2009

boyfriend sent those pictures to other students at both his and Jesse's high schools. That's Problem #3. The photos were forwarded further, and verbal and physical taunting began at both schools. She was called *slut, whore,* and *skank* by her peers; she was taunted by phone, text, and on MySpace; objects were thrown at her at school, at graduation, and at parties. Problem #4. The school knew about the harassment, but didn't stop it. Problem #5. In May, 2008, Jesse went on local TV to tell her story, in an attempt to end the problem and to prevent it from happening to others. That takes guts. Unfortunately, the damage had been done. By July 2008, Jesse couldn't take any more and committed suicide. Big, irrevocable Problem #6.

Let's consider the problems one at a time and what might have been done differently:

- ▪ ***Problem #1*: Nude Photos Were Sent**. Jesse sent the pictures herself. Lots of kids do these days, not just 18-year-olds in their first serious relationships. There are 10-year-old middle school boys and girls sending nude pictures of their body parts to classmates they've *never* dated, to express their *interest* in dating [We used to say *"Wanna go to a movie?"*].

  Jesse could have used more inner strength and self-respect at this point – to be able *not* to press the *Send* button, even if many around her had done so with no apparent damage. To help her access those qualities and think twice before sending, she could have used the stabilizing influence of her peers. Surrounding yourself with girlfriends who "get it," who can think clearly, with self-respect and self-control, is the most protective thing a child can do. Jesse also needed the stabilizing support of adults. See the next problem.

- *Problem #2:* **Adults Didn't Know Or Weren't Paying Attention**. Could her parents have done more? Were they even aware what sexting was, much less that their daughter was *doing it*? Her mother only became aware that there was a problem quite late, when the school notified her that Jesse was skipping classes. Jesse had only told her mom part of the story, not revealing the true depth of her hurt and despair.

  What about the school? Were they aware that students were sexting? Did they provide education to their students on the risks? Preferably these discussions start **before** the school learns there's an ongoing sexting problem. They could have helped Jesse focus on the fact that, once you press *Send*, that picture is *completely, irrevocably* out of your control. Forever. And you're depending on the emotional self-control of *everyone* else not to forward it. Forever.

  Teens have always hated needing adult help, but we need to pry open the tiny communication window between adults and teens a bit more. Kids [both the target and her friends] need to learn to ask for help earlier. Adults need to move in closer to teens, ask kind-hearted questions and make themselves available. There's no simple solution, no magic wand, but we must keep adjusting our behavior until we get better results.

- *Problem #3:* **Lack Of Emotional Self-Control**. In a moment of emotional upset [anger, sadness], the ex-boyfriend lost emotional control and forwarded the nude pictures, reasonably aware of, and fully intending, the potential for damage to Jesse.

These are kids in their first serious romantic relationships. It is virtually 100% certain that those first relationships won't last, and *will* result in breakups with hurt feelings. **We need to teach our kids how to handle those inevitable feelings, to break up *kindly and with dignity*, despite the hurt, and *not* to lash out in anger – physically, emotionally, or electronically.** This is, again, an opportunity for surrounding adults to play a preventive role.

That boy had no idea of the full downstream consequences of his thoughtless act; he most certainly did not envision Jesse's suicide nor did he envision the dramatic, negative toll it would take on his own life. A huge lawsuit, school and job opportunities lost, a permanent police record. That boy needed supportive peers and adults around him too, *before* pressing *Send*.

I don't think anyone could have imagined the full magnitude of the negative consequences, but once again, when you go too far down the road, it sets other wheels in motion and you end up someplace you never expected. That's chaos theory. So don't start down that road. If you make a mistake and hurt someone, there ARE consequences, whether or not you intended it to go so far. A few teens have even ended up with police records and permanent designations as sex offenders in the aftermath of forwarding nude pictures of their under-18 girlfriends.

- *Problem #4:* **Peers Failed To Support Jesse And Increased The Damage By Viewing And Forwarding The Photos And Insulting Her**. It would take an almost superhuman act of willpower to resist the temptation to look at an email that you *know* contains nude photos of a teen classmate. Perhaps if we could stop for a moment before opening the email and think about how we would feel if we were about to open a nude picture of *ourselves*, and know that, if we opened it, *everyone* in our school would open it too, we might be able to summon the strength to do the right thing and delete it. Press *Delete* and don't forward it. And certainly don't talk about it. And have some empathy for someone in that position, even if she contributed to it herself. And don't call someone a slut or whore. Just don't.

- *Problem #5:* **Lack Of Sufficient Adult Intervention By The School, Once It Was Aware Of The Problem**. Jesse reported the problem to her school and was referred to the school resource officer, a city police officer, who told her that, since she was 18, and she initiated the photos herself, there was little that could be done.[11]

  Apart from the legal issue, adults at the school missed a big opportunity to provide guidance and leadership here. This was a chance to help a kid who was in trouble [really two kids – the boyfriend was in trouble too]. The school community could have come together to support *both* kids, and help everybody [Jesse and her ex, their friends and frenemies, and the adults at both schools] learn a lot about the volatile mix of relationship breakups and technology. When adults fail to step in, the impact zone grows bigger.

Problem #6: **Jesse's Suicide.** There is no way back from this, not for Jesse, not for her family, not for the boyfriend, not for any of the active and passive bystanders who are scarred for life by being part of this tragedy.

---

[11]M Thomas, "Teen Hangs Herself After Harassment For A Sexting Message, Parents Say," CourthouseNews.com, Dec 7, 2009

The problem of sexting is overlaid on a background of teens routinely being exposed to overtly sexual material. Parry Aftab of Wired Safety cites statistics showing 40% of teens have sent or posted sexy material, 50% have received sexy material, and 44% of boys surveyed have seen sexual images of girls from their own school.[12] I'd guess the actual figures are higher. It's easy for teens, swept away in this sexual riptide, and spurred on by developmentally normal teen hormones and curiosity, to not fully understand the risk. Teens are typically terrible at thinking through consequences.

Yes, there will be some sex and a huge amount of sexual curiosity on the teen menu – there always have been – but adults need to guide teens, talk to them more [yes, it's uncomfortable], help them overlay their growing sense of sexuality with some adult perspective on both the beauty of the connection they're about to grow into AND tempering it with some knowledge of today's risks and pitfalls.

It's easy to do the forensic look back, to identify in retrospect the warning signs and missed opportunities, and see clearly what the most supportive behavior on all parts might have been. **But what is *most* important is the carry-forward – how we use this tragic, avoidable loss to change the way we scan for, identify, and handle these situations, in order to minimize the number of Jesse Logan-type suicides and the eddies of destruction that spin out from these incidents. All the people**

---

[12]M Celizik, "Her Teen Committed Suicide Over 'Sexting'," Today.MSNBC.MSN.com, Mar 6, 2009

who played a role here – the bully, the target, the active and passive bystanders – were complicit.

In the wake of Jesse's death and other, less catastrophic sexting cases, there has been some effort to introduce legislation to criminalize sexting. A teen who sends a sexy picture of herself could be charged under child pornography laws. **I think there's a real risk that we'll drive the problem underground – that kids will be *less* likely to report it if the penalties are that great. Again, the road to containing the problem involves less punishment and more *prevention* –** helping kids understand the risks, emotional *and* legal, and guiding them to the skills of emotional self-control, respect for self and others, and empathy. If we rely solely on enforcement, we'll be too late.

Students Bully Teachers

Online criticism, gossip, and slander of teachers by students demonstrates one of the classic cyberbullying dynamics – the less powerful person in the relationship strikes back in covert, passive-aggressive ways, retaliating in a troubled relationship or trying to equalize the power imbalance. As with peer bullying, things get said online that a kid [or an adult] would never have the guts to say face-to-face, especially to an adult teacher.

Online teacher rating sites, like all online information, have their benefits and risks. Kids can post their experiences with teachers and professors, for the benefit of future students. It's not all bad. Kids post *lovely* comments about teachers they adore: *"Miss Evans was my favorite teacher this year. She read to us about artists' lives while we worked on our art projects. I'm so sorry she's leaving. Come back soon, Miss Evans!"* And with the benefit, comes the risk, which we have to guide our kids through. Like Jesse Logan's boyfriend, kids do not realize that the words they write about a teacher, including made up stories about a teacher having a sexual relationship with a student, can ruin 20-year reputations in an instant.[13]

In February 2007, 19 high school students at Robert Hall Catholic Secondary School in Caledon, ON, Canada, were suspended for comments they made about their principal on Facebook.[14] Angered by a new school district policy banning cell phones and personal electronic devices at school, these kids took out their frustration with a shocking string of sexually crude invective directed at the principal. Not only was this a completely disproportionate response, it was a totally ineffective approach to engaging school administrators in what should have been an important discussion about appropriate use of cell phones on school property.

Technology: Handle With Caution

Speaking of boundaries and limits for appropriate use of electronic equipment, schools and school districts are confronting the burgeoning use of cell phone and personal music players, and their occasional [or frequent] misuse and theft.

---

[13]L Ferran and S Netter, "Former Teacher Says Life 'Ruined' By Student Sex Claims," ABCNews.go.com, Oct 22, 2009

[14]"Students Suspended For Cyberbullying Their Own Principal," CTV News, Toronto.CTV.ca, Feb 13, 2007

Some districts have responded with a blanket "no electronics" rule. I find that problematic for several reasons: (1) It's inflexible, (2) They're missing a great opportunity to work on boundaries and balance, and (3) It's potentially dangerous. Here's why.

When you listen to the kids who survived Columbine, you realize what a crucial safety link their cell phones were. Cell phones provided the *only* direct information police and parents had about what was going on – how many kids were hurt, where the injured were, and where the shooters were as the crisis unfolded. What if those phones had been sitting in school lockers when they were so desperately needed during the emergency?

Here's another opportunity to teach balance. Keep your cell phones off during class hours. Yes, you may check your messages at lunch. But no texting during class. No Internet access or texting during tests. Mistakes will be made – with the opportunity for some good-humored consequences. One of my daughter's high school teachers told me it was his policy to answer personally any kid's cell phone that rang during his class. He told the caller the student was not available, that the student was in his class right now, and by the way, that this cell phone just became *his* [the teacher's] for 24 hours, so call back after that. A kid without a cell phone for 24 hours is a communications emergency! It almost never happened twice – the kids knew it was three days for a second offense. At the end of the year, my daughter called her friend's cell phone on purpose while both girls were in his class. The teacher took the phone, then saw it was my daughter calling. Everyone had a good laugh.

It's a good opportunity for adults to lead by example and clean up our own behavior around cell phones. I know we've *never* seen any adults using cell phones inappropriately – texting during boring meetings, texting while driving, calling people from public places [coffee shops, restaurants, standing in line], talking long and loud about things those of us in audible range would rather not know, dialing as soon as the airplane wheels touch down on the runway: *"I'm in Chicago now!"*.... Enough said!

Electronic Snooping – Should We Or Shouldn't We?

It's very tempting to snoop through a child's written or online diary [chat logs, email, texts, Facebook pages], either to "ensure compliance" or when you suspect there's a problem brewing. I do not recommend it, except in the most dire of circumstances. **First, kids need some privacy for many reasons, including having the ability to make some small mistakes without everyone knowing**. This generation of parents knows much more about the comings and goings of their kids than did previous generations. Before cell phones, parents had no idea where their kids went or how to contact them if their destination changed after leaving the house. I don't need or want to know *every* detail of my teen's life.

Second, and far more important, our relationships with our kids are [or should be] based on trust and mutual respect. When your child discovers that you've been snooping [and they almost certainly will], unless there is an *extraordinarily compelling* reason for snooping – major drug or alcohol use, cutting, worries of suicide, other self-harm, or plans to harm another person – you will damage your relationship with your child in ways that will take you *years* to rebuild. If you treat your child in a distrustful manner, his most likely reactions will be to: (1) passively close you out even more, (2) actively hide information from you, and (3) possibly seek out worse friends and activities to "justify" your view of him as untrustworthy.

If you think you need to snoop in your child's chat logs, your first step should be to raise your care and concerns directly to your child – often. Working with your child face-to-face may not solve the problem directly, but it will give your kid a lifeline to know her parents are right next to her, all the way, and will make it much more likely that she will reach out to you or you can reach in to her so you can decide together when and if you need to bring in outside help from a doctor, therapist, the school, etc.

Cyberbullying Action Items

While it's an ongoing challenge to keep up with the pace of innovation in cyberspace – for good and bad – *it's our responsibility, as adults, to know enough to demonstrate guidance and leadership in this area, too.*

Summarizing the main steps adults can take to fight cyberbullying:

- **Adults must set an example**: clean up our own behavior and stop adult cyberbullying.

- **Keep the Internet connection in a public place** where kids know that adults will pass by frequently.

- **Home and school must share oversight responsibility** for kids' Internet safety and cyberbullying prevention.

- **Evaluate cyberbullying as part of systemic bullying, not just as the "flavor of the month."** Strategies to curb cyberbullying must involve plans to curb face-to-face bullying as well. Set, teach, and enforce appropriate standards for face-to-face and online conduct.

- **Educate kids about the risks of sexting.** Coach towards more emotional control in the face of emotional upsets, romantic breakups, and friendship breakups.

- **Adults should keep abreast of evolving technology,** not as experts, but well enough to supervise kids.

- **Focus on prevention,** with consequences for misbehavior:
  - Monitor frequently
  - Intervene early
  - Learn from mistakes

- **Consider carefully whether criminalizing cyberbullying may drive it underground,** further delaying adult knowledge of incipient problems until they've reached crisis level.

- **Develop guidelines and boundaries for technology use** that take advantage of the best tech features.

- **Set flexible, consistent rules for technology use** [eg, clear guidelines for when and how you may or may not use cell phones in school, rather than a blanket "no cell phones" policy]. Expect and welcome some mistakes, with reasonable consequences. Don't remove privileges permanently. Give kids the opportunity and encouragement to try again. Express confidence, aloud, that this is a learning process, and adults struggle with appropriate boundaries too. Review your family's technology policies once or twice a year, and be prepared to adjust as your children's needs change and as technology changes, too.

Cyberbullying's danger comes primarily from *within* us or from friends and colleagues we know well. The solution must come from within, too. We must continually upgrade our knowledge and practices to keep pace with developing technology. We must evaluate new tech products and platforms with the questions, *"How do we use this with safety and respect?"* and *"What are the limits we need to set for child/teen/adult use?"* With consistency and practice we can enjoy the enormous benefits of technology, while minimizing the risks of us becoming faceless stalkers lurking inside our own computer screens.

6

How To Tell
The Difference Between …

We still need a few more tools to move forward with clarity. We often have trouble knowing where to draw the line, where an activity crosses over from being fun, equal, and reciprocal, to cruel, mean-spirited, and damaging.

The problem can lie with the activity itself, or with the language we use to describe the activity or the behavioral boundaries. Our words are often vague or mean one thing to one person and something quite different to another. When we use the same word over and over, but in different contexts, kids can become confused. We're confused, too. For example, what's the difference between good teasing and bad teasing? What does *"Don't tease your sister"* mean?

Teasing vs. Taunting

We use the word "teasing" to encompass a full spectrum of actions, everything from good-natured, give-and-take banter between close friends to malicious, intentionally hurtful "teasing" of an overweight child about her body size or shape.

Following Barbara Coloroso, for consistency and clarity, it's important to differentiate clearly between these extremes, by using completely different words. We can make a distinction between **teasing**, the acceptable, humor-based, equality-based version and **taunting**, the mean-spirited, one-sided, power-imbalanced bullying version. Side by side, let's compare the two.[1]

The defining differences between teasing and taunting are:

Teasing	Taunting
✓ **Roles can swap**	✓ **1-sided, power imbalance**
✓ **Not meant to hurt**	✓ **Intended to hurt**
✓ Keeps dignity of all	✓ Humiliating, demeaning
✓ Only 1 part of relationship	✓ Cruel, bigoted
✓ **Laugh *with* not *at* target**	✓ **Laughing *at* target**
✓ Both parties laugh	✓ **"Disguised" as a joke**
✓ Humor in voice	✓ Harms self-esteem
✓ No harm to self-esteem	✓ **Continues *especially***
✓ **Stops when someone gets hurt or says "Stop"**	**when target is upset or says "Stop"**

- Can the roles reverse? Can I ever tease you, or are you *always* teasing me?

- Is the intended outcome to hurt the target?

- Is there humor in the interaction? On *both* sides?

- When the teasing goes too far, and it occasionally does, does the teaser back off and offer an apology or does the teasing intensify? If the teasing continues or intensifies, that's taunting, not teasing.

---

[1]B Coloroso, *The Bully, The Bullied, And The Bystander* (Toronto: Harper Collins, 2002)

Sometimes well-intentioned teasing can go too far and cross the line into taunting. We see this happen frequently with siblings. Things start off fine, with both parties enjoying the give-and-take, verbal or physical. It continues for a while, but then something changes, and suddenly it's not fun anymore for one of the participants, often the smaller, younger, or weaker one [but not always]. From that point forward, it is increasingly unpleasant for the target – for now the roles have changed, and there are, indeed, a bully and a target, if only briefly. How long it takes for the taunting to stop is a reflection of the underlying relationship between the two and the recognition by the bully that she is hurting the target.

That inflection point, that line crossing, where the situation changes from teasing to taunting, is what I call the "Ouch!" point. When we are the target, we can feel that "Ouch!" point – because we get hurt physically or because our feelings get hurt. In either instance, there is an accompanying reaction in our body – we gasp, our stomach sinks, we pull back, tears burn our eyes, we start to feel an impotent rage, sometimes all of the above. It usually shows in our face or our body language.

We can teach kids to become more aware of the "Ouch!" point. They can learn to use their words or their bodies to communicate that information more clearly to the other person. *"Ouch!," "That hurts," "Stop now. For real," "Please stop," "I'm done,"* putting a hand up as a *STOP* signal, are all indicative of crossing the line and a clear message that it's time to back off and cool down.

The request to stop needs to be honored. We need to do a better job teaching kids to watch and listen for the "Ouch" point when they play with or talk to others. Knowing what it feels like to be on the receiving end, as a target, we can learn to recognize that look on someone else's face or the reaction in their body when we inadvertently go too far.

We can teach kids how to recognize a serious *"Please stop!"* request and insist that everyone must stop – immediately – when they hear it. It's most effective to choose one phrase or one word, used consistently, to mean *"Stop it now. No kidding."* It should be very clear and easy to recognize when it's time to stop. It's good practice for home and school to use the same *"Stop Now!"* phrase for consistency.

Sports: Life Lessons In Bullying Prevention

Team and competitive sports provide many opportunities to recognize and practice staying away from the [bullying] "ouch" point [there are lots of other, non-bullying "ouch" points in sports]. Sports teach many important physical and emotional life skills – focus, concentration, goal-setting, persistence, teamwork, how to work effectively with teammates you may not like, how to give and take feedback, the need for practice, and the need for physical and mental resilience – just to name a few valuable skills. Coaches have a great chance to demonstrate and teach valuable leadership skills, both on and off the playing field.

Adults can learn a lot about bullying prevention from sports. Let's look at sports through our bullying lens, at the important sports skills we can apply to bullying prevention and, going the other way, the important bullying prevention skills we need to use in teaching honorable, admirable sports behavior.

While we've already talked about individual coaching styles and offering feedback in constructive, non-humiliating ways, there's more. Clean coaching, where players are taught to see opposing team members as human beings, not just obstacles, is a crucial contribution to being able to draw the line between competition and bullying. It's a challenge to learn how to balance the cascade of emotional brain chemicals, as you focus in on your goal, to give it your all, yet retain the finesse and self-control to remain aware of emotional and physical boundaries.

It can be done. Players learn, with practice, to improve their sport-specific skills and follow the rules in the playbook. We must also make certain to provide enough complexity and practice opportunities in our **emotional sports coaching**, helping players learn to expect and handle the brain chemical cascade that can impair clear thinking. **It must be *key to our coaching* that we always remember, *no matter the provocation*, that the other team is composed of human beings**. This value must be central, repeated, and demonstrated often. We might lose a few decibels off our competitive extremes, but the benefit will have a far-ranging impact, both on and off the sporting field.

Tattling vs. Telling

Here's another language problem. We've raised our kids to honor an imperfect code of silence – *"Don't tell on your brother,"*

"Don't tell on your friend." Then something dangerous happens and the first thing we ask our kid is, *"Why didn't you tell someone?"* The culprit here is not the kids; rather, it's the language and the imprecise way we describe our value system.

If we were clearer about which situations need an adult's help, and gave kids more chances to practice, we'd get better results. Consider Coloroso's distinction between *tattling* and *telling*:[2]

- **Tattling** – Gets a child into trouble

- **Telling** – Gets a child out of trouble

The key is to start young and use these words consistently and often. We must help kids learn to tell the difference *themselves*, so they no longer need adult arbiters. Ask and guide kids often enough and they will eventually internalize the difference. Asking a child *"Is that tattling or telling?"* puts the responsibility back on the child to reflect on both the seriousness of the problem and the underlying motivation behind the tattling or telling.

Yes it's slow and it's inefficient. The first 100 times you ask kids the difference they may need your help sorting the complexities. Just add it to the list of things that are inconvenient and inefficient about raising and teaching kids, guiding them into adulthood!

This raises a serious question: What "secrets" are OK to keep? It can be complicated – sometimes you need to get a kid *into*

---

[2]B Coloroso, *The Bully, The Bullied, And The Bystander* (Toronto: Harper Collins, 2002)

trouble to get him *out*. The line is not always clear and the decision not always easy. Today's "OK to keep" secret may transform into a malignant problem needing adult intervention next week. Choosing different language can help us here, too. Make a distinction between keeping someone's *privacy* [good] and keeping a *secret* [bad]. Even with clearer language, we need to be alert to the potential for harm, to ourselves or to others.

Think about Dawn-Marie Wesley, who killed herself after struggling to "handle" her tormentors without adult help, and Jesse Logan, whose sexting led to her suicide. Jesse kept most of the details of her torment at school and her increasing emotional pain from her mom. Kids and adults need to learn to keep watching these inherently unstable situations. If someone had "told" [not "tattled"], these tragedies might have been prevented. Don't wait for the crisis.

Let me be clear. While we certainly need to monitor, **most of all we need to not engage in the tormenting behavior in the first place**. It isn't enough to monitor a Dawn-Marie daily, to see if today is the day she can't take any more. **We need to know, inside us, when it is the wrong thing to do. This is about how we treat other human beings**. When you're thinking it might be "fun" to video your college roommate having sex and then post it to the Internet, your next thought **has to be**, "*But I won't do that because it would be wrong.*" Saying *"I had no idea he would be so upset he would kill himself by jumping off a bridge"* is clearly not nearly good enough.[3] As a backup, and until

---

[3]Associated Press, "Rutgers Students Mourn Classmate," WashingtonPost.com, Oct 1, 2010

everyone has internalized kinder boundaries, knowing when to call for adult help is a valuable safety skill.

Bullying vs. Conflict

Another stumbling block to bullying prevention is the commonly misunderstood distinction between bullying and conflict, and the frequent misapplication of conflict resolution tools or skills to solve a bullying problem. Put simply, **you cannot use conflict resolution tools to solve bullying problems**. It is, at best, ineffective. At worst, it can be explosive. Let's see how and why.

Again, the language we use is part of the problem. For a while, we were labeling everything a conflict. Now too many problems get a bullying label. We need to do a better job understanding the differences, so we can identify each one properly, and even more important, so we can choose the best tools to solve the problem.

Let's look at the key differences between bullying and conflict. We know that bullying is characterized by a persistent, one-way power imbalance, with the power in the hands of the bully, who has an underlying intent to harm the target. In contrast, **conflict is characterized as a difference between approximate equals**. The roles can reverse. One example of a simple conflict is a situation with a classroom that has one computer. Let's say that today Sean is on the computer and Amanda can't get on, even though she needs to finish her math challenge. It's a problem for Amanda today, but it's a problem that could reverse, if Amanda were to monopolize the computer for a long time tomorrow. It's a problem between approximate equals, although Sean temporarily has control of a resource that Amanda would like to use.

Conflicts are solved by some form of negotiation. Negotiation involves compromise, requiring each party to give up a little to arrive at a solution where everybody gets *most* of what they want, rather than everybody getting nothing or one person getting everything and everyone else left with nothing. For example, Amanda and Sean and their other classmates could work out a schedule, with fairness and some flexibility, giving everyone access.

The Danger Of "Let The Kids Work It Out"

Conflict resolution is a valuable skill for kids to learn. It's never too early to start developing the skills of problem solving and compromise. I highly support the idea of *"Let the kids work it out for themselves"* for conflicts, but it's **only after they have sufficient training and lots of experience that they *can* work it out by themselves. In too many cases kids are left on their own to work out problems that are beyond their maturity or ability.**

Training in conflict resolution skills begins with developing solution options. William Kreidler, one of the pioneers of kids' conflict resolution, developed a terrific chart that I have used in many classrooms, camps, and homes.[4] We reproduce it here:

---

[4] W Kreidler, *Teaching Conflict Resolution Through Children's Literature* (New York: Scholastic, 1994)

Problem Solving Choices

Build trust Work together Solve the problem Put it off Get help Skip it	Talk it out Listen to each other Share Take turns Compromise Make a peace offering Say *"I'm sorry"*

This chart works equally well with young and older kids. For younger kids, use fewer choices to get them started. Use pictures with words for preliterate children.

The goal is autonomy, not needing a parent or teacher to sort out every problem, but it takes time to train these skills. As with teaching teasing vs. taunting and tattling vs. telling, it *only* takes about 100 times, with adults walking the kids over to the chart and saying, *"Hmm, which choices would work best for this problem?"* before the kids can do it themselves. Unfortunately, I haven't found any shortcuts between the first time and the 101st, but it's worth it! One day you'll realize that the kids are walking themselves over to the chart to decide. Soon after, they won't need to see the chart.

As kids mature, they can delve more deeply into the reasons behind the conflict, analyzing the causes and the step-by-step dance between characters that builds or dismantles a conflict. The core techniques in our kids' drama curriculum emphasize learning how to construct and deconstruct conflicts, as kids learn to tell or write a story or create a play. Conflict makes life interesting!

The hidden agenda: While kids are learning the nuances of the interaction between their dramatic character and others, they are also increasing their ability to understand and handle conflict and complex interpersonal relationships in real life.

The only downside: Once kids have become encouragingly self-sufficient in identifying conflicts and solutions, they may be tempted to use those skills on everything! When you have a hammer, all the world looks like a nail. This simplistic approach can create problems. Let's see why it's important to distinguish between conflict and bullying.

Conflict Resolution Makes Bullying Problems Worse

"Let the kids work it out for themselves" is *never* a solution to a bullying problem. No matter how skilled the kids are at conflict resolution, negotiation and compromise are *not* solutions to bullying and will not protect a child from further attacks.

Here's the take-away: To ask a kid who is *always* on the bad side of the bully, who never has the power, and is always on the receiving end of trouble, what he's going to *give up* to make a situation work out is unjust and just plain wrong. Further, it clearly communicates to the target a deep adult misunderstanding of the dynamics and inequities of the bullying relationship. It implies that adults, however well-meaning, are not able to help the kids solve this problem. It gives a clear message to the bully too – that bullying is tolerated, and that it may be possible to get the target to give up *even more*, including his self-respect. This is the final straw for many weary targets. This is where they leave the school, club, or team, or even worse, take matters into their own hands and come back with guns blazing.

Conflict Or Bullying – Which Is It?

I was called into a school to help with an emergency bullying problem. [Schools don't seem to call me when everything's going fine!] A child on the softball field had chased another child, trying to hit him with a baseball bat. Needless to say, all the adults jumped to disarm the child with the bat. This seemed like a huge bullying issue. Now what to do?

It's easy and very tempting to "treat the emergency" in front of you, but if you jump to a solution too fast, you may miss the most important contributing factors. Be patient and look beyond the obvious. Sounds easy, but everyone wants a quick solution when one child's about to break another child's bones with a bat.

The background: Two teams were out on the playground, one playing soccer, one playing softball. The soccer ball kept crossing into the softball area [it was a small playground]. The softball kids asked three or four times for the soccer ball to stay on the soccer side. The last time the soccer ball came over, one of the softball players lost it. Unfortunately, he was also holding a bat at the time. Start the chase, cue the adults.

Here are some interesting questions:

- Where were the adults as this situation was building? Why did no adult intervene sooner?

- Why did the softball kids have to ask three or four times for courtesy from the soccer players? Why did the children not comply with repeat requests? Why could the kids not settle this amongst themselves, without the bat?

Did the kid with the bat need to work on self-control? Absolutely. **But the bigger problem and the only solution is for adults to do a better job monitoring the playground actively, and not leave kids too long in situations that test them beyond their ability to endure, beyond a child's level of emotional self-control. Catching these problems early preserves the option for a small correction.**

A final note on conflicts: Conflicts left unresolved over a long time can develop into one-way power differentials that become systemic bullying or just big, long-standing, intractable conflicts. If Sean *never* lets Amanda use the computer, he's crossed the line to bullying. Adults must invest the time to help kids develop conflict resolution skills, teach them the difference between bullying and conflict, give kids more precise language [and use it ourselves], and step in earlier and more often, to avert large problems of either type – bullying or conflict.

7

Bullying & Respect: The Key Connection

We keep circling back to respect. Respect is a foundational issue, especially for teens, who are, by definition, at a formative time for self-concept. We need a healthy balance of respect for self and respect for others. And while our focus is on children and teens, as with the rest of this book, most of our discussion of respect applies directly to adults too.

How Are Bullying And Respect Related?

One aspect of my bullying prevention work that has really inspired me has been my collaboration with high school girls through the Girls' Respect Groups program. These young women have contributed so much to the impact of our programs by sharing their own experiences with bullying – as bullies, targets, and bystanders. When adults hear, directly from kids' mouths, about the heartache, the damage, and the guilt that bullying can cause, adults get motivated to act.

The longer my team and I worked on bullying prevention, the more clearly we saw that underlying all bullying is a lack

of respect – for yourself and for others. Kids [and adults] with a strong sense of self-respect don't need to put others down. Kids who respect themselves don't seek the friendship of bullies. They will not stand by and watch others being bullied, either. Strongly anchored self-respect helps kids be resilient when other people act badly towards them. Nobody likes to be on the receiving end of unkind or unfair bad-mouthing, but a person with a robust sense of self-worth is more likely to let it roll off his or her back and less likely to feel the need to respond in kind, with words, fists, knives, or guns.

Inspired by understanding this connection, we dug further and began to focus our preventive efforts even earlier. How could we stabilize kids' self-respect at an earlier age? Later in this chapter, I'll tell you more about Girls' Respect Groups, a truly inspiring program these high school girls created to lend a helping hand to middle school girls. But first, let's talk about why respect is so important.

Respect: A Big And Underappreciated Life Influence

Respect drives many of life's important decisions. Respect influences the friends we choose. A teen with shaky self-respect will choose very different friends than a teen with strong self-respect. Parents often recognize when a child is surrounding herself with the "wrong" friends, but we misunderstand the cause and effect. We often ban the friends, thinking that if we remove the child from the "bad influence" her behavior will improve. The problem is much more than just the behavior, but because the behavior is the most visible thing, that's often where parents focus. Unfortunately, it's the child's *underlying lack of self-respect* that drives the friend selection in the first place.

Banning the friends usually results in the child sneaking around to see the friends, which creates two new, *genuinely dangerous* problems. Now my kid's lying to me and I don't know where she is when she goes out – a *really* serious safety issue. Equally bad, it creates the precedent of my teen lying to solve a conflict with me, which can create a cascade of other related problems. Frankly, the *least* problematic response my child will likely have to my banning her friends is for her to find an equally "bad" set of friends to replace them with. Back to Square One, and I *still* haven't done anything to stabilize her weak self-respect, which was the original problem.

Respect also influences how we approach school and work. Do we show up physically? Do we show up mentally? Do we approach school and work with an open, inquisitive spirit? Do we bring our best? The teen years are not always known for commitment to academic achievement, but a kid grounded in self-respect is much better equipped to focus and work harder to improve her skills and marks when needed. Even though my daughter's favorite "class" in grade 12 was her first period "spare" [no class], she rose to the occasion and improved her grades when she knew colleges were looking.

Respect influences the challenges we accept or avoid. Self-respect encompasses the strength to feel you're still worthwhile, even when you don't feel completely capable, knowledgeable, or confident. If our self-respect is small or shaky, we end up needing to stay within a very small comfort zone, and we're always trying to support and prop ourselves up. We need an endless amount of emotional propping up from other people in our lives too.

Lack of self-respect undermines our resilience. At every stage of life, we need resilience to help us bounce back from life's unexpected side trips and from our inevitable mistakes. Low self-esteem is a lifelong adult risk factor for depression, and depression is both a cause and an effect of lack of resilience.[1] Nathaniel Branden, a specialist in the psychology of self-esteem, calls positive self-esteem "the immune system of the spirit."[2]

Lack of self-respect limits your choices and can keep you living in a very small world. We can be unwilling to try new things – a new language, a new job, a hard biology class, a new romance, a new city – or lack the courage to break away from bad relationships or bad jobs. These things are hard enough to do even *with* solid self-respect. Our fear of looking different, uneducated, stupid, or awkward can keep us living inside a constrictingly small circle.

We may fail to notice a lack of self-respect in preteens or teens while they're still largely under adult supervision. But when they

---

[1] U Orth, RW Robins, KH Trzesniewski, J Maes, and M Schmitt, "Low Self-Esteem Is A Risk Factor For Depressive Symptoms From Young Adulthood To Old Age," *J Abnormal Psych*, 118(3), Aug, 2009

[2] N Branden, "Articles And Essays," NathanielBranden.com

step out into the real world as young men and women – into their first jobs and apartments, and life in college or university – look out. Remember the tsunami? The ability to make good decisions is so seriously compromised in these young adults with poor self-respect, they're not even aware of the damage they're inflicting on themselves. We've seen scary examples: a young woman at college made a porn movie of herself in her dorm room and posted it to the Internet. Then she showed it to friends when they dropped by, asking, *"Do you like it? Do I look good?"* She obviously had no idea about the emotional and potential physical danger she was putting herself in, or the long-term damage she was inflicting.

That's the problem that led to Tyler Clementi's death too: kids' lack of respect for themselves *and* for others. Kids who don't know the boundaries for the appropriate treatment of others aren't going to suddenly "get it" when they move into a college dorm with virtually no adult guidance. There's danger ahead – and they can't see it coming. In addition to the wrong and cruel-hearted way they treated Tyler Clementi, I'm sure the college kids who filmed him had no inkling how profoundly and irrevocably *their* lives would change in the instant following their bad decision.

Carry that sort of behavior forward a few years and there's *"Lack Of Self-Respect: Las Vegas."* The owner of the Bunny Ranch Brothel, a legal brothel near Las Vegas, boasts that 1,500 women a month apply to be prostitutes there; even more during the recent economic crisis. How have women so lost their way that so many consider prostitution to be a viable, even a desirable, career objective?[3]

I'm the middle-aged daughter of women who, just one generation ago, *fought so hard* to give women equality in our work and personal lives. The right to be treated with equity and respect, to have access to jobs, to be paid equally [still working on that one], to qualify for mortgages, to be treated with equality in our personal relationships. **It makes me heartsick to see North American young women**, who are largely unaware of the magnitude of the struggle that gave them the freedom they take for granted today, giving away all that hard-earned equity ["equity" in both the "equality" sense and in the real estate sense "owned and free from encumbrances"].

Today's young women get role model images from music videos, where half-naked women are men's accessories. **Girls and women need to be the central characters in their own lives, not background players in the lives of others. Boys and men need to have valuable, self-fulfilled lives, too, but not at the expense of women.** Strong self-respect helps you feel valuable in jobs and relationships, confident to grow into new skills as needed, and capable of recognizing when to say *"No."*

Self-Respect: What Is It?

Here are some essential elements of self-respect:

- I have a realistic sense of my strengths and weaknesses.

---

[3]Dennis Hof Interview, *Dean Blundell Show*, The Edge 102.1, Toronto: edge.ca, Jul 13, 2010

- I accept myself the way I am right now, with imperfections.

- I am entitled to be treated with respect, by myself and others, *just because I am a human being*.

- I feel worthy of respect from myself and others.

- My sense of self and self-respect are robust enough to withstand the bumps and bruises of life. I can fail a test, survive a relationship breakup, or receive other tough feedback without coming unglued. I take responsibility for my contribution to those outcomes. I know when I need to study more or do better – and I'm *still* a valuable human being.

- I feel and show respect for others. I care about fairness and equity for all, especially those with less capability or power.

- I feel worthwhile *without* needing outside approval. It's always nice when other people appreciate what you do and who you are, but it's not needed. Neither kid nor adult behavior should be driven by needing the approval of others.

- I feel worthwhile *even [and especially]* in the face of mistakes, shortcomings, and challenges that reveal my lack of knowledge, experience, or ability in certain areas.

- I apologize genuinely and quickly when I hurt someone.

- I don't bolster my own self-respect at the expense of others, nor do I flaunt my physical beauty, intelligence, toughness, money, or material goods to "prove" to others [or myself] that I am valuable.

- I can earn additional respect or regard for my additional accomplishments – if I learn, share, create, or build something.

- My self-respect helps me to know when to stop chasing relationships that aren't working, when people are treating me disrespectfully, and when the personal cost of the compromise required to maintain a relationship is too high. [Hmmm, good adult lesson too.]

- Even though I am happy with who I am and accept myself as I am today, I still want to learn, grow, and change.

Self-respect based on these principles is a strong scaffold on which a child can build a sense of **competence and confidence** over time. Competence and confidence reinforce self-respect, and they come from **experience** – the opportunity to have *many* occasions to build things, do things, learn things, help others, overcome obstacles, redo things that didn't go so well the first time, to try new things under the watchful eyes of adults, and later on one's own. Confidence and competence come from having both the technical skills *and* the emotional skills to handle the stress of finding ourselves in uncharted or challenging territory. **There is no substitute or shortcut for building one's own competence and confidence directly, and although the encouragement of others is always welcome and valuable, it is no substitute for life experience.**

When our children are learning to walk, we can encourage them to be brave or fearful, to persist despite the inevitable bumps and falls, or to give up and just wrap themselves with more padding and insulation after each fall. We cannot, however, walk for our children or convince them that walking is a skill that they don't need.

Contained in this simple example is the basic template we can apply to the entire range of complex skills our kids need to develop – physical, intellectual, and emotional – in order to become capable, caring, happy, connected, independent adults. **We need to provide safe[ish] opportunities for kids to practice, encourage them, show them how to protect themselves when we're not there, and teach them how to learn from and not get disabled by mistakes.**

Sometimes it's the *parent* who gets disabled – or overly fearful – when a child makes a mistake. It's a reflexive tendency to protect a kid so he doesn't make the same mistake again. That's where a parent's overreaction can become a child's disability. There are many times, especially as parents of teens, when we have to help our children learn what they need to learn from mistakes or insist that they make repairs, then hold our breath while we make the space for them to venture out and *possibly make that same mistake again.* Ugh. Add *that* to the list of "Things I Wish I Had Known Were In Store *Before* I Decided To Become A Parent"!

Life sometimes presents us with extra obstacles. Kids can have physical, emotional, or learning disabilities that make "learning to walk" much more of a challenge, either literally or metaphorically. That's a real challenge for adults coaching kids, with or without disabilities, and builds on the previous point: How do we [as parents, teachers, coaches, etc] balance our own desire to protect, ease, and insulate with our children's need to accomplish as much as they can on their own, to build resilience and resourcefulness?

Whatever the child's native ability, adults can disable a child by protecting him too much from the physical and emotional challenges of the real world. In life we *all* have strengths and weaknesses, more or less apparent, and we all need to work to develop our skills to reach our highest potential. Frankly, we almost never get rid of our weaknesses. We must learn both to play to our strengths and *manage* our weaknesses.

Self-Respect? Self-Esteem? What's The Difference?

Disentangling self-respect from self-esteem can be tricky. The terms are often used synonymously.[4] To eliminate confusion and nit-picking, let's consider them to be interchangeable, congruent concepts. I'll use "respect" and "self-respect" for our discussion, with one exception, in the next paragraph.

Well-Meaning Adults Can Erode Kids' Self-Respect

For more than a decade, adults have been overly focused on propping up kids' self-esteem, with some downsides we hadn't expected. I use "self-esteem" here because it's commonly used in this context. Adults overpraise kids for insignificant

---

[4]Merriam-Webster.com

contributions, or for doing things that are the bare minimum expected, falsely thinking they're building self-esteem. *"Sean, you're breathing so well today. That's just awesome." "Sandra, it's so great that you didn't hit your sister all day yesterday."* Then we fail to applaud accomplishments that *really* required a lot of work [academic, physical, or emotional] or showed a lot of improvement. We also focus too heavily on school and sports achievement and too little on the development of kids' emotional skills and care and concern for others.

Finding the right balance can be difficult. We *do* want to be interested and appreciative of the effort kids put into their first art attempts. We *are* grateful when kids learn to make their beds or help us clean up in the kitchen. And we're truly thankful when a kid *doesn't* hit her sister! But let's not overdo it. Save the big kudos for the big accomplishments.

Just to be clear, we *should* thank a child who contributes to the everyday work of running the house, but everyone in the house should be *expected* to contribute to that work. A quick *"Thanks, that was a big help"* is enough recognition. Fawning all over a kid for emptying the dishwasher or folding some clothes doesn't build self-respect. What it often means is that we're not asking our kids to help out with housework enough, and we, as parents, end up being *too* grateful for little things. We've all been in that situation, but don't confuse that with building self-respect.

There can be complex challenges to nurturing a child's self-respect. A kid who is profoundly discouraged by struggling academically at school needs skillful handling by all the adults around him. The lack of self-respect can be both a cause and a result of the school issues. We must beware of shovelling useless praise at kids who know they did nothing special, or even worse, telling kids they're doing great or OK when they're clearly not. [Yelling makes it worse. Obvious, but often used by frustrated parents.]

Social promotion, passing kids who are failing in school to the next grade, is a misguided attempt to preserve a kid's self-respect. Passing a kid who's struggling just gives you a kid who's even *less* prepared for the next academic level, and will struggle even more to meet the increased challenges. We can get a much better result when we identify a kid who's having difficulty and say, *"Hey, I can see you're really struggling. Do you know why or can we help you find out? Can we help you get the support you need to pull yourself up?"* And then actually give that child the close supervision, support, and retraining he or she needs to close those learning gaps and proceed to the next grade.

Many studies of social promotion have focused on picking the "better" of two bad alternatives: (1) fail the child, without providing individualized help to fix the deficit and meet the educational goal or (2) promote the child, again without providing close, individualized support. There is a third option. **Repair the deficit. Catching the child early is key – before too much damage has been done to the child's self-respect** and we're facing the uphill struggle of *also* restoring their curiosity about learning and their willingness to reengage. That's a much harder job than "just" building stronger math skills. Intervene when there's only one deficit, not three.

Wouldn't a kid feel happy and proud to know *"Wow, I was really messing up in school, but people came to help me. I worked hard, I pulled myself up, and I passed 10th grade!"* [Even if it took an extra year.] Isn't that a much more valuable, enduring lesson in tenacity and resilience for that child? That's the kind of experience that prepares him to face similar challenges in the future, academic or not, with self-confidence and determination, based on a history of overcoming obstacles – because he took responsibility and dug deep when times were tough? The ability to look yourself squarely in the eye and say, *"I made a mistake. I can do better."* And then do so. **That's a mature kid showing self-respect in action.**

It's also useful for kids to see early videos of their heroes, to see how expert singers, athletes, or other role models developed their skills through practice, hard work, study, and determination. Kids think hockey and figure skating heroes were born with blades on their feet, hat trick-ing and triple Lutz-ing as soon as they could walk. Watch their practice tapes and you'll see how much time they spent falling on their butts. Kids need to know that excellence and accomplishment come with work.

Self-respect comes from within ourselves much more than from the outside. Adults should watch for opportunities to involve kids in situations and activities that *genuinely* challenge them to grow and contribute, building competence, confidence, and self-respect the old fashioned way – with hard work.

Avoiding Self-Respect Inflation

Kids know what's good and what's not, when they've tried their hardest or when they've only performed with mediocre effort. We're not fooling them when we over-praise them for inconsequential or minor accomplishments. There are several unintended negative consequences to adults over-praising kids:

- **Excessive praise devalues the *real* work that kids do.**

- **Excessive praise leads a child to distrust the words of the praiser.** When a child really does something remarkable, the child thinks *"Last time she told me that folding my socks was fabulous. How do I compare my National Merit Scholarship or Ontario Scholar designation to that?"*

- **Excessive praise weakens the child's own internal ability to perform accurate self-assessment.** *"Did I or did I not just do something great?"* Kids need to know, by themselves, when they've done their best job. Sometimes you're the only person who pats yourself on the back for a job well done – and that should be all we need.

We all can benefit from realistic feedback on our skills and performance and some guidance about where we need to grow. That's called teaching and learning – and it happens in school, work, and life. It's a *good* thing. In real life, we all get messages, perhaps too frequently for comfort, telling us that our current skills either are or *are not* good enough for our current environment, job, or situation. We get those messages about all of our life skills – study skills, sports skills, social skills, management skills [time or people], emotional skills, and stress-handling skills, to name a few.

The message *"You need to improve and do better,"* though painful to receive, is very valuable. It opens the door to the opportunity to work with experts, mentors, and peers who can teach and guide us to the next level of expertise. Much of human evolution and experience is built on the good fortune of having the people who went before us turn around and offer us a helping hand. That's why the denigrating, disdainful, humiliating feedback seen in "American Idol," "Survivor," "The Apprentice," and other "let it all hang out" reality shows is so damaging, in ways that I fear we don't yet fully appreciate.

The Preteen And Teen Years: Disrespect Overload

Being a preteen or teen is tremendously destabilizing – physical, social, and emotional factors combine in a triple negative of self-respect erosion. When you really look, with adult eyes, at the enormous level of disrespect levelled at teens from the outside, it's no wonder they struggle with self-respect. Kids whose sense of self-respect is unstable are easy targets for bullies and other misadventures in life.

Self-esteem drops for both boys and girls in adolescence, starting from equal levels at age nine. Self-esteem for girls, however, plummets twice as far as for boys.[5] Here are some of the influences undermining our teens' sense of self:

---

[5] R Robins & K Trzesniewski, "Self-Esteem Development Across The Lifespan," *Current Directions In Psychological Science*, 14(3), Jun, 2005

- **Middle school is the peak of bullying**, especially relational bullying, undermining friendships and confidence.

- **Peer conformance pressure is at its peak**. Kids' main objective through middle school is *"Don't stand out!"* It's hard to be self-confident when you're always looking on either side of you to make sure you don't step out of line. And the line can be very harsh and unforgiving.

Mean Girls, a 2004 "comedy" about high school girls' cliques and "friendships," has a lunchroom scene where one of "The Plastics" [Remember the real-life "Populars"? Not making it up!] tells Lindsay Lohan's character, new to the school and eager to fit in, *"You can't wear a tank top two days in a row, you can only wear your hair in a ponytail once a week, and you can only wear jeans on Friday. And we always ask the other girls before we invite someone to join us at lunch. I mean, you wouldn't buy a skirt without asking your friends if it looks good on you, right?"* to which clueless Lindsay says, *"You wouldn't??"*[6] She quickly learns the rules of "Girls' World."

And while you might think that's "just" a movie, real life in Girls' World is shockingly similar. A 15-year-old girl in Surrey, England, lost her standing in her group overnight by not wearing a skirt on the designated day. *"They haven't spoken to me since, even though one in particular has been my best friend since primary school."*[7]

In a case of life imitating heartless art, "Burn Books" from *Mean Girls*, in which girls write mean things about other girls in their class or school, started popping up in many

---

[6]*Mean Girls*, Director: M Waters, Paramount Pictures, 2004
[7]A Hill and E Helmore, "Mean Girls," *The Observer,* Guardian.co.uk, Mar 3, 2002

middle schools after the movie was released.[8] There are literally step-by-step instructions on the Internet for how to make your own Burn Book, complete with suggestions for how to lie if your parents or teachers find it: *"Have a cover plan if you're caught. Say that you found it and were going to hand it in to the school or something plausible like that. A good way to make this even more believable is putting an entry for yourself in the book. Just don't make the handwriting recognizable."*[9] On the day I saw that entry on the Internet, 109,000 people had read it before me.

- **Girls lose interest and confidence in math**. After 30 years of building girls' math skills, girls and boys now demonstrate equal math abilities.[10] Nonetheless, adults are still steering girls away from math and math-intensive disciplines, and girls are living down to our expectations.

- **The teen years are full of conflicting, hypersexualized, and unrealistic body image issues**. As family physician Leonard Sax said, *"Girls are losing what psychologists used to call middle childhood: eight to 12 years of age, the age of Pippi Longstocking and Harriet the Spy, the time for girls to have adventures and develop a sense of who they are as people without worrying whether they're hot."*[11] Young boys feel the pressure too, the need to develop six-pack abs, leading to rising rates of boys' eating disorders and anabolic steroid use.[12]

- **The media showcase impossible goals for perfection, for boys and girls**. Dove Soap started its *"Campaign For*

---

[8]M Varadi, "Kids Have To Watch Their Backs," *Toronto Star*, Jul 17, 2004

[9]"How To Create A Burn Book," wikiHow.com

[10]J Hyde, S Lindberg, M Linn, A Ellis, and C Williams, "Gender Similarities Characterize Math Performance," *Science*, 321(5888), Jul, 2008

[11]K Fillion, "Inside The Dangerously Empty Lives Of Teenage Girls," Macleans.ca, May 3, 2010

[12]S Boodman, "Eating Disorders: Not Just For Women," WashingtonPost.com, Mar 13, 2007

Real Beauty" in 2004 to enlarge our narrow, stereotypical view of women's beauty.[13] Dove highlighted some of the problems in *Evolution*, a one-minute video showing a fresh-faced teen model, with acne, arriving at a studio to get prepped for a photo shoot. In fast-forward mode, dozens of people hover over her, doing hair and make-up, transforming her into a perfect Glamazon with wind-swept hair and flawless skin.

That's just the beginning. Her photo then goes to Photoshop, where her lips are made fuller, her eyes bigger and wider set, her eyebrows more arched, and her neck slimmer and longer. Then you see that super-retouched photo on a city street billboard. And we wonder why girls and boys have an unrealistic view of beauty??!

As an aside, Photoshop is an amazing and powerful piece of photo editing software. It needs to be used with its own set of limits and boundaries.

- **Teen clothing – baby girl or hooker? Thug life or squeaky clean? Shopping for teen clothing is a minefield – for parents and teens. There is far too much overly and overtly sexualized clothing for boys and girls**. Thongs for preteens, padded push-up bras for 10-year-olds, underwear showing through and over your clothes, for boys and girls, half-naked girls as accessories in music videos. How's a self-respecting teen to balance being fashionable without looking like a prostitute or a thug? And how to pick boyfriends or girlfriends that don't look like prostitutes or thugs?

- **Those confusing, often unrealistic external images are superimposed on the naturally occurring body**

---

[13]CampaignForRealBeauty.com

confusion that comes with the teen years. Teen bodies change so rapidly that it's hard to tell what you look like or what looks good on you from moment to moment. As an adult, think how you would feel if every month you were a different size – taller, heavier, arms longer, legs longer, hips wider, chest or breasts bigger, feet bigger. How could you possibly have a strong sense of your body image? It's crazy-making.

As an adult, I can go into a clothing store and have a reasonable idea which clothing would look good on me, even without trying it on. If I had to reevaluate that image every month, I think I'd go nuts. It's not all negative – it's also very exciting and fun to suddenly be adult-sized and have a whole new world of clothing options open to you. I didn't think about it that way when I was that age, but from an adult perspective, I have a lot more empathy for the confusion and the destabilizing process teens go through.

- **Adults Frequently Treat Teens With Disrespect**. Been in a store with teens recently? How were they treated? There's a grocery store near my house, across the street from both a middle school and a high school. For a while, there were signs on the doors: *"No more than four students at a time in the store,"* then *"No students at lunchtime or after school."* Nice.

  Do kids need to be taught manners and supervised until they are able to act appropriately in public places? Yup – kids are usually much better behaved when they're eight than when they're 15! There is some backsliding, but a little extra adult supervision, clearly expressing our expectations, and adult follow-through go a long way towards helping kids behave in ways that garner respect from others – which becomes self-perpetuating.

We need to treat kids with more respect, *especially* when they're struggling to act appropriately. Would you behave better towards the person who sneers and growls at you or the person who looks you in the eye, thanks you for your business, and wishes you a nice day? Wouldn't you feel just a little guilty if someone treated you decently and respectfully, when you *didn't* fully deserve it? **That's the kind of inner turmoil you want to create inside kids, the grain of sand that produces a pearl from the oyster.**

Here's where parents and schools can step in to solve a problem. Working with local merchants, parents and teachers can show up in stores, at lunch and after school, insisting on and guiding kids to appropriate behavior. The ability to conduct yourself appropriately in public is a skill every bit as valuable as math. Teens should be *encouraged* to go into stores and learn the skills of appropriate behavior, with adults there to provide the visual reminder, *"Yup, we're watching"* [with a smile, please]. People live up or down to our expectations. There should be consequences for mistakes, but we should set our standards high, make them clear, and keep expressing our expectations and optimism that our kids will grow into them.

Convenient? No. But failing to give guidance, set limits, and teach when it's needed only makes the problem worse. Pay now or pay later. Adults can't be everywhere. If we invest the time to teach and train early, we won't need to do so much monitoring and punishing later. Our goal is to help kids internalize their own standards for appropriate behaviour.

Every school, home, and community has different strengths and different problems. Pick your own problems and work on them. We need to reopen our eyes and our hearts to the many simple solutions that have always been right in front of us. Fix the problem while it's easy.

Kids' Self-Respect: Lack Of Adult Guidance

It is NOT easy guiding preteens and teens into adulthood – especially because they are often so unwilling to seek guidance from or be guided by adults at this time. They know they still need you and they hate that they still need you, even though they still love you [very deep down]. Parents and teachers of teens suffer through many unpleasant moments. Teens also suffer through those unpleasant moments, even though they'd rather have a tooth pulled than admit to an adult that they're suffering too. Teen angst is often expressed in a conflict-seeking, combative manner intended to keep adults at arm's length. Ironically, at the time they most need a hug and someone who loves them to stroke their head, they are the most unapproachable. It's like trying to love and hug a porcupine.

Unfortunately, when the going gets tough in the teen years, many adults, both parents and teachers, pull back and pull away from kids, just when they need the love and attention the most. And while I'm not advocating staying in abusive relationships, with your teen or anyone else, it's a real challenge to persist in playing a parental or guiding role to someone who is actively discouraging you. But like it or not, easy or not, that's a parent's job, even though I didn't fully realize that was in the job description when I signed up. [Who did?]

I often felt, during my daughter's teen years [and I could be wrong], that she thought that if she was snarly enough every time my husband or I asked her to do the dishes, even when she knew it was her turn, she hoped we would eventually stop asking and leave her dish-free. It was irritating and frustrating to try to figure out how to get her to contribute, and I'm sure it was irritating and frustrating to her when we asked and insisted [also known as nagging, no matter how polite we tried to be]. Frankly, it would have been much easier to do the dishes ourselves.

While my method in that instance may have been clumsy or faulty, along with many other things I could have done better as a parent, I offer it as a simple example of the very complex dance that we frequently do with our kids. Often when they most seem not to want us, they really need us. Part of our job as adults is to insist that kids contribute to the greater good and to set boundaries on their behavior, even when they'd rather we left them alone and it's certainly easier, in the short term, to do so. The goal of raising an adult who has strong self-esteem AND contributes to the lives of others is worth the friction.

Here are some surprising stories of bad adult choices and lack of adult guidance:

- **Parents Lying To Win**. To help her 6-year-old daughter win Hannah Montana concert tickets, a mother "helped" her write an essay saying that the child's father had died in Iraq. Fortunately [or unfortunately, not sure which way this one goes], he hadn't. The mom said, *"We did the* *essay, and that's what we did to win ... We did whatever we could to win."[14]*

This was *not* an instance of lying or stealing because your kid needs chemotherapy that you can't afford – this was for *Hannah Montana tickets*!!! When an adult is willing to stoop to this level for two Hannah Montana tickets, what is she teaching her kid? And while this seems particularly egregious, we have all had our own equivalents, times when we had opportunities and incentives to shave the truth or conveniently look the other way. Problem is, our kids are watching, and especially in the teen years, they are sensitive to issues of justice, fairness, and truth [even if they don't always act that way]. Parenthood and working with kids present many opportunities to re-examine our own principles and the consistency with which we adhere to them.

- **Clothing Wars – Part 1**. Teens, parents, and schools often clash over standards for dress, both in school and out. It has always been a tough job for parents – every generation of kids pushes the envelope for dress, music, and risky behavior. As adults, we are well prepared to guide our kids through the time period *we* grew up in, and not nearly as comfortable or capable guiding our kids through the challenges of *today's* teen minefield.

  The way we dress communicates how we feel about ourselves to the world. Teaching kids to dress appropriately is another part of a parent's job, but there are a lot of parents ignoring or outsourcing their responsibility.

  To avoid conflict, parents are increasingly giving their teens complete decision-making control for clothing

---

[14]Quotations, *Time Magazine*, Jan 14, 2007

choices. Parents are also hiring professional image consultants to teach their teen girls to dress appropriately.[15] While the skills of a make-up artist or an experienced friend can help a teen learn how to apply make-up skillfully, in shades and amounts that suit her, parents shouldn't abdicate all responsibility for teaching kids how to dress.

Parents belong in the "war zone" of the clothing store dressing room with their preteen kids. Many a nuclear explosion has erupted in dressing rooms as we taught our kids how to buy jeans – not too tight [or baggy], not too low, no butt cleavage or underwear showing, squat down to test, etc. [Nag #78 on "Mom's Greatest Hits."]

Then we back off and let them buy jeans on their own, clearly stating that any jeans that fail the appropriate dress test must be returned. Expect a few mistakes and set your return policy. [Who pays if the jeans can't be returned? Hint: Make sure you *can* return the clothes! Who takes the jeans back to the store? If you haven't discussed it, the parent takes the first hit. Future mistakes are out of the child's pocket and time.] Don't forget the discussion about shirts [How low? How short? How tight? How thin?], pants, dress clothes, and dressing for hanging with friends vs. visiting Grandma.

- **Clothing Wars – Part 2.** Making the most-viewed list on YouTube in May 2010 was a video of seven-year-old girls competing at the World of Dance Competition, dressed in lingerie and dancing to Beyoncé's "Single Ladies," complete with booty shaking and crotch grinding. Seven-year-old girls. These girls were all extremely talented dancers for their age, but where was the adult guidance in

---

[15]C Alter, "The Minor Makeover," *Washington Post,* WashingtonPost.com, Jul 11, 2009

deciding whether their costumes were too revealing or their dance moves too sexy or age-inappropriate?[16]

- **Clothing Wars – Part 3.** Thong underwear for elementary school girls? Abercrombie & Fitch thought it was a great idea in 2002. When you're 10 years old, your butt belongs in your underwear, not in a thong with the words *"eye candy"* on it.[17] Endlessly creative, A&F introduced push-up bikini tops for eight-year-olds in 2011. Are you kidding??

- **Makeup For Babies?** Walmart recently introduced anti-aging cosmetics for eight to 12-year-old girls.[18] Just stop.

Adults are unwittingly guiding kids towards sex too early, pushing them prematurely out of childhood into adulthood, teaching them that they and their bodies aren't good enough without padding, makeup, and 6-pack abs.

There is hope. Even when the adults have little sense, sometimes kids step in to fill the gap. Heidi Medina, cheerleading captain of Central High School in Bridgeport, CT, went to the Bridgeport Board of Education to say that their cheerleading uniforms were too skimpy, revealing the cheerleaders' midriffs even when their arms were at their sides. *"I am embarrassed to stand up here dressed like this. Is this really how you want Bridgeport to be represented?"*[19] Thank you, Heidi. Here's hoping we'll catch up soon. Wait for us.

---

[16] J Berman and S Netter, "Young Girls' 'Single Ladies' Dance Sparks Controversy On Internet," ABCNews.go.com, May 14, 2010

[17] J Robinson, "Abercrombie & Fitch Catches Heat For Preteen Thongs," *Minneapolis Star Tribune,* StarTribune.com, Jun 18, 2002

[18] "Walmart's 'Anti-Aging' Makeup For 8-Year-Old Girls," Yahoo.com, Jan 27, 2011

[19] C Smith, "Connecticut Cheerleaders Want Uniforms With More Coverage," ca.Sports.Yahoo.com, Oct 5, 2010

Dating And Self-Respect: Older Kids, Bigger Problems

The problems of poor self-respect and failure to set appropriate boundaries show up very clearly in the growing epidemic of dating violence. In 2008, the Liz Claiborne Foundation's study of Tween & Teen Dating Abuse revealed that among kids *11-14 years old*, 62% felt they had friends who were in verbally abusive relationships. Among kids *ages 13-14 years old,* 20% said they had friends in *physically abusive relationships.*[20] That is a bad way to start off your dating years. If you already accept, at ages 11-14, that it's not unusual for you or your friends to be in abusive relationships, it substantially ups the odds that you will end up there.

Premature focus on dating and sex is another area crying out for adult guidance. We need to rethink whether it's even appropriate for 11-year-olds to *be* in dating relationships. There is way too much and too early of a preoccupation with "dating" – too early a focus on romantic partners before kids are emotionally ready. While younger kids have always hungered to be older, scanning for info on the adult world by eavesdropping on the activities and conversations of older siblings, surprisingly, much precocious behaviour in *today's* kids is prompted by *adults*. Today's parents unthinkingly allow kids to dress and act in inappropriately "mature" ways. It is **not** "cute" to have "Juicy" written on the butt of a four-year-old or adorable that a six-year-old is wondering who her "boyfriend" will be for Valentine's Day

---

[20]Teenage Research Unlimited, "Liz Claiborne Inc And National Teen Dating Abuse Helpline Study On Tween & Teen Dating Abuse,"LoveIsNotAbuse.com, Feb, 2008

in grade 1. Please think and please stop. Kids need *friends* in grade 1, not boyfriends or dates.

Precocious preoccupation with romance and sex can lead kids down dangerous roads which they are ill-prepared to navigate safely. Not only is there a huge loss of childhood, but 11-year-olds do not have the emotional maturity or life experience to handle the intensity of one-on-one romantic or sexual relationships. Even more dismaying to adults is the emerging trend towards casual, relationship-free "hook ups" for preteens and teens. It's not a new development for 11-year-olds to be interested in romance, but in the past, "romance" for 11-year-olds did not include blow jobs.[21]

The alarming casualness with which today's teens and young adults often approach sexual encounters is very worrisome, for both girls and boys [and the people who love them]. We are hearing of teen girls having multiple sex partners in a single evening, often in public view, at a party. Oral sex for all the guys at a party [Google "chicken party"]. Remember the young woman mentioned earlier who made her own sex video, then posted it online and showed it to her friends and acquaintances? Some girls may think of that as sexual self-empowerment. *That's not sexual empowerment – it's self-imposed sexual **slavery**, the complete opposite.* At some point in their lives, those girls will understand what they've done and pay the price for treating themselves with so

---

[21]L Duberstein Lindberg, R Jones, J Santelli, "Non-Coital Sexual Activities Among Adolescents," *J Adolescent Health,* 43(3), Sep, 2008

little respect and value – they've given away their own power and have betrayed themselves.

The news isn't any better for young men. While at first it may seem that the availability of no-strings-attached sex is a dream come true, there's a price to be paid. Easy access to online pornography is disabling young men from having emotionally committed relationships with real women who aren't porn actors. Some of the early research on this is starting to appear, but we don't need to wait for the long-term studies to know that this is a big downstream problem in the making.

With so much emphasis on sex and sexuality, our kids are in danger of thinking there's nothing else about them that's important. They're so focused on developing their sexual personae, that they're neglecting the rest of what makes humans unique, valuable, and admirable.

As a parent, I know that someday my child will decide to be intimate with another person. I am not going to be there to tell her whether this is the right time for her, or whether she has chosen the right partner. It will be her decision, as it should be. But what I *can* do, as a parent, is to help her have the strength and self-knowledge to know that she is not a party favor and her body is not a party favor, to be handed out casually. I can help her understand that she should look for a partner who is loving and supportive, who cares about her as a human being, who makes her world bigger, not smaller, who looks out for and protects her, and that she should feel that same way about her partner.

Begin this discussion early, even if it seems impossible to believe that your child might be considering sexual activity. No matter how young your child is, it's almost guaranteed that her peer group includes kids who are sexually active. Although your child might be a bit too young to understand the full import of this discussion [you'd be surprised], you'll be opening a window of inquiry in her head. She needs to know what's right for her and have a chance to think **before** she gets in "the impact zone." She'll think about this repeatedly, each time with more maturity, as she approaches readiness for an emotional commitment. Boys also need parental guidance to view their bodies and their relationships with respect.

If you don't know where to begin, you and your teen can both read [separate copies of] a book girls love, and that inspired the creation of the Girls' Respect Groups program. *Respect: A Girl's Guide To Getting Respect & Dealing When Your Line Is Crossed*, by Courtney Macavinta and Andrea Vander Pluym, is a book that every girl, every parent and teacher of a girl, every boy related to a girl, and every boy who'd like to be a friend or boyfriend to a girl [think that covers it] should read. In a fun, lively way, Macavinta and Vander Pluym help girls think about how to build friendships and later romances, based on respect, and how to fix, if possible, relationships where respect is lacking. Your girl will be able to use these important ideas as a standard against which possible relationships can be measured.

Girls' Respect Groups affect boys, too. Girls grounded in self-respect demand respectful treatment from the boys around them. Boys who read the **Respect** and **Girls' Respect Groups** books will gain insight into the challenges that teen girls face and have a better understanding of how to build friendships and romances, in that order, anchored in mutual respect.

Similarly, supportive books and programs for teen boys are valuable to both boys and girls. BAM! [Boys Advocacy and Mentoring, BAMGroups.com] and the Boys To Men mentoring program in the Toronto District School Board are examples of programs that are anchoring for boys and educational to girls.

Dating Violence: Danger Ahead

For kids not grounded in their own sense of self-worth, there are even bigger problems looming when they enter serious, adult-style relationships in their late teens and early 20s. In one high-profile case, popular and well-known singer Chris Brown, 19, beat up his girlfriend, equally popular and well-known singer Rihanna, also 19 at the time.[22] Let's look at this situation through a self-respect lens.

Abusive relationships, especially relationships with physical abuse, do not start out that way. It's a slippery slope of increasingly bad behavior, sometimes by both parties. Abusive romantic relationships are one kind of adult bullying relationship, building over time, and increasing in severity. Many factors contribute to

---

[22]"Brown's Alleged Victim Was Girlfriend Rihanna," *CNN,* CNN.com, Feb 09, 2009

abusive relationships and this is not intended to be a comprehensive discussion of the scope of the problem. Rather, it is an effort to identify and single out the aspects of dating violence that are related to poor self-respect and to bullying.

Why did Rihanna not get out sooner? How and why did she not recognize the warning signs? Didn't her friends see it? Her family? After the beating, why didn't she cut all ties to Brown? Even after pictures of her bruised face were all over online and traditional media worldwide, Rihanna supposedly went back to Brown briefly, ostensibly at the urging of friends. [Side note: Who leaked the pictures of a 19-year-old at the lowest moment of her life? Shame on you.]

A woman in an abusive relationship has many problems and weaknesses – and right up near the top of the list is damaged self-respect. Why do you stay in a relationship where someone treats you so badly? Why do you think you're not worthy of peace and safety?

Equally problematic and equally shaky is the self-respect of the abusing man. A man whose self-respect is strong doesn't beat up women, or anyone else, no matter the perceived challenge or provocation. He is strong enough to not let himself get pulled off-center or lose his cool, even when someone's bugging him or behaving badly.

Here's what's so interesting about this from a self-respect perspective. By anyone's standards, both Rihanna and Chris Brown should be pretty high on the self-respect scales, given what both have accomplished in their very short lives. Rihanna had developed a stunning amount of adult competence by age 19. She had taught herself to sing and dance well enough to be paid [a lot] to perform. She'd acquired the stage presence and technical expertise to perform in front of tens of thousands of people, millions when televised. Think about the hours of practice needed to become competent and comfortable doing just that. In addition, she had learned how to record CDs, how to work in a professional music studio with other professional musicians, how to hire agents, publicists, assistants, and stylists, maybe how to buy a house and a car. She should have been able to look around, survey herself and her 19-year-old life with a lot of satisfaction, and think *"Wow, look how much I've learned and done! I'm not done yet, but damn, I'm good!"*

And yet, despite her extraordinary accomplishments in so many areas, this young woman suffered from shaky self-respect. **The message: even accomplished, capable women [and men] can lack self-respect and the result can be catastrophic.**

The Rihanna situation, being so public, has some interesting, additional twists. Without proper adult conversation around the topic, teen girls could take away the idea that dating violence is to be expected and accepted. *"If it happens to Rihanna, it must be OK if it happens to me."* This dangerous message was reinforced when Rihanna went back to the relationship.

Yet Rihanna dug deep, ended the relationship, and after a period of seclusion, talked on national TV about the pain and the personal growth she'd experienced.[23] She had felt moved by the opportunity to stand as an example to her fans – many of whom are girls and young women – to speak out about the dangers and risks of dating violence. That took a lot of maturity and guts.

Adults can support kids as they get ready for healthy romantic relationships by starting early to ground boys and girls in self-respect and respect for others. We can help kids learn the positive skills of building friendships first, and delaying romantic relationships until they're more emotionally ready [age 60?]. When kids start romantic relationships, in their mid-teens, adults can help them learn the skills and self-discipline to treat one another kindly and with respect during breakups.

We can teach kids to recognize the warning signs of an abusive relationship. *"No, 60 phone calls and text messages a day is not cute. It's needy, controlling, and possibly leading to something much worse. Get out!"* We can give them safe people and places to go to when they need to exit a relationship. If you think it's hard for a child to admit she has a 6th grade bullying problem and needs adult help, it's even harder for a young woman to admit to her friends or parents she's having serious problems in an adult romantic relationship.

As I was writing this book in May 2010, we learned of the shocking, violent beating and murder of 22-year-old University of Virginia student Yeardley Love by her boyfriend George Huguely,

---

[23]D Sawyer, "20/20: Rihanna Speaks Out In Exclusive Interview," ABCNews.go.com, Nov 5, 2009

also a 22-year-old UVA senior. Huguely and Love had been in an abusive relationship for at least a year, fuelled by his rage and drinking problems, which were widely known to their friends and lacrosse teammates. He reportedly yelled at her frequently, called her dozens of times a day, and blamed her for his problems.[24] Friends described him as out of control and violent when drinking.

How could she have missed the warning signs? Why did she stay in the relationship? Why didn't their friends and family speak up, to either or both of them? When you put yourself on this road, how do you know what day is the day the Chekhov gun on the wall gets used?

Girls' Respect Groups: Girls Helping Girls

It's not all bleak – there's some good news. While there always has been and always will be some experimentation, angst, and instability during the teen years, there are also encouraging and inspiring ways to keep kids more connected and grounded. Earlier in this chapter, I talked about working with high school girls. One team of girls I worked with was keenly focused on finding ways to help middle school girls get through the anguish of the middle school years.

Together we created **Girls' Respect Groups**, an after-school program for middle school girls that is led by high school girls. GRG puts middle school girls directly in contact with teen girls –

---

[24]A Canning, E Friedman, and S Netter, "University Of Virginia Murder Suspect George Huguely Had History Of Violence," ABCNews.go.com, May 6, 2010

the people they most want to talk to, listen to, and be like. These kind-hearted high school girls share their experiences and offer a helping hand through the rough spots of middle school. It's **Girls Helping Girls** in action, bringing out the best in both groups of young women. Learn more at **GirlsRespectGroups.com**.

Girls' Respect Groups is just one example of programs which support kids through a difficult period of change. It's not about using any particular program, or using my program, or reading the right book. It's about clearly demonstrating to kids that we value respect. We can create places where adults, teens, and preteens work together, breaking down barriers and supporting one another with love, laughter, and limits, rare commodities in the teen years. GRG has some crucial ingredients that anchor respect for young women and the boys around them, but you can work to create nurturing environments with these characteristics in your own homes, schools, and communities with or without a specific program. There is so much work to be done out there; it is much bigger than any one program. **We must help one another**.

What's unique about GRG**? It's led by teen girls. Teen girls do this job best. How unusual is it for a teen to have a job as the *best* qualified? One of our teen leaders said, "It's a chance for teens to turn heads for the *right* reason for a change!"** I agree! GRG calls out the leadership skills in every teen girl.

GRG treats teens with respect and gives them opportunities to shine. GRG was developed by real teens. The book we wrote together, *Girls' Respect Groups: An Innovative Program To Empower Young Women & Build Self-Esteem!*, [25] will help you train empathic teen leaders and contains the curriculum for the GRG Middle School Program.

Why is a program like GRG so great? It's positive, preventive, and respectful. It builds community, it builds capacity within the community. It teaches helping and volunteering. It sets out a road map for good behavior, before the bad is encoded. Most of my bullying prevention work consists of me [or others] saying "*Stop it!*," trying to correct bad behavior, often long-entrenched. In contrast, GRG is so easy, so inexpensive, and opens so many other positive doors.

The "secret" behind GRG is NOT the GRG program itself. Six weeks in an after-school program isn't a magic wand. What GRG does that's REALLY important is build supportive networks of girlfriends, both at the middle school and high school levels. These girls encourage, support, and stick up for one another, spreading the message of respect long after the formal program ends. It encourages kids to take responsibility for their own character and moral development, choosing loving, supportive friends, and insisting on respect from themselves and from the people around them. Loving, supportive friends will also tell us, kindly, when we've made a mistake and crossed the line.

---

[25]L Blumen, N Evans, and A Rucchetto, *"Girls' Respect Groups: An Innovative Program To Empower Young Women & Build Self-Esteem!,"* (Toronto: Camberley Press, 2009)

This is the real benefit of GRG and other like-minded programs. It's not just a program "applied" to girls. It's an eye-opening education, a chance for girls to press the reset button on respect, to move forward with strength and share that strength with others around them.

Here's just one example: Natalie Evans and Anne Rucchetto were my teen co-authors on *Girls' Respect Groups: An Innovative Program To Empower Young Women & Build Self-Esteem!* They helped create the GRG program and became published authors before graduating from high school! More important, they've contributed so much to so many girls, running GRG programs, training GRG leaders, and sharing their knowledge and hearts through the GRG book and the GRG website. Anne and Natalie are extraordinary young women, who are perfect *everyday* examples of the amazing things teens can do, given a chance!

A firm anchor in self-respect and respect for others can help kids ride through the tumultuous teen and young adult years. The key is to build in the preventive protection of a robust sense of self-respect starting in the early years, so it's strong enough to withstand the ups and downs of adolescence and the new challenges of emerging adult life and relationships. Adults can guide kids through the emotional rollercoaster of teen and young adult relationships, teaching kids the warning signs of abuse and how to exit an explosive relationship early and safely, *before* it happens to them or their friends. Learning from Jesse Logan's experience, we must teach kids how to behave with emotional self-control and kindness through breakups and other heartbreaks, and most importantly, *adults need to clean up our acts*, our own relationships, so we can lead by example and speak with authority to our teens.

Kids who are grounded in self-respect don't need to bully others to maintain their emotional state or demonstrate their social power. They don't need to change friendship alliances every two seconds. They don't require constant reassurance of their social standing or importance. Kids who are grounded in self-respect walk away from frenemies and relationships based on disrespect, directed at them or at others. They can ride through conflicts with friends without freezing them out or slamming them on Facebook.

Only when our kids are emotionally strong and self-confident can they do the right thing. The time to build that strength is early, in preparation for the challenges that will inevitably come.

8

Is It Bullying & What Should I Do?

As we've talked about bullying, we've recognized how hard it can be to identify. Well-meaning, experienced adults can be standing *right in the midst* of bullying and be clueless. By the time we *do* see it, it's often very late and a lot of damage has already been done. What else can help us identify bullying at an earlier stage, so we can intervene easily and change the trajectory towards a better outcome?

How Can I Tell If A Child Is Bullying?

If you think a child or a group of kids is actively ringleading bullying activities, put on your detective hat and glasses and spend a few days to a few weeks investigating. A 360° assessment should connect info from school and home, including after-school programs.

Here are suggestions for how to proceed and what kind of information can be useful in a 360° assessment:

- **Intervene Early. This is the single most important thing adults and other kids can do, for *all* bullying problems, whether you are dealing with bully, target,**

or bystander. Ask questions; indicate your genuine interest in the developing situation. Be pleasant and positive, not punitive. Tell as many observers as possible to keep a pleasant eye out for trouble. Lots of smiling and nodding – not the "Sopranos"-style threat, *"I'm watching you,"* pointing your fingers towards your own eyes, then towards the possible offender. Keep it positive, but make sure they know you're paying attention.

When bullies and bully-supporting peers know that adults and other kids are watching them, and won't accept intolerant behavior towards others, they are much more likely to disband. It's like sticking your finger into the midst of a whirlpool – you disorganize the current and cause it to flow off in another direction.

If peers are going to confront a bully about change, it should be a group effort. Today's environments are too unpredictable for a single child to be a lone confronter. Ultimately, we want our environments to become safe enough that a single child has full confidence to caution another with a word, a gesture [keep it clean!], a quiet shorthand for *"Check yourself. You're over the line."* End of discussion, problem solved. But until we achieve that safety goal, we need to make sure that kids are protected when they take a courageous stand against bullying.

- **Dig Deeper**. Resist the temptation to focus on the first or most obvious symptoms. As we've discussed, very frequently the real problem is much more complex and involves more actors than seen at first glance. Take the time to learn more before formulating a solution. **Investigating below the surface is the second most**

important thing adults and other kids can do, for *all* bullying problems.

- **Watch Peer Relationships**. Listen to kids' conversations with friends – how they talk to one another. How do they talk about kids who *aren't* there? This is particularly revealing. Kids talk most freely in the presence of adults while the adult plays a background role – driving kids to activities or sitting at your desk at the front or back of the classroom. Be a fly on the wall.

- **Ask Other Adults – Teachers, Coaches, And Parents**. Ask if they're aware of any brewing problems. Share your concerns. Even when there isn't a specific problem to be solved, other adults can be a good source of information about whether a child has social collaboration skills. *"Does my child/this child work well with other kids?"* Parents can learn a lot by asking that question of teachers. *"Does she exercise leadership with restraint? Does he know when to step back from active leadership and adopt a supporting role? Does she work well in teams and in group settings? Is he inclusive of other children?"*

- **Ask The Kids Directly**. Sometimes it's that simple – just ask. Even when your kid says *"Oh, Mommmmmm"* [insert eye rolling here], you've opened the door to a discussion and made it easier for a child to come back to you later, when *she's* ready.

- **Watch For Children With Strong Personalities**. Many child bullies are kids with strong personalities – **and great leadership potential**. They're just using their personal power in bad ways. Our job, as the adults around those kids, is to gently push them back onto the right road. Adults can help these kids find a positive focus for their energy and persuasive skills. They need the help of their peers too, to insist on behavior change AND to keep these kids as friends while they learn to soften their rough edges. There are some amazing examples of transformation when those kids find their stride.

- **Watch For "Unintentional" Bullying.** *"We were just kidding," "It was just a joke," "She knew we didn't really mean it."* Don't let those lame excuses throw you off the track. Adults are often diverted from further action, especially the consequence stage, by the apparent uncertainty of whether they're dealing with bullying. **Whatever the intent, the goal is to help kids become aware of, and responsible for, the effect they have on others.** An apology and a change of behavior, at an adult's insistence, can lead the way to a permanent change of heart.

- **Share Info With Other Teachers, Coaches, And Parents.** If a group of kids is having significant friendship issues, lasting more than a week or two, every teacher and support person in the school should be made aware of it. Those kids should have watchful eyes on them *everywhere*, including at home. At school, watch those kids at recess, listen to them in the cafeteria or gym. Watch the hallways between classes and the locker rooms. Give the bus driver or bus guard a heads-up too. Make sure parents know. Sometimes parents see the problem first; if so, touch base at school to see if the problem's showing up there too. Share information between home and school. Ask one another what you can do to help out. **Build collaboration between home and school, not animosity.**

Under the watchful eyes of many adults, kids get the message that we're paying attention and behavior problems will diminish.

In fact, our silent, watchful gaze puts direct pressure on kids to work it out, while our verbal coaching helps kids learn the friendship skills needed to smooth it out.

Action Plan: If A Child Is Bullying

If you've identified that a child is bullying:

- **Intervene Early. There is no more effective strategy, no easier time, and no easier way to solve these problems than to catch them early.**

- **Make A Plan**. Outline *in writing* a short list of changes you'd like to see. Suggest some tools and techniques the child can use to accomplish those goals. Include weekly check-in dates [set frequency as needed]. A 30-second check-in lets a child report progress, get some encouragement, and lets him know that you're paying attention and *it's still important*.

- **Ask For Change**. Ask for the child's help and cooperation. Ask what you can do to assist her as she works towards those goals.

  Be Consistent And Insistent. Be insistent on change. Be clear about what behavior you *do not* want to see anymore and, even more important, what behavior you *do* expect to see. Be very clear and give several examples, particularly "better choices" from a previous real problem.

- **Be Prepared To Sustain Frequent Low-Level Monitoring For Months**. Come back to the written plan after one, two, and three months for a progress review. Be encouraging, recognize effort and progress, and set the next set of goals. It can take less than two minutes to do.

- **We Can Go Far Beyond Solving The Immediate Problem**. Remember Dylan Beckham who defended an autistic classmate against bullying? Once the problem was solved in his classroom, he set his sights on the school, then the community, building commitment, enthusiasm, and pride.

- **Ask For Help From Home Or School**. Share the plan with parents and teachers. Each person should state clearly what they will be contributing. Parents and teachers, approach one another as colleagues, with support: *"How can I support that change at home/at school?"* No one leaves the meeting without an assigned task.

Identify the behaviors that need work. Start small, working on one or two items at a time. Let the child know you're there to help and that you expect effort and improvement. Be clear that you anticipate mistakes too – with apologies and repair. Mistakes are part of change and learning. Change takes time. **Kids need to know we mean it when we say we're insisting on change.**

Bullies Gone Wild: Too Little, Too Late

Not intervening can lead to tragedy or permanent harm. Unchallenged, little bullies become more adept and powerful, leaving a tornado path of destruction, swirling peers and adults in their wake. A 12-year-old Virginia girl accused a teacher of sexual molestation when he threatened to discipline her for her bullying behavior on the school bus patrol.[1] Fearing the loss of her coveted positions in several school activities, she lashed

---

[1] T Jackman, "Fairfax Teacher Found Not Guilty Of Molesting Girl," *Washington Post*, May 27, 2010

back in the way she knew best – lying and manipulation. The teacher ended up on trial for molestation. While acquitted by a jury in less than an hour [one juror said there was no evidence, no real case], this teacher lost a year of his life defending the charges and suffered permanent damage to his reputation.

This interesting story has several contributing factors that built on one another:

- A little kid with a lot of power, accustomed to bullying the kids and adults around her with lies and threats.

- Overzealous political correctness, with adults trying to be sensitive to a girl's charges of inappropriate sexual advances by an adult in power.

- A legal system that quickly solidifies those accusations, perhaps not allowing a young girl, who might have made a dreadful mistake by making a false accusation in the heat of the moment, the opportunity for adult-supported, quiet reflection and a chance to rethink or repair.

- A man with 20 years' experience as a teacher and soccer coach, a father of three who "treated students the way he treated his own children, picking them up, twirling them around, laughing and joking."[2]

Each ingredient on its own might step us *just a little* over the unacceptable line. But they combine at a sudden flash point, creating a complete mess, with no way to press the rewind button. Unfortunately, the only way to stop events like this from spiraling out of control and to contain the damage is to diverge

---

[2]T Jackman, "Fairfax Teacher Found Not Guilty Of Molesting Girl," *Washington Post*, May 27, 2010

from the path, long before the final incident. It's hard to tell which exact incident will be that flash point incident.

The solution: we need to not play it so close to the edge all the time. Some "firewall" actions, to keep the damage from building and spreading:

- **Stop the bully sooner.** That was not the first occurrence.

- **Kids and adults need an internal compass, a conscience that won't allow us to fling accusations or untruths that could hurt someone else's reputation or feelings.** In today's reality show format, where you give the fastest, cruelest criticism you can think of, lying [intentional or accidental] is just a small additional escalation. We have become too accepting of lying as a means to achieve our goals. Adults and kids need to reclaim a commitment to their own personal integrity.

- **We need to reestablish a BIG gap between acceptable and unacceptable ways of treating people** – what's too rude or too much of a lie, even if it seems entertaining or makes your own life easier for a while. Bullies can be extremely adept social manipulators. We need to recognize and stop that behavior early, long before it takes on pathological twists.

- **We need to be careful about being too politically correct,** so we don't rush to judgment over accusations against a teacher with 20 years of experience helping kids. We should also be very, very careful to give a child enough space to back down and retract. These kinds of accusations take off in a whirlwind and it's hard to stop the tornado once it's in motion.

- **That said, in today's world, a teacher should be smarter than to leave himself so open to accusation** by "picking up and twirling" 12-year-old preteens, boys or girls. Laughing with kids is great, but adult behavior with kids should be kept within appropriate boundaries. We are their parents and teachers, not their peers. We, the adults, should not be playing it so close to the edge, either.

How Can I Tell If A Child Is Being Bullied?

Now let's look at the problem from the other side. How can we identify – and assist – a child who's a bullied target? If we're lucky, other adults or kids will notice the building blocks of this problem before it reaches a crisis. Even if our first heads-up is a sad and discouraged child who asks us for help, there's much we can do to identify the contributors to the situation, in preparation for making an effective action plan.

The following symptoms can serve as red flags when a child is being bullied. Some are more obvious, some less so, but what you're really looking for are changes, patterns, and clusters of symptoms. These red flags suggest it's time for the "detective hat and glasses":

- **Stress Symptoms**. Is the child irritable, sad, or angry? These can be hard to distinguish from normal teen temperament issues [sigh]. Biting nails? Having nightmares?

- **School Refusal**. Is attendance becoming a problem? Even if a child is still attending school, does she have frequent headaches or stomachaches? Are the stomachaches only on weekdays? If you have headache-free weekends, that's a clue that something's going on at school. May not be bullying, but it's a signal to investigate further.

- **Slipping Grades.** The problem could be bad study habits or a shift in interest from academics to social life, but it could also be distraction or worry about friends or other unhappiness that makes it hard to concentrate on school. Intervene early with support on this one, before the child digs too deep an academic hole. Obviously, school refusal and slipping grades often go hand-in-hand.

- **Ripped Clothing Or Bruises.**

- **Damaged Or Lost Books, Backpacks, Or Money.**

- **Sudden Loss Of Interest In School Activities Or School Friends**. This could be a symptom of being cut off by former friends.

- **Sudden Loss Of Interest In Being On The Computer.** Could be a symptom of cyberbullying.

- **Sudden Loss Of Interest In Answering The Phone, Especially The Cell Phone.** Could be text message bullying. Teens are usually all over their cell phones. When a teen lets the phone ring or buzz, unanswered, repeatedly, I get curious.

- **Not Eating Lunch.** Where do the kids eat lunch? Are the social structures flexible? Can kids eat lunch with a variety of kids or are the social structures so rigid that kids must eat with the same people every day or face social exclusion? Not eating lunch can be a reaction to anxiety symptoms, eg, stress nausea, fear of physical interference in the lunch room [food thrown at you, tray knocked out of your hands, threats to hurt you later], or social humiliation. Safer to skip lunch.

- **"Unrelated" Behavior Changes.** You know your child. There will be *lots* of behavior changes through the teen years; most are normal, if not desired. It can be a full-time parental job to sort through and deal with the changes!

  That said, the appearance of angry or depressive behavior should be investigated. Pull out your phone and text your kid: *"sup? u stressed? can I help?"* Even if you get no answer, you've perhaps opened the door to a later conversation, or at least let your child feel that you're noticing and open to talk. [Don't be surprised if you get the snarly girl or vacant boy response – that's part of the teen years too.]

- **Alcohol And Drug Use Or Cutting.** These symptoms usually manifest later. Be aware that girls sometimes cut as part of a social club, not only in response to their own internal pain. Some say they cut **to** feel pain.

Not everything is bullying and even one, two, or three of these symptoms isn't proof of bullying. But you should have your radar tuned to notice changes in behavior. If your child or a child in your class starts behaving differently, you should be asking why.

Earlier I shared a story about a child who never used the boys' room at his elementary school, for fear of bullying. He came home to use the bathroom. When my daughter began middle school, she started coming home desperately needing to use the bathroom. My antennae went up. Was it bullying? A quick investigation showed no cause for alarm. School finished at 3:15

pm and the kids' bathrooms closed at that time, but there were sports [and lots of water] after school, so by 5 pm... Worth investigating, glad there was no problem. [Note: We requested that a bathroom remain open.]

Talking To Teens: Anyone In There?

Can we know for certain what's going on? We can't, and many of our kids would rather endure intense physical or emotional pain than confide in an adult, especially a parent. All we can do is be alert to changes, ask a few, non-interrogation-style questions, and try to be available when asked.

That can be tough during those prickly teen years. For most of the teen years, my daughter thought *any* question I asked her was an interrogation. Me: *"How are you?"* Val: *"Why do you want to know?"* Real life gives me all the head-scratching examples I've ever needed! Kids are usually on better behavior with their teachers and other adults outside the home, but I've been left scratching my head over kids I'm not related to, as well!

Here are a few suggestions that have helped me navigate these difficult waters. They're useful whether or not your child is having bullying problems.

Despite a child's outwardly discouraging stance, make yourself available to talk or hang out non-verbally. Try to keep yourself approachable, so a child who *does* want to talk feels welcome, or at least not discouraged. Kids will often want to talk at your *least* convenient time. The bedtime chats of early childhood are gone; parents of preteens and teens may have to stay awake till 1 or 2 am to catch their teens in the mood to talk!

It's useful to remember that (1) teens really need adults, (2) teens *hate* needing adults, and (3) teens *really hate* finding themselves in those situations where they're forced to admit they still need us and our help. **This internal conflict can lead to very puzzling behavior**. It can produce uneven, unpredictable, almost irrational behavior at home, on top of "normal" teen volatility. A teen who's just had an open-hearted conversation with a parent, asking for help solving a bullying problem that's beyond her ability to solve, may feel *too* emotionally open and vulnerable. How does she handle it? By picking a big fight with you and closing the emotional "window."

Even though your brain may understand what's going on, it takes a lot of emotional maturity and self-control for a parent not to get frustrated and discouraged and walk away from a kid who is fighting with you when you're trying to help them. Just keep remembering that this volatile behavior is really a symptom of the pain he's feeling. It's tough for everyone. Similarly, a kid who has to hold back tears or confront humiliation on a daily basis can barely hang on to her emotional control until she gets home. Asking *anything* of a child so on the edge [*"Please pass the salt"*] can be enough to cause the floodgates to open. Again, they're showing their pain in the environment where they feel safe. Don't take it personally.

A kid with a stronger personality is more likely to exhibit anger or argumentativeness under stress; a gentler personality tends to exhibit symptoms of depression. No hard and fast rules, but, as a parent or teacher, it helps to understand what you may be seeing.

Your own personality may influence your response to your child's challenging behavior. If you have a stronger personality yourself, for example, you may be triggered to respond angrily when a child seems to challenge you with his anger. Or you may not feel empathic when your gentler child withdraws into depression. Be careful that your own behavior doesn't become an add-on to the drama. Same caution, with roles reversed, if the parent is the one with the gentler personality.

Set boundaries on bad behavior – you don't have to take abuse, even while you're trying to provide a safe space for your child to unload emotionally. Manage your own emotions – don't melt down yourself. Remind yourself that it's often when children [and adults] look the *least* lovable that they need our love and help the *most*.

Don't feel that you have to be an expert – on child psychology or bullying prevention. *"Don't worry, we'll figure this out together"* is reassuring to a child. Then follow through, and keep making yourself available to love, support, and problem solve.

Action Plan: If A Child Is Being Bullied

When a child comes to us with the admission that they're being bullied and need our help, it's time to hurry up … and go slow. As adults, especially parents, our first instinct is often to jump in and rush to a "solution." There are several problems with that knee-jerk, instinctive reaction: (1) It can prematurely close the conversation about what happened, (2) It can incorrectly communicate to the child that he is too weak or powerless to solve the problem, and (3) We are likely to race off with the wrong "solution."

Here are some tips for helping a child who is being bullied:

- **Reassure The Child.** Be clear that it's not his fault, he's not alone, and you will help.

- **Hear The Story.** Be gentle and quiet as the story unfolds. Ask open-ended questions that encourage conversation: *"Tell me about it," "Is there more?," "What happened next?"* Resist the temptation to finish sentences if the child's slow to speak, resist the temptation to jump in with solutions at this point until the whole story is out. [These are my weak areas. Apologize and offer to try again if you blow it.] Make a few notes if you have some good ideas you don't want to forget while your child is speaking.

- **Assemble The Facts**. Print and collect any email, voice mail, or text messages. Document other physical evidence. Take dated pictures of bruises or property damage. Start a notebook or write the story, with names and dates, on a computer.

- **Decide If This Is A Problem With Immediate Danger**. This can be very hard to tell – trained experts often get this one wrong. Ask your child. The danger may be from others [eg, escalating physical bullying, risk of ambush or beating] or from the bullied child [feeling seriously depressed, hopeless]. **If, together, you and your child** feel there is immediate danger, then bring the problem immediately to the appropriate authorities – the police, the school, or a mental health professional.

- **Problem Solve With The Child.** If the problem doesn't seem to be immediately dangerous, ask the child if he'd like to take a little more time to try to solve it, with some new ideas and with you backing him up. Sometimes, we rush in too soon to solve a kid's problems, and **despite our best intent, we inadvertently communicate that we think the child is too weak or too powerless to solve the problem on his own.** This can reinforce or exaggerate his own feelings of helplessness or tendency to feel like a victim.

  Give the child a chance to tell you things he's tried that have or have not worked. Problem solve other ideas that might be tried over the next two weeks or so.

- **Give The Child Words To Use Or Actions To Take.** We can help a child who is being targeted by giving her strategies or exit lines for safely extracting herself from a potentially dangerous situation, *without losing face*, crucial in the teen years. *"I'm leaving," "I'm outta here," "This is ridiculous," "Bye," "No, thanks, I'm in training," "Gotta go – soccer"* [help your child find her own words], are all designed to slightly tilt the playing field back in favour of the target, giving her the opportunity to exit without seeming to run away. We can also give a child some coaching on safety ideas, making sure she finds a friend to walk with after school or go out with to recess. Talking with your child about how to recognize when it's time to call an adult for help will help her be prepared.

- **Often, We Give Our Kids Ideas They Can Grow Into.** There have been times when I asked my daughter, *"Do* you think you could say…?" and she would reply, *"I could* **never** *say that."* Two weeks later, I'd hear her saying it to someone on the phone. Think of it as leaving the breadcrumb trail for our kids to follow, and don't be discouraged if they reject your ideas when first offered. That's also part of them hating to need you. Don't expect to be thanked, either [until your kid is 40].

- **Set A Short Time Limit To Try Some New Strategies** – two weeks. If a child can start to solve a big problem like this, under his own steam, backed by a caring adult, it's tremendously empowering. If nothing has changed after two weeks, it's time to escalate. If you're the parent, call the teacher. If you're the teacher, time to tell the child's parents, bring it forward to staff meeting or to the principal. Check your school board's policy. You may be required to notify parents or principal once a child makes you aware of the problem.

- **Keep A Log**. Use dated entries to describe meetings, phone calls, action steps, plans, or further evidence of bullying and any improvements or additional problems.

- **Talk To Other Teachers**, **Coaches, Parents, Other Adults**. Is there additional information available to help guide your understanding of the situation or assist in developing a targeted plan of action?

- **Develop A *Written* Action Plan With Specific Steps And Deadlines.** This is perhaps the most important step and the one that is most overlooked. It doesn't need to be detailed, but it does need action items, who's doing each step, and a next check-in date. *"You do this, I'll do that, and we'll talk in 10 days. I'll call you after school on the 18th."* Then make **sure** you follow through.

Much dissatisfaction between teachers and parents arises at this point, when plans tail off and nothing happens. It's not important to have the perfect plan. Start somewhere. If Plan A doesn't help in 10 days, develop or modify into Plan B. Plan C. It's the effort and attention that count.

- **Improve Communication Between School And Home**. You can earn a lot of positive support, and dismantle that adversarial relationship between home and school, just by providing regular updates and the opportunity to discuss and collaborate.

- **Stay Polite But Don't Stop Working On It**. *Do not bully your kid's teachers or principal*, but do not be deterred. This problem MUST get solved, and someone needs to be the driving force behind it. The school needs to know if the initial improvement has or has not been maintained. While the school should be actively monitoring the situation, the student and parent are often more acutely aware of what's going on. Change will take some time [see the next point], and we need to keep pushing it along.

  Parents, it helps to remember that teachers can view an upcoming meeting with you with worry or dread. Prepare to stay on your best behavior, even if you get triggered. Enter the meeting as a friendly colleague – bring coffee and muffins to an after-school meeting with a teacher who's had a long day. Teachers, the same applies to you. Be sympathetic to the anxiety a meeting with the teacher causes for parents. Most stressed of all is the parent who is also a teacher, maybe in the same school as her own kids!

- **Commit To Low-Level But Active Monitoring For Three To Six Months**. Bullying problems do not yield to magic wand solutions. It took a while for the problem to reach this stage of crisis and it will take a while to solve it. **An entire environment must change, along with all the individuals in it. The problem often looks much better quickly, because adult attention drives the problem underground. Expect it to resurface several times**, each time less bad than the time before.

Mistakes will be made, but we're looking for a positive trend line. If you're not seeing progress, check in with all involved players, assess the current obstacles [new or existing], modify your action plan, and keep working on it. Follow up with regular check-ins with all parties, via phone, email, or in person. Keep notes to track progress and new problems. **When kids know that adults are paying attention and they really mean it, changes will happen**.

For teachers or parents who think this approach is too time-intensive or too much work: How much time do you spend now, dealing with bullying and other disruptive behavior problems in your school, program, or home where bullies reign? It's worth the investment in time to reground kids in the commitment to treat one another with respect. Reestablish that bullying is not permitted, and that we are *all* responsible for intervening early when someone needs help or crosses the line. It can take seconds to fix a problem: *"We don't treat people that way in this school. We treat everyone with courtesy and respect – whether you like them or not."*

The results will be evident and the time invested well worth it. Straight talk – it will take effort, commitment, and time to

press the reset button on an environment where bullies rule, but a year from now you'll be astounded at the magnitude of the change. In an environment of respect, helping, and consideration, where mistakes are caught early, and the kids monitor themselves and one another, adults will spend much, much less time on discipline issues of **all** types. Adults will also be surprised by the rapid **academic** progress students will make. You will also breathe a breath of fresh air in an environment with much less stress and much less adult peer bullying. You may find you actually enjoy work again!

If you cannot get your whole school involved in this effort, then just reclaim your classroom, your after-school programs, the places where you have the most influence. Start there, improve your own world and your influence will spread. Same thing if the problem's at home.

Problems And Pitfalls

When the bullying's invisible, what do you do? What if there are no adult firsthand witnesses? Adults often get stuck here, in the *"We need to see it to act"* framework. This does not mean installing more security cameras. Whether or not you've "seen it," you need to get actively involved at this point, with an investigation plan that engages most or all of the school faculty and staff. There also needs to be a specific, concurrent plan to keep the targeted kids safe. Educate the targets, make sure they're buddied up at recess, lunch, and after school, with adult eyes watching targets and bullies. Bystanders need engagement, too, with a restatement of school [or home or community] values: **we protect and take care of one another and we stand up to deflect bullying**. Everyone is accountable, everyone is responsible. Consider adding incentives or penalties for not helping someone in need, until kids internalize the new values. Choose ideas that meet the needs of your environment.

Go back to the targeted kids and ask for more info. Has the problem changed? Even if you don't have direct evidence, working with the kids in question – bullies, targets, bystanders – gives the strong message that adults are nearby and are watching. **A major cause of failure to solve bullying problems is our own lack of follow-through**. After a bullying problem raises its head, there's typically a flurry of activity, several meetings, promises to look into it, promises to "take care of it," and then … nothing. What happened to all that well-intended energy?

The written action plan is key, even just one Next Step with a date. Don't leave a meeting or end a phone call without summarizing the Next Steps and setting a date to check in by phone or in person. Then **follow through** – do what you said you would and make the follow-up call or email. Even when you don't have significant progress to report, it builds goodwill, and it provides the starting point for the next Next Step. Put it on the calendar – a quick review every week or two. Decrease the check-in frequency as the situation stabilizes.

Should A Bullied Kid Leave School?

That's such a tough call. Nobody wants to see this happen, but there are situations when it's the only realistic option. Leaving a school because you can't solve a bullying problem [or any problem] is bad at both extremes:

- **It's bad to yank a kid out of school too soon.** If we cut and run at the first sign of problems, it can communicate that we think the child is too weak or incapable of solving the problem. It can set up a habit of running from adversity, which really undermines a child's resilience and encourages him to perceive himself as a helpless victim.

  Most parents don't rush in and physically remove a child from school immediately, but, with the best of intent, we sometimes "take over" the problem so completely that it can have almost the same effect on the child. If indeed we do end up removing a child from the school, he can have a tough time making the adjustment to a new school with his confidence severely undermined. It's a difficult balance to monitor.

- **It's also bad to let a child stay too long, suffering in a school that cannot or has not acted quickly and strongly enough to ensure the child's physical and emotional safety and to stop the bullying permanently.** Remember Dylan Theno, who was tormented through junior high and high school. His mother finally realized she had to take Dylan out of school to save his mental health. Surviving parents of kids who've committed suicide often wish they had realized the seriousness of the situation sooner and changed schools or homeschooled.

If adults take the problem seriously, react more quickly, and intervene earlier, we could avoid most school withdrawals and a lot of the damage that trails after. But we're not close to doing that reliably, yet. **Bottom line, if you've asked for help and the school [or team or friendship] does not move fast enough to ensure a child's emotional and physical safety, remove the child from that environment.**

Do We Need To Intervene For Every Little Thing?

Should adults step in EVERY time we see something a little unkind? No, but a lot depends on the state of the current environment, the context in which the event is set. If the environment has many problems, with frequent stepping over the line of respect and courtesy, and we're trying to press the reset button, then yes, we need to intervene *every* time we see behavior we don't like, probably for months, less intensely for a year, and at a low level forever. We need to help the kids lower their radar zone, to start to become conscious of their own behavior and the actions of others. Awareness is the first step to change. It will take more than one reminder for the kids to believe that we're serious about change. **If we want change, we need to act as if we mean it. The worse the situation is when we start, the more work we have in front of us. Next time, don't let it get that bad.**

Watch for the storm clouds – don't wait until it's already raining. We need to do a better job monitoring incipient bullying, getting a better handle on situations as they build, so we can intervene before someone is suffering. We need simple reporting systems to track incidents, so multiple teachers don't each see one incident and fail to realize that they're looking at a much wider pattern of harassment. Use a log. Review incidents at staff meetings. Are we seeing the same cast of characters showing up in multiple incidents?

Develop a consistent intervention approach and train new, part-time, or volunteer teachers and staff – new or young teachers, coaches, camp counselors, and appropriate school volunteers [lunchroom and recess supervisors, student teachers, educational assistants, student "shadows," etc]. Be clear with them how to react and how to intervene in ways that promote courtesy and respect for others.

Here's an incident that started me training camp counselors. One morning, I walked into a summer day camp classroom. On the blackboard was the message *"Joe's a big fat loser."* Given what I do, you can imagine my first reaction was to start erasing, while I'm saying, *"Kids, kids, kids, I'm sure you can think of some other ways to have fun with one another."* Turns out Joe was the group *counselor*, not a camper. In some intergroup rivalry, encouraged by the camp, campers from another group had come into Joe's group's homeroom and written this *"Oh, yeah??"* style message on the classroom blackboard, dissing this group's counselor.

Joe was 19, an admirable young adult with a good heart, working to provide leadership and sports training to kids. It wouldn't ruin his day to see that mean-spirited but insignificant message on the board. This small moment, however, represents a HUGE guidance opportunity. The way Joe handles this will set the tone for these kids for months to come. **Joe is not just a counselor, he's a role model**. As a teen, he's admired and his behavior copied by the 20, 50, or 100 younger campers he deals with every day. He sets an important example for his campers. They learn from him what it means to be a cool teen. They scan him constantly, like a high resolution scanner downloading *"Joe 1.0"* software for later use.

Unfortunately, Joe's greatest strength is also his potential weakness. His youth, which enables him to forge a strong connection with his campers, won't have prepared him to think through the importance and the subtle implications of his reactions to this situation.

There are 3 basic ways to respond to this challenge:

1. **Retaliate and up the ante. Not a good choice**, even though give-and-take and friendly competition are hallmarks of camp and sports. In this case – *and this is key* – *"big fat loser"* means the kids have crossed the line, turning a game into a personal attack. It's just gone from teasing to taunting. It would be inappropriate, in this case, to escalate with meaner words or deeds or even a completely friendly arm wrestle for dominance. **Continuing to escalate once the line has been crossed, with no mention of the boundary, gives the signal that this is acceptable behavior. It will repeat**. Subtle but important. If, instead, the blackboard message had

said *"Explorer Team Rocks! Meet us on the soccer field and we'll prove it!"* there's no problem. Go for it.

2. **Blow it off, erase the board, and say nothing. Slightly better.** While not escalating, it doesn't use the teaching moment.

3. **Note it, set the boundary, and offer an example of how to handle it better next time. Best choice for behavior shaping.** *"Hey guys, we've crossed the line here. That's a personal attack. No problem, it happens when we get our competitive spirits on, but let's remember we're all human beings here. How about a volleyball spiking contest instead?"* Simply, directly handled. End of issue.

And while I've minutely analyzed this situation, don't underestimate the impact of how Joe handles this on his younger, admiring campers. That's where adults who train camp counselors have an important opportunity to teach Joe, and other counselors, to recognize these situations and to handle them routinely in a manner mindful of the influence they have on their young charges.

The most important thing we can do is intervene early, while the problem is fairly small and the solution easy. Here's a time when I should have done better. My daughter had a great group of girlfriends through middle and high school, some of whom had been friends since preschool. In grade 7, they were getting interested in boys. One of the girls, Alyson, started "dating" a boy from school, Marcus [not sure what 7th grade "dating" is; I'll leave that with you]. After a while, they stopped dating. Another girl from this close circle of friends, Jasmine, decided she liked this boy. Jasmine went to Alyson and asked her if it would be OK if she liked Marcus. Alyson said it would be OK.

Turned out, it wasn't OK. Once Jasmine and Marcus started to hang out, Alyson started bad-mouthing Jasmine; pretty soon many girls in their group were shunning Jasmine. The ones that weren't shunning her looked away and didn't stop it, either. This went on for months, getting worse.

These were young kids, in their first romantic relationships. They are bound to make some mistakes as they step into the "adult" roles of dating and romance. Is it a bad idea to date your best friend's former boyfriend? Oh yeah. Even if you ask if it's OK? How mature and polite that she actually asked! Better than most adults, who also make this same mistake. With life experience, you learn it's a very bad idea to date your best friend's ex-boyfriend. Even years later! This would have been a great place for some adult guidance – a big "PASS" on dating the ex-boyfriend AND some guidance about having emotional self-control after the breakup, despite provocation. All the girls in this group could have learned from this.

Back to the story. When I found out about it, you can imagine our conversation at home. *"Moooom, you CAN'T say anything!,"* *"Well then, you better, Val. This isn't right."* I left it in Val's hands for a while and I called Jasmine's mom, who filled in some details and told me how upset Jasmine was. I told her I had put pressure on Val, and I was prepared to talk to the other parents and the girls' teacher. Jasmine's mom asked me not to call the others just yet, to see if the girls could work it out. I agreed, and it seemed to improve [checking with Val and Jasmine's mom].

A few months later, it reemerged. Expect this. When kids realize that adults are watching, it drives the problem underground for a while. It almost always recurs, at least once.

Stories came back to me about group projects at school where Jasmine was either excluded from meetings or the meeting was set for a time when Jasmine was away at a hockey tournament. They made it hard or impossible for her to contribute, then told the teacher that Jasmine had done no work on the project.

I stepped in. I met with the teacher, asking if she was aware of the girls' exclusion and bullying happening in her class. She said she hadn't seen anything, but now that she knew, she would look for it. We agreed to talk the next week. I also called several of the parents and asked them to speak to their kids.

A week later, I spoke to the teacher. She said, *"I'm looking for it and I can't find it."* She was a kind-hearted, empathic teacher with more than 20 years of teaching experience. I couldn't have asked for more skilled assistance – she was a teacher, a woman, a parent who really "gets it," she had been warned that it was going on, and she was actively looking for it – and she still couldn't see it. This is a perfect example of how hard it can be for adults to spot kids' bullying. The kids don't want you to see it.

That weekend, most of the girls and their parents attended a performance by one of the girls in the group. At intermission, I spoke to the girls. *"This has to stop right now,"* I said. *"She asked if it was OK. It wasn't. These are your first romantic relationships. Mistakes get made. You have to forgive one another, learn from it, and move on. Are you going to lose your girlfriends over it?"*

It stopped that night. They healed the relationships, and they're all still good friends, seven years, several boyfriends, and a few friendship bumps later. I give Jasmine credit for being a big enough human being, at age 13, to accept their apologies and move back into the friendship circle. We can all learn from that.

While I was very happy at the outcome, I felt stupid and disappointed with myself for not intervening sooner. I [we] let a kid suffer when the [easy] solution was in reach all the time. Especially given what I do. I learned from that experience.

The take-away lessons:

- Even good kids with good friends can have bullying in their midst. In fact, girls' relational bullying *frequently* involves good friends.

- Experienced adults [parents and teachers] often have trouble catching bullying in the act. We can never know the whole story, but that shouldn't stop us from intervening. Even if we couldn't see it, we knew it was going on.

- **Intervene early**. Give the kids a little time, but move right in. Kids are suffering every day we look the other way.

- It takes so little to stop it, especially in the early stages. When kids know adults are watching, they behave better.

- We need to teach kids the skills of emotional self-control in all areas of life. When they're old enough to start dating [even thinking about it], we need to give them some specific coaching in that area, too.

Once we start looking, we can see many ways to lightly inject our adult influence. We can provide preventive guidance to kids, setting limits and boundaries, helping them internalize good behavior standards. We can be on the alert for incipient bullying, do a better job of intervening earlier, dissolving small problems, and preventing them from building into big emergencies. Handling it at this stage takes hardly any time at all. In this environment, the kids themselves will become ambassadors of goodwill, solving or bypassing social conflict, welcoming new students, campers, teammates, and friends. That's when we know we've done our job as adults – when our kids are doing most of our work for us!

Imagine how our daily lives could look and feel when we work, study, and play in communities like that!! In this vastly improved environment, we can be much more effective dealing with the [fewer] remaining problems – we'll be able to assess situations earlier and better and improve our abilities to develop flexible, accountable action plans that monitor our progress and reaffirm our commitment to paying attention until the problem is fixed.

9

Bullying & The Law

If you do what you should not, you must hear what you would not.

BENJAMIN FRANKLIN

This chapter's focus on bullying and the law will encompass the laws we make at the school and community level, as well as the laws enacted by legislative bodies and the justice system. We will look at both prevention-focused and enforcement-related issues.

At present, we are relying on the law to do things it was never designed to do and therefore cannot. We need a clearer idea of how and when to use laws effectively and how to construct and enact new or amend existing laws so our efforts to use them to backstop bullying prevention will be successful.

This chapter is not intended to be a comprehensive state-by-state or province-by-province review. Nor is it a systematic review of case law. Rather, it will highlight some strengths and weaknesses of our current systems, so you'll know the questions to ask, the places to start looking, and the ways to start pressing for change in your own systems.

I'm grateful for and this chapter benefits from the assistance and perspective supplied by Judge Janet Thorpe, a family court judge from Orlando, FL. Judge Thorpe speaks from her experience within the legal and judiciary systems, highlighting recent relevant cases. She also discusses a newly enacted Florida anti-bullying and harassment statute, considered a model piece of legislation and a template for crafting new, bullying-specific legislation. Judge Thorpe and I often agree, although we approach from different perspectives. I take full responsibility for my comments, as an outsider to the law [as opposed to an outlaw], and thank Judge Thorpe for her willingness to juxtapose her reasoned, thoughtful comments with mine. I've tried to make clear which thoughts are hers, which are mine. Despite any differences, our mutual goal is to provide protection for children who cannot protect themselves. We have worked together to elucidate some of the stumbling blocks in our current systems and to highlight the framework and tools to begin the process of bringing our laws and guidelines into better consistency and, more important, more effectiveness.

Is Punishment The Answer?

Our current systems focus far too much on the enforcement and punishment end of the telescope. Punishment without prevention puts us on a much longer path to the changes we're trying to make – we're working with one hand, perhaps both hands, tied behind our backs. It's like trying to get someone to stop shooting a gun by trying to catch the bullets as they leave the gun barrel. We're looking at the wrong end of the gun. *We need to unload the gun.*

There *is*, however, a role for punishment and consequences. There *should be* consequences for mistakes and bad behavior, even unintentional. Life is full of consequences. Swear at your boss, you lose your job. Yell at your boyfriend a lot, you damage or lose the relationship. Hit someone's car, intentional or not, you pay the repair bill.

Part of the challenge is to rebuild our commitment to individual and group responsibility. Mistakes sometimes happen, despite our best intentions. We occasionally hurt or damage others, without realizing or meaning to. We must take responsibility for our mistakes and repair the damage we've caused to someone else.

The problem is, we've become afraid of mistakes; afraid to step up and take ownership of making them, and then to take responsibility for repairing them. Mistakes are actually *good* – up to a point. Barbara Coloroso said, *"You want your kids to make lots of mistakes when they're cheap."*[1] Mistakes are our best teachers. We need to develop more tolerance for viewing mistakes as learning opportunities, not as experiences to avoid and deny. When kids hear parents trying to deny or weasel out of their own or their kids' responsibility for hurt or damage, it teaches kids to do the same.

---

[1] B Coloroso, *Kids Are Worth It!* (Toronto: Penguin Canada, 2003)

Adults can also go overboard in the other direction – assuming **too much** responsibility for kids' mistakes. Parents who rescue kids from their mistakes do kids no benefit. Adult smoothing over, adult-to-adult apologies [instead of the errant child apologizing], adults paying for damage repairs out of the parent's wallet [rather than the child's] – these well-meaning efforts actually *disable* children from learning to take responsibility for their actions. When your teen damages your car [count on it], they may not be able to afford the entire repair bill, but a portion should be repaid to parents through some combination of the teen's money, extra work done around the home, and paid work outside the home. Be responsible for your mistakes at home and it's easier to take responsibility in the outside world. Mistakes are cheap lessons that help us create insurance policies, so we don't keep making the same mistakes in more serious forms.

Along with too little focus on prevention and the fear of mistakes, we also suffer from **lack of discipline**. Discipline doesn't mean punishment, it means *learning*; the learning that helps us build emotional skills, self-control, and conform to both our inner principles and the external laws and guidelines that help us live in society.

Unfortunately, lack of emotional discipline, lack of preventive efforts, and avoidance of responsibility create a dangerous combination deficit. It keeps us riding too close to the precipitous edge, ignorant that we're approaching a "chaos theory" flashpoint, where, once we've crossed the final, invisible line, we suddenly end up someplace we never thought we could go.

After Every Crisis: A Cry For More Laws

Predictably, the outcry after Tyler Clementi's death has focused on needing to create tougher laws to outlaw the bullying of gays. **This is much too narrow a view of both the problem and the solution**. There are two things wrong with this approach: "gays" and "laws." Let's look at each.

Gays. Tyler Clementi's bullying is not "just" a gay issue. **This is fundamentally an issue about how we treat *all* human beings**. By labeling this a gay issue, we ironically trivialize and marginalize the importance of the problem. By labeling it "gays-only," many people will think *"Not my problem."* Instead, when we have principles that are woven into our universal culture and individual hearts that we treat ALL human beings with respect, then *all* gays, *all* women, *all* teens, *all* blacks, *all* Muslims, *all* teachers get treated with respect. No question. No exception. No mincing. No slicing into small categories. No dicing. No fooling.

Whether you "like" or "support" a gay lifestyle is irrelevant. Like someone or not, agree with their choices or not, **we are obligated to treat everyone with respect.**

Laws. Laws won't stop kids from videotaping a roommate having sex and posting it to the Internet, gay or straight, any more than laws stop teens from drinking. Can we catch every person using technology inappropriately and prosecute them? Even 50%? **The laws need to be on the inside, as well as on the outside.**

As we'll see shortly, when the "little" laws are not taught on a family or school level, then the "big" laws [made by the legislature and the judiciary system] have not and will not protect those who need it, even vulnerable kids. Just the opposite. As our society moves further away from standards of personal integrity, personal accountability, apology, and repair, the "big" laws increasingly get subverted into a game, the object of which is to see if you can slither out from your responsibility due to some technicality.

Further, looking to the legislature to enact laws to solve this problem is **another example of passing the problem to someone else**. When we do that, we are saying, *"This is not my immediate problem, and I am not contributing to the solution."*

We cannot expect the law to fulfill a function it was never designed to do. It's not the law's job to *build* kids' ethical characters, helping kids internalize the difference between right and wrong. **It is the parents' job, aided by other adults who guide and shape kids, to teach behavior and ethics.** Such teachings are certainly in keeping with our laws, but **our own internal codes of ethical behavior should always far exceed the minimum responsibilities placed on us by the law.** We must commit to the time it takes to set, teach, practice, and enforce behavioral limits for ourselves and our kids.

The laws are like the out of bounds markers in downhill skiing. They catch you when you've gone seriously off course, but the best line down the hill is considerably inside those markers.

Prevention helps us find our best behavioural line. We should only use the law as the last resort. By the time we call on the law for help, the damage has already been done.

Let's start by looking at the "big" laws, our statutory laws, then we'll focus on our "little" laws, the rules that govern us at the family and school level.

Bullying And The Evolving Law
Judge Janet Thorpe, Ninth Judicial Circuit, Orlando, FL

All laws enacted by either the State or Federal government can be viewed as legislative behavior modification, seeking either to encourage or discourage specific behaviors. While I'm speaking from a US perspective, Canadian law is comparable in many key areas. A reactive law dissuades behavior by threat of penalties and criminal punishment. Consequences for civil action, set by statutes and case law, can involve monetary damages, specific performance, and declaratory actions. Preventive legislation frequently encourages behavioral compliance through governmental monetary inducement or safe harbor protection [eg, schools are required to set up a Safe Schools Program or they won't receive their Title IX funding].

Few laws currently on the books were specifically designed to deal with bullying. Claimants and attorneys have been required to attempt prosecution through the specific application of narrow aspects of existing laws. While frequently not "successful" or as straightforward as we would prefer, these cases have been, piece by piece, building a road map for how to [and how not to] prosecute bullying cases successfully. They are guiding us in our evolution towards the enactment of bullying-specific laws.

Days after the Columbine massacre, the US Supreme Court handed down an opinion providing leverage for bullying claims based specifically upon sexual harassment. In *Davis v. Monroe County Board Of Education*,[2] the Court found that Title IX, under narrow circumstances, provided a private right of action against a school district which failed to provide a school environment that was safe from sexual harassment for a 10-year-old girl. That recourse is narrowly restricted; only where (1) the school receives federal funds [all public schools in the US]; (2) acts with deliberate indifference; (3) to known acts of harassment in its programs or activities; and (4) the actions are so severe as to bar the student from getting an education.

Once school officials have been notified, failure to put a stop to sex-based bullying can result in significant financial liability for the indifferent school. Despite the ruling's narrowness, the creation of the private right of action in the *Davis* case has proven a useful legal weapon for parents of bullied students and a motivator for school officials to abandon their apathy.

More recently, in *Patterson v. Hudson Area Schools*,[3] a federal jury in Michigan awarded $800,000, under the provisions of Title

---

[2]Davis v Monroe County Board Of Education, 526 US 629, 1999
[3]Patterson v Hudson Area Schools, US District Court, ED Michigan, Case No 05-74439, leagle.com, Feb 12, 2010

IX, to a student named Dane Patterson who was subjected to four years of escalating, sexually based bullying which culminated in a sexual assault. School officials, while aware of the problem, proved ineffective in protecting the plaintiff from his bullies and providing a safe learning environment.

Hudson Area Schools motioned the court to set aside the verdict. While pending, the case was quietly settled out of court. The timing was fortuitous. Within 24 hours of the confidential settlement, the US District Court trial judge granted the motion, set aside the $800,000 jury verdict, and dismissed the case with prejudice. By settling, the Hudson Area Schools [or perhaps, its insurers] minimized their financial exposure from this case, which could have included an award of five years of plaintiff's attorneys' fees, in addition to the $800,000 jury award. Although the court's determination was moot for Dane Patterson, and certainly disappointing to his supporters, it is instructional for future litigants. It specifically details the judicial expectations as an evolving road map for pursuing bullying and harassment claims under Title IX.

The same gender, student-on-student bullying to which Dane Patterson was subjected certainly met the more stringent threshold of "extreme student misconduct," but unfortunately was not found to be "so severe, pervasive and objectively offensive that it deprived him of access to the educational opportunities provided by Hudson Area Schools" [Note: The sexual assault was prosecuted separately and successfully]. Nor did the Court find the bullying pattern sexual in nature, required in order to hold the school district liable under Title IX. Additionally, certain evidence presented at trial apparently was markedly different than allegations set forth in the initial trial court and appellate pleadings.

Patterson failed to prove to the satisfaction of the trial judge two essential components of his Title IX claim. First, Patterson's counsel failed to show the "*deliberate indifference*" of the person with actual knowledge of and authority to stop the harassing conduct. As trial testimony revealed, the school did, indeed, follow up with every student Dane Patterson identified as having harassed or bullied him. The students specifically reprimanded ceased their offensive conduct, but other students stepped in and the bullying continued. The trial court did not seem concerned that the school's efforts were *ineffective* at stopping four years of pervasive bullying of Dane by a large and ever-changing cast of classmates. Future court opinions must address whether such inefficacy and a school's failure to try new approaches to stop sexual harassment or bullying should constitute deliberate indifference under the Title IX standard.

The second determination for future litigants to address more effectively is whether hostile conduct, such as Dane Patterson experienced, meets the definition of sexual harassment [rather than "just" bullying], if it's based upon the victim's demeanor or behavior not conforming to stereotypical notions of masculinity or femininity. This interpretation would be analogous to that used in the past decade's Title VII hostile workplace and sexual harassment litigation.[4] The US Supreme Court has previously

---

[4]Michelle Nichols v Azteca Restaurant Enterprises, 256 F 3d 864 (9th Cir 2001) at 874

held that there is no basis for distinguishing the circumstances under which offensive or abusive conduct amounts to harassment "based on sex" in Title VII and Title IX claims.[5] Thus, the history and case law of Title VII has laid the groundwork for similar sexually based bullying claims brought under Title IX.

It's only a matter of time until gender-based harassment, including that predicated on sex-stereotyping, will be covered by Title IX – if the harassment is sufficiently serious that it limits a student's access to educational opportunities. Eventually, a US Appeals Court or Supreme Court opinion will address this issue, drawing from the already established interpretations for sexual harassment under Title VII.[6] *Patterson v. Hudson Area Schools* could have been that appellate case, had it not been settled.

The volume of cases against school districts with jury verdict damages or settlements under Title IX is growing, both in number and size of award. Parents and children who believe that schools have acted with deliberate indifference to sexually based bullying can now have their claims addressed by a court. School districts are waking up to their monetary exposure under Title IX. Plaintiffs' attorneys are recognizing a new and lucrative practice area. Lawyers have begun to advertise aggressively for bullied clients, in order to bring Title IX claims. This type of litigation is attractive to plaintiffs' counsel for several reasons: (1) Complainants have an immediate right of recourse to the courts. Unlike some federal legislation, Title IX does not require any

---

[5]Franklin v Gwinnett County Public Schools, 503 US 60 (1992) at 75
[6]Montgomery v Independent School District No 709, 109 F 2d (D. Minn. 2000) at 1081 is a non-precedential district court opinion

administrative remedies to be first exhausted; (2) There is no limit on the size of jury verdicts; (3) Punitive damages can be assessed, if appropriate; and (4) As most plaintiffs are juveniles, the Statute of Limitations is tolled [ie, the clock stops ticking] until they reach the age of majority, which can be years after the alleged bullying or harassing conduct occurred.

These factors expose public school districts to great financial risk over a long period of time. As a result, these claims will cause school district insurers and risk managers to realize that anti-bullying policies will not be sufficiently protective, if not followed up with a commitment to action. Eventually, school personnel will be required to ensure adequate levels of "eyes on" adult supervision of students, during and between classes and supervised activities [eg, monitors in locker rooms, teachers in hallways and stairwells between classes] to prevent liability under Title IX. We can anticipate changes in school behavior to minimize the schools' financial exposure.

Title IX could become a powerful remedy in those cases where a school district can be held liable because its administrators knew or should have known that sexually based student-on-student harassment was occurring and they did not take immediate, *effective* action to protect the bullied target. Although this is a narrow slice of the pie, it highlights the way laws may be used to bring pressure to bear on people and organizations, to **prevent** bullying by creating safe environments with consistent monitoring and rapid, effective response to calls for help.

Using Title IX to prosecute bullying and harassment cases, however, has its limits. Title IX was never designed for this purpose. Litigants have been forced to search for existing laws on the books that might, under the properly narrow circumstances, provide a protective wing. If our intent is to prosecute bullying and harassment systematically, consistently, and effectively, then we need different laws, created specifically for that purpose.

Florida's "Jeffrey Johnston Stand Up For All Students Act"[7], officially titled Florida Statutes, Section 1006.147, "Bullying and Harassment Prohibited," is among the first.[8] It was passed in 2008, in memory of a 15-year-old Cape Coral, FL, boy who killed himself after years of bullying. The law "prohibits the bullying or harassment of any student or employee of a public K-12 school during any school-related or school-sponsored program or activity or through the use of data or software accessed by a computer, computer system, or computer network of a K-12 public educational institution."

The Florida Department of Education was required to develop a "model policy" and transmit it to all school districts. Each district was required to adopt its own bullying policy based on the statutory guidelines, develop and comply with investigation and reporting procedures, and report annually on implementation. This multi-faceted approach should provide a more consistent method for identifying and reporting bullying behavior.

---

[7]BullyPolice.org/Fl_Law
[8]Florida Statutes, Sec 1006.147 et seq

The statute defines bullying as "systematically and chronically inflicting physical hurt or psychological distress on one or more students" and provides an inclusive, but not exhaustive, list of conducts that constitute bullying:

- Teasing

- Social Exclusion

- Threat

- Intimidation

- Stalking

- Physical Violence

- Theft

- Sexual Or Racial Harassment

- Public Humiliation

- Destruction Of Property

Harassment includes any "verbal, written or physical conduct that threatens, insults, or dehumanizes any student or employee" and includes harassment committed electronically or with the use of computer software, both from within the school and from remote locations. The conduct must be sufficient to place the student or employee in reasonable fear of harm for himself or his property, and sufficient to interfere with the student's school performance, opportunities, or benefits.[9]

---

[9]Florida Statutes, Sec 1006.147 et seq

School policies are additionally required to include a description of the behavior that *is* expected of students and employees, the consequences for bullying, and the consequences for retaliation [wrongfully and intentionally accusing another of bullying].

The law protects students, parents, volunteers, and employees who report bullying promptly and in good faith. They are granted immunity from civil actions resulting either from the reporting itself or from the failure to solve the reported bullying problem.

The Florida Department of Education modified its School Environmental Safety Incident Reporting System [SESIR] to include the reporting of bullying and harassment. In this manner, bullying and harassing behaviors are monitored at the school district level, including those occurring on school transportation and at school-related activities, creating a consistent, permanent data base for all to utilize for prevention and improvement. Year-by-year progress can be assessed, within and between districts.

Access to Safe School funding is contingent upon Department of Education approval of a school district's bullying policy and provides further incentive for compliance. As a model anti-bullying law, the expectation is that the Jeffrey Johnston Law will effectively thwart bullying behavior in Florida schools and will serve as a template for legislation elsewhere.

This new law requires schools to respond to all bullying incidents rapidly and with deliberate intent, including cyberbullying, off-campus bullying, and the incitement or coercion of others to bully.

The consequences for violating this law include school disciplinary actions and, where appropriate, referrals for criminal actions.

Florida extends the reach of the Jeffrey Johnston Law with its existing criminal code for cases where conduct rises to criminal level [eg, assault, battery, stalking, or harassment]. In addition, Florida has several statutes prohibiting hate crime, including Florida Statutes Section 775.085, which increases criminal penalties and triples the monetary exposure in cases based on race, color, ancestry, religion, sexual orientation, national origin, mental or physical disability, or advanced age of the victim.[10]

Jeffrey's Law was implemented for the 2009-2010 school year. A first-year report was issued in January 2011, and year-over-year comparisons should be available in January 2012. We must monitor progress within and between schools, and modify our behavior and laws accordingly. Enacting a new law is the beginning of the work, not the end. We can only make progress if we keep asking *"How are we doing?"* and make adjustments to laws, policies, and behaviors as needed. Not needing to use the law is the best indicator of success.

The following elements found in the Jeffrey Johnston Law should be included in any bullying prevention legislation:

- **Definitions**. The law must clearly define its terms.

- **Requirement For Model Policy**. Legislation should mandate responsibility to a governmental agency, most likely the Department of Education, for the development

---

[10]Leg.State.FL.US/statutes/index

and issuance of a model policy. Technical advisories should be issued to guide school districts through the interpretation and implementation of the law. The adoption of a model policy should provide safe haven for school districts where local policies require approval to avoid school funding lapses.

- **Bullying Prevention Content**. New statutes must establish a strong standard for the duties and rights enunciated. It must send the message to students, parents, and the public that bullying behaviors are not acceptable. The policies and procedures must give parents of students who have been bullied recourse to address their claims.

- **Learning And Prevention.** Preventive activities should include implementation of grade-appropriate anti-bullying curricula. Counseling services should be provided to the bully, target, and bystanders after bullying incidents.

- **Reporting Of Incidents**. School crime reporting should be uniform and consistent. State or local law should require centralized reporting. Consider nationally mandated reporting requirements to ensure uniformity.

- **Investigation.** A procedure must be outlined for the prompt investigation and verification of all claims, including anonymous reports. Unsubstantiated reports and warning signs should be logged and monitored as situations develop.

- **Notification**. The statute must require that the parents of both the bully and the target be notified when a violent or bullying incident occurs, including reporting to criminal authorities, as appropriate.

- **Discipline**. There should be clearly delineated procedures and consequences for children who bully and for intentional false reporters.

- **Immunity.** Prompt, good faith reporting of bullying should be immune from civil liability.

If all, or a majority, of the above elements are included when drafting anti-bullying legislation, the end product should prove effective in modifying harassment and bullying behavior and in creating safe[r] school environments.

The reality is that bullying incidents do not belong in court. Once parties are in litigation, the damage has already occurred to the victim, and all involved [except maybe the attorneys] have already lost. Lawsuits alone cannot stop bullying. Creating lasting change requires more than a legalistic approach. Bullying is a community issue, and schools are a critically important part of the solution. We need to create school environments that actively discourage bullying and harassment. The law is not intended to teach kids ethical standards and boundaries; it merely establishes society's minimally accepted behavior standards.

The Limits Of The Law: An Outsider's View
[Back To Lorna]

As an outsider to the law's inner workings, I'm much more pessimistic about the law's ability to intercede successfully and the ability or willingness [possibly both] of the people behind the laws to close loopholes and bring justice to terrorized, tormented kids.

Relying on the law to protect kids from bullying has not worked. It has not and will not prevent the bullying from occurring. Help is too far away for most victims of bullying. If you've read any of the case law on bullying, you would be sick to your stomach reading about kid after kid after kid who has suffered years of torment with virtually no help, then gets dragged through the courts for three to five years more, with every detail and humiliation made public, only to have the vast majority of cases dismissed or reversed on appeal, after several trips through the court's revolving door. Even if a case were "successful" after this harrowing journey, the damage to the target cannot be undone or repaired through monetary damages, jail time served, or a permanent criminal record for the bully. There is no rewind button. If you need to invoke the law for protection, you've already lost.

Not only has the law not protected these kids from the humiliating, soul-scarring indignities they have suffered at the hands of other kids [and sometimes other adults], but the courts have not validated the legitimacy of desperate victims' calls to stop the torment and call the perpetrators to account. There's virtually *always* some technicality about how the law was written or how the defense was crafted, which has allowed bullies – child and adult – to remain unaccountable for the damage inflicted and the wake of destruction trailing both the perpetrators and the targets. **When we fail to hold bullies – and the environments**

that permit bullying – accountable, we are sending a loud, unmistakable [although silent] message that bullying is, in fact, permitted and accepted.

I could have filled this entire book documenting cases where justice has been miscarried, while still "obeying the law." Educate yourselves. Do some more research and reading. To get you started, here is just one example where I believe "the laws" [big and little] have gone very wrong. Let's look in more detail at the human side of *Patterson v. Hudson Area Schools*:[11]

- Dane Patterson was subjected to relentless physical and emotional bullying at school from grade 6 to grade 9. He was pushed around in school hallways, called *"queer," "faggot," "gay," "pig," "man boobs," "Mr Clean"* [no pubic hair], slapped by a girl when he came to the assistance of another girl she was bullying, then taunted by a teacher in front of the class – *"How'd it feel to be slapped by a girl?"* [The above list was excerpted from the court filing, as are the crude taunts below].

- Patterson estimated he was called these names more than 200 times in grade 7 alone. His gym clothes were thrown in a toilet and urinated on, his locker defaced with epithets and hand-drawn pictures of a penis entering a rectum, his planner defaced with *"I ♥ penis," "I lick it in the ass," "I ♥ cock."* Patterson's parents met with school officials multiple times each year. His only peace: when he hid out in the resource room – for all of 8th grade. He was not permitted to hide there in grade 9. The bullying began anew.

---

[11]Patterson v Hudson Area Schools, US District Court, ED Michigan, Case No 05-74439, leagle.com, Feb 12, 2010

- **But wait, there's more**. Harassment escalated to sexual assault in May 2005. Patterson's parents filed a lawsuit. From the court filing: *"After Friday night junior varsity baseball practice, DP [Patterson] was sexually assaulted by a fellow teammate, LP, in the locker room. LP stripped naked, forced DP into a corner, jumped on DP's shoulders, and rubbed his penis and scrotum on DP's neck and face. While the assault was occurring, another student, NH, blocked the exit so DP could not escape."* Although the assault was reported, the assailants were permitted to play the upcoming game.

  "After the sexual assault, the varsity baseball coach, Jeremy Beal, held a team meeting with both the junior varsity and the varsity baseball players. At the meeting, Mr. Beal informed the players that they 'should not joke around with guys who can't take a man joke'."

- **But wait, there's less.** Of course, every intimate detail of the abuse and the assault was recounted in the filings and in open court. That alone would be enough to retraumatize anyone, much less a child or teen. By now, this poor kid must be the poster child for PTSD [Post Traumatic Stress Disorder].

- **The verdict:** Three verdicts, actually. (1) The first time through the system, the case was dismissed, for failure to satisfy one of the three elements for Title IX claims, deliberate indifference. On appeal, the Sixth Circuit Court of Appeals reversed in January 2009, remanding the case back to district court for trial. Around we go again. (2) This time the ruling was in Dane's favor. He was awarded $800,000. Hudson Area Schools motioned to set aside the verdict or for a new trial. (3) The case was set aside, thrown out, with finality, in July 2010. Elapsed clock time since entering the court system: *five years*. With an out of court settlement, the Patterson case does not provide a precedent for successful prosecution of bullying or harassment cases under Title IX. [In a separate action, Patterson's assailant, LP, was found guilty of assault and expelled from school. The assisting student, NH, was suspended.]

The court concluded that because *"the harassment to which Plaintiff was subjected in sixth, seventh and ninth grade constituted bullying, not sexual harassment,"* and since *"Title IX protects [against] only harassment or discrimination based on sex, it must as a matter of law dismiss Plaintiff's cause of action."*[12] Back to Square One. Did you notice that 8th grade was omitted? That was the year in the resource room.

Traumatic enough? How much childhood and time were stolen from this boy? Was justice served? What effect will this have on Dane going forward? *"I don't know how you get back eight years,"* Dena Patterson said. Her son has been so emotionally damaged, he can't even go away to college and live in a dorm with other students. *"We said it was worth standing up. We don't want another student, another parent to endure what we have seen."*[13]

- I hope you feel as sick reading this as I felt writing it.

The news from Canada is no better. While at present perhaps slightly less litigious than their friends to the south, Canadians are increasingly turning to the courts to adjudicate intractable bullying problems, in school and out.

---

[12]"Patterson v Hudson Overturned," Cyberbullying Research Center, cyberbullying.us, Aug 11, 2010
[13]P Walsh-Sarnecki, "Court Awards Bullied Student $800,000," Hearts4Autism.org, Mar 9, 2010

A London, ON, family filed a $3.7 million lawsuit against the London District Catholic School Board, charging that their 11-year-old son was repeatedly bullied at school, before finally receiving a blow to the head so severe that the fracture required three metal plates to stabilize the bones.[14]

The Ottawa, ON, Catholic School Board is being sued by the parents of a 10-year-old girl, charged with failing to protect their daughter from repeated acts of bullying at school, despite several requests for aid from the girl's mother, via phone calls and meetings.[15]

Bluewater District School Board in Owen Sound, ON, about 120 miles north of Toronto, was recently sued for $35 million in combined damages from four lawsuits brought by a group of families charging that their children were repeatedly bullied by teachers and children at district schools. Named as defendants were five teachers, three principals, two students and their parents, and one vice-principal.[16]

Consistent among the cases is the long-standing, repetitive recurrence of the incidents, the failure of the schools to stop the bullying even after notification by students and parents, and the widespread, commonplace knowledge, within each school, that these kids were being bullied. Also tragically common are the deep, long-standing psychological scars carved

---

[14]K Dubinski, "Parents Sue Over Brain Injury," *The Sault Star*, SunMedia.com, Oct 4, 2008
[15]J Sadler, "Bullying Lawsuit Could Set Precedent," cnews.canoe.ca, Feb 16, 2010
[16]L Nguyen, "Families Sue School Board," NationalPost.com, Oct 2, 2010

into the victims, both by the actual incidents and by the sinking knowledge that neither peers nor adults would stop the torment.

Laws must, by their very design, be written in an extremely narrow and specific manner, to avoid accusing innocent people. **This specificity, however, creates huge loopholes for bullying, wherein we are evading our moral and ethical responsibility and failing to keep kids safe at school and in our communities, while *technically* obeying the letter of the law**. We cannot console ourselves that we are "in compliance with the law" while vulnerable kids are being traumatized as we look the other way.

Aren't Schools Required To Keep Students Safe?

Are schools required to keep their students safe? One might think so, but the prevailing evidence says otherwise. Negligent supervision claims fail. Lawsuits against individuals [teachers, administrators, or school board trustees] are typically dismissed summarily. Most lawsuits brought by parents against school boards are dismissed on a variety of grounds:[17]

- **School has no legal or constitutional duty to protect a student in their care from harm caused by a third party, even another student at the school. Part 1.** In the Columbine situation, a suit against the school district, county, and police, brought by a student shot in the head, was dismissed, *despite* advance knowledge of the planned assault, *including the date*, by school officials and the on-site police officer.

---

[17]J Grim, "Peer Harassment In Our Schools: Should Teachers And Administrators Join The Fight?," Barry Law Review, 10, Spring, 2008

Apparently, "the student was unable to show any underlying constitutional violation by the law enforcement officers, county or school district, or that they owed a higher duty of care to the student because of a special relationship. In addition, the armed students, rather than the law enforcement officers, county or school district, were the 'moving force' behind the suing student's injuries. Thus, the student's claims against the law enforcement officers, county and school district were dismissed."[18]

- **School has no duty to protect a student in their care from harm. Part 2.** Despite being required to attend school where children are, by definition, deprived of the protection of their parents or caregivers, and schools are assuming that responsibility *in loco parentis* [in place of parents], there is still apparently no requirement or responsibility for schools to protect the children in their care. Courts *"decline to hold that compulsory attendance laws alone create a special relationship giving rise to a constitutionally rooted duty."*

  Apparently, or should I say unbelievably, "the restrictions imposed by attendance laws upon students and their parents are not analogous to the restraints of prisons and mental institutions. The custody is intermittent and the student returns home each day."[19] **So we're required to protect prisoners and institutionalized mental health patients from one another … but not our children??**

- **Courts find the schools immune**, as state or provincial agencies, even in cases where a student was clearly harmed.

---

[18]Ireland v Jefferson County Sheriff's Department, 193 F Supp 2d 1201 (D Colo 2002), Journal Of Law And Education, Jan, 2003

[19]Doe v Hillsboro, TX Independent School District, US Court Of Appeals, 5th Circuit, 94-50709, caselaw.findlaw.com, May 27, 1997

- **The school couldn't foresee the incident**. A student bully demanded lunch money from a student in the cafeteria. When the student refused, the bully physically attacked him. Despite an extensive, documented history of the bully's aggressive behavior towards other students – six previous disciplinary incidents for the bully, including multiple incidents of fighting – the school was held not liable. *"None of the previous incidents involved attempts to take money from food trays in the school's cafeteria"* [on Wednesday October 15 at 11:37 am, when the victim was wearing a blue shirt....]. Can we split more hairs? Actually, yes: *"The school district didn't have notice that the bully posed such a danger to fellow students."*[20] I can't imagine what more they needed in the way of notice.

- In the Dane Patterson case, Hudson Area Schools successfully countered that the school could not foresee that student LP would sexually assault Dane. LP had no prior history of assault, on Dane or other students. And while that may be true, the inability of Hudson Area Schools to stop the ongoing bullying harassment of Dane Patterson created and maintained a culture where bullying was permissible, where each act of harassment paved the way to the next level down, where numerous students felt it was an accepted part of the culture.

- A grade 10 cosmetology student was attacked with a razor by a female classmate, requiring 100 stitches to her face. The razor came from a cosmetology tool kit issued by the school and permitted to be taken home, despite being *"an operational act of negligence on the part of the teacher and contrary to the school's zero tolerance policy [for weapons]."* School: not responsible. The event was

---

[20]Smith v Half Hollow Hills Central School District, 349 F Supp 2d 521, District Court, ED New York, Dec 6, 2004

not foreseeable.[21] Great. The one time we could benefit from a zero tolerance policy, they found a way around it.

■ Yikes [my legal opinion].

While these are just a few of the thousands of examples, they are illustrative of the kind of legal loopholes and "hide the walnut" attitudes that allow adults to continue to evade their moral and ethical responsibility to safeguard children in their care. **We cannot continue to turn a deliberately blind eye and be ignorantly unresponsive to the warning sirens of students with multiple offense disciplinary histories, then open our mouths in a wide "O" of surprise when the same students attack yet another student under the school's care.** Under the school's nose. Or when a persistently bullied target comes back with an AK-47 and cuts down a swath of students in the library. Under the school's nose.

Look for these legal loopholes and close them. The Jeffrey Johnston law is just a first step. I'm certain loopholes will be found there, too [hopefully smaller than the previous sinkhole-size exits]. It will likely take several rounds of legislation until we have effective anti-bullying laws. **In the meantime, until the loops are closed and the laws more directly effective, if we can't figure out how to fulfill our *legal* obligations to our children, we must have the courage to step up to our *moral* obligation to safeguard our kids. Teachers, lawmakers, parents, we can and we must do better than this.**

---

[21]Mason v Metropolitan Government Of Nashville, Court Of Appeals Of Tennessee, 03C-234, TNcourts.gov, Jan 6, 2005

Bernard James, law scholar at Pepperdine University in California, suggests that educators, and by inference the legal system, are interpreting their mandates too narrowly. *"Educators are empowered to maintain safe schools. The timidity of educators in this context of emerging technology is working to the advantage of bullies."*[22] Although he was writing specifically about cyberbullying, the point is well-taken and applicable to bullying in general.

As we strive to do better, close loopholes, clearly articulate responsibilities, and intervene early, before people or events get out of hand, **these tragic and almost ludicrous examples illustrate *exactly* why laws aren't the protective panacea we long for**. Is Rutgers responsible for Tyler Clementi's death? Were school or dorm representatives aware of prior privacy violations, inappropriate Internet video postings, homophobic face-to-face or other bullying? After only three weeks on campus? Perhaps not, but now that sex-and-tech incidents are commonplace, schools and parents must shoulder the responsibility to provide clear, pre-emptive guidance. And while our instinctive reaction after a horrible misadventure or tragedy may be to look for someone to blame legally, **laws can never fully enumerate the myriad specificities required to determine liability**. Someone can always figure out a technicality through which it's possible to slither out of the legal responsibility. **But evading our moral responsibility to keep one another safe is another matter.**

---

[22] J Hoffman, "Online Bullies Pull Schools Into The Fray," *New York Times,* NYTimes.com, Jun 27, 2010

Little Laws, Big Problems

Let's turn our focus to the school or local level and look at a few of the legal loopholes there. At first, it might be hard to see the connection between these "small fry" examples and the harrowing Dane Patterson case, for example. I encourage you to see, even on this smaller level, the evasive tactics, prevarication, and hairsplitting, which seem to [but don't] absolve adults of their responsibility to keep kids safe. These are the building blocks of the bigger problems we've just seen – lack of action breeds more of the same, and when kids see adults permitting bullying and ducking their responsibility when caught, they learn fast. The real lessons we're supposed to learn get lost in the misdirection.

The bus driver who did nothing to help Si'Mone Small, the 7th grader beaten up on a Florida bus, was defended by both the school board and the bus company. *"You're on dangerous liability grounds when you touch a student, so they have to be very, very careful when they intervene and touch a student,"* said Duval County, FL, Superintendent John Fryer. This was not a case of sexual interference; rather, it was an opportunity to help a kid in physical peril. The parents of the bullies: *"Our boys did community service and are now going on with their lives"* and *"Sorry, but my son had never been in trouble before or since."*[23] Not very apologetic.

The burden of proof always rests on the target. At present, that seems an insurmountable burden. Must every child log and

---

[23]G Tuckman, "Caught On Tape," *Anderson Cooper 360, CNN*, May 20, 2005

document every single incident of verbal, physical, and relational harassment that occurs, in perpetuity, to present a sufficiently convincing dumpster full of evidence, to be able to prove the existence of a systematic, pervasive pattern of bullying and the equally systematic, pervasive pattern of adults and classmates looking the other way?

The process of enacting laws is necessarily detailed, specific, and slow. Laws will always lag behind our current knowledge and understanding. We need to keep updating and upgrading – our knowledge and the laws – but there will always be a big gap between what needs to be enforced and what is enforced. How effectively is bullying prosecuted now? That's why prevention remains key.

Laws: Ineffective Quick "Fixes" To Messy Problems

Despite knowing the limitations inherent in the design of the law, we pass responsibility to the law to outlaw certain behaviors. We have school and community laws that "outlaw" cyberbullying, with specified penalties if you're caught. There is still too much cyberbullying to call those any of those laws successful.

Laws have been enacted in school systems in Canada,[24] the US,[25] and England[26] outlawing snowballs – making and throwing them [insert audible sigh]. Outlawing snowballs is a convenient, but not effective, solution to the ages-old problem of helping kids

---

[24]"Students Fight Rule Banning Balls In Schoolyard," *CBC News*, Jan 20, 2010

[25]L Fulbright, "Sledder Hurt In Accident May Be Arrested," *Seattle Times*, Jan 09, 2004

[26]"Parents Angry After Pupils Sent Home For Breaking Snowball Ban," *London Evening Standard*, Feb 09, 2007

find a balance. We're back at the line between teasing and taunting, safe play and dangerous play. Where is the boundary? Who's responsible for establishing and enforcing it? It seems much clearer and easier, at least initially, to "simply" outlaw all snowballs and take it off our plate. One Canadian school even outlawed balls that could be used as the inner core of snowballs.

It is initially somewhat harder, and takes more adult time, to help kids learn safe play with snowballs. Think it through:

- No embedded rocks or ice

- Keep it below the waist

- Stop when someone's had enough and says "Stop"

- No snowballs at passing cars, etc

What happens when mistakes are made? How do we identify the mistake-maker? It can be hard to identify, in a school yard of flying snowballs, whose snowball had the ice in it.

There are big downstream benefits of letting children and adults struggle with these little problems. As we encourage kids to sort through the small complexities of the snowball issue, we are building the foundation for how they approach larger life issues. What are the basic guidelines for safety? You broke the rules today? Sorry, sit out recess tomorrow inside. Can't tell whose snowball has the ice? Everybody stays in tomorrow. We'll try again the next day. **The willingness of adults to permit enough wiggle room for kids to grow, make mistakes when they're small, and have the chance to try again soon** *pushes* *the responsibility onto the kids* to internalize appropriate behavior standards, for their own moral development and for the benefit of the entire group. And it's the kids who need to learn this. The adults already know [well, ...].

The kids need to sort through the texture and complexity of these social "rules of engagement." It prepares them to tackle the next level. Do we cheat on tests? Do we run from a party where the police have been called when there are two unconscious, drunk teens in the backyard? Do we report or try to stop tomorrow's planned ambush of an unsuspecting kid? Film our roommate having sex?

We do need laws. But we also need to instill in kids, at the front end, the internal knowledge of the difference between right and wrong and the societal value of treating other human beings with respect. Those are the "laws" that will keep us safe.

Police In The Schools: What's Their Role?

Some communities are struggling with rapidly rising behavior problems, mostly at the nuisance level, but some much more menacing – drugs, gangs, weapons, assaults, in-school shootings and stabbings. Even if the shootings are "just" interpersonal conflicts gone wrong, rather than a Columbine-style whole school assault, it's frightening and stressful – for teachers and students. Even if your school doesn't have those issues, having those problems at nearby schools or community centers makes parents, teachers, and school administrators understandably nervous.

Enter the police. Toronto brought in armed, uniformed police to 27 high schools in September 2008, citing the goals of school safety, breaking down barriers between teens and police, and hoping teens would be more likely to report crimes to officers they've come to know.[27] Six months later, the schools reported a "very positive" result; they "absolutely wanted to continue" the program. Participating schools saw suspensions decline 17%, with a 16% drop in criminal charges.[28]

Sometimes you get the right answer for the wrong reason. While it's easy, in the short term, to turn over responsibility for discipline to an armed guard, I have concerns about this approach. Does the need for an armed guard in the lobby make the schools [feel] *safer*? **What happened to the authority of adults without weapons?** Does intimidating students help them internalize the right behavior standards? When do you need a second guard, a third? Will there ever be enough guards, metal detectors, suspensions, punishments?

Armed guards *could* be used, *briefly*, to help pull a chaotic school, mid-emergency, back from the edge of crisis. The police presence would indeed get everyone's attention. That could provide enough breathing space for adults to step back in with a *different* plan to press the reset button and reestablish permanent equilibrium at the school. "Different" means (1) not relying on the permanent threat of armed guards in the lobby and

---

[27]C Kim, "Armed Police Officers Coming To A High School Near You," *Etobicoke Guardian*, Sep 10, 2008

[28]T Shephard, "High Marks For In-School Police Officers," *Globe And Mail*, Feb 05, 2009

(2) different from the plan in place before the guards, because that clearly wasn't working, either.

I fully support teens and police developing less adversarial relationships, but there are many more positive ways to accomplish that, rather than through an armed, uniformed police presence. Bring the police in *unarmed and out of uniform*. Have local police and firefighters run after-school programs showcasing their other skills and leadership talents – basketball, auto mechanics, carpentry, basic home repairs, electrical, plumbing, fitness, weight training, or nutrition and cooking. **There is a huge need for capable, grounded men to work as mentors with teen boys – that's how you build respect and relationships.** It's like "Boys' Respect Groups" – it matters less the specific choice of activity and more that you're creating a network of "Boys Helping Boys."

Zero Tolerance: Friend Or Foe?

Zero tolerance policies were intended to demonstrate our strong commitment to identify and stamp out the more egregious forms of misbehavior. The intent was also to simplify and clarify the rules: *"If a child hits another child, he gets a 1-day suspension," "If a child brings a weapon to school, she gets a 2-week suspension and an education program,"* etc, and to provide consistency within and between schools and school boards when handling similar problems. All great goals, but the day-to-day results of these policies have played out somewhat differently.

Zero tolerance tied principals' hands and took away the benefit of their knowledge, experience, and discretion to handle situations in a somewhat customized manner, based on the history and the players. The standardized penalty formula now needed to be followed every single time.

It also apparently took away much of our common sense and created some excessive penalties and almost-humorous over-reactions by adults responding in the name of zero tolerance:

- The Prince William County, VA, school board's 20-page behavior code "outlines 47 categories of misbehavior and 26 possible punishments. The list of 39 banned weapons includes guns, poison gas, darts, and wallet chains. The zero-tolerance policy applies to possession of items from drugs to Sony Walkmans."[29]

- A 3rd grade boy was suspended from school for pointing a chicken finger "gun" at a classmate and saying *"Bang, bang!"*[30] The school had a "no weapons" policy and the child was found to be in violation – armed with a chicken finger.

- There have been several incidents where elementary-aged boys, kindergarten to 2nd grade, ages five to eight, have been suspended for kissing a female classmate.[31]

Bigger kids, bigger problems:

---

[29] D Cauchon, "Zero Tolerance Policies Lack Flexibility," *Education News*, USAToday.com, Apr 13, 1999
[30] "Student Suspended For Chicken Finger Gun," *CBC News*, cbc.ca, May 31, 2001
[31] N Onishi, "Boy In Harassment Complaint Is Linked To Other Incidents," *New York Times*, NYTimes.com, Oct 4, 1996

- Lindsay Brown, a high school senior and National Merit Scholar from Estero, FL, missed her high school graduation after a kitchen knife was spotted in her locked car at school. She had moved the previous day. Arrested for the felony charge of possession of a weapon on school property, Lindsay spent a day in jail. Even 1,000 community emails requesting that she be permitted to attend graduation fell on deaf ears.[32]

There are some real dangers to this type of inflexibility, the downstream consequences of which are often not recognized until later. Zero tolerance and similarly rigid, punishment and consequence systems have several weaknesses:

- **Adults are always "in charge," with all the rules.** That puts kids in the position of always looking to adults to determine right from wrong. Kids need to (1) internalize their own knowledge of right and wrong, (2) be able to contextualize it, and (3) use good judgment to evaluate and apply it to each situation, even without a rule book.

- **If adults are the arbiters of rules, then kids feel free to misbehave *until* they get caught** or until a rule is created that outlaws that particular misbehavior. Kids need to be able to choose appropriate behavior, **whether or not an adult is watching.**

- **Excessive punishment *seems to* "remove" a child's need to make amends for damage or harm done.** When a kid is turfed out of school for pointing a chicken finger, the adults around him get agitated and upset, with reason. Problematically, the adults' focus is diverted to the

---

[32]"Zero Tolerance In Schools News Articles," Florida Department Of Juvenile Justice, DJJ.State.FL.US, Aug 27, 2010

excessive and unrelated nature of the punishment, instead of staying focused on the real problem.

While the adults are in a tizzy about a five-year-old being suspended for kissing a girl, there is an important lesson being missed. That child needs to be encouraged to take responsibility for his actions and apologize to his classmate for hurting or frightening her, even if that was not his intent.

- **Worst of all, disproportionate or unrelated punishment defeats the real learning.** The real lessons needing to be learned by the five-year-old kissing boy are important and should not get lost in the uproar. Beyond the apology to his classmate, that child needs to understand the meaning of "No Means No" and keeping your hands to yourself, on a kindergarten level. He will certainly need to understand "No Means No" on a 6th grade level, a 12th grade level, and a college level too, as time goes by.

The chicken finger kid needs to understand and internalize that pretending to have a gun, and pretending to point and fire it at another student, is a bad decision in a school that's really serious about no weapons. Even if it was a chicken finger. Make a better choice next time.

It's interesting to note that this was the second suspension for the chicken finger kid. The first time, he pointed his *finger* and said *"Bang."* Did someone sit with him during the first suspension and talk about making better choices? Don't know. Clearly he hadn't learned enough or practiced enough to keep him from making the same mistake twice. It's easy for adults to confuse the suspension with the learning opportunity. Sometimes you do need both, but the learning is usually more important and accomplished more directly without the suspension.

Even if you *do* sit down with a child after the first problem and help him understand and work on impulse control and how to make a better choice next time, **there is no guarantee that he won't make that mistake a second time**. Kids are kids. [Let's not start again on the adult self-control issue, even when *we* know better!] Some kids "get it" immediately; other kids need those "100 Reps" we talked about in conflict resolution training. **If adults miss our opportunity to guide kids, however, we are virtually guaranteeing that kids *will* need 100 repetitions.** And we'll have to be there every time.

We can also see the pitfalls of excessive and unrelated adult reaction to kids' misbehavior. Let's look at a situation where an adult might have spanked a child – for speaking rudely to an adult, for example. The main reasons for not hitting children are: (1) it hurts and demeans a human being, (2) it doesn't teach the lesson we want to teach [*"Don't swear at your mother"*], and (3) the lesson it *does* teach is: *"When I get big, I can win by physically overpowering someone smaller."* Wrong lesson.

Hitting a child or relying on other, over-reactive punishments, might seem to "work" in the short term, but it just drives the behavior underground. It will return. When you hit someone, they're usually so angry at you for hitting them [or over-penalizing], the *last* thing on their mind is internalizing the behavior-changing lesson [*"Wow, I really feel bad for swearing at Mom. I hurt her feelings. She didn't deserve that."* or *"Oops, I swear a lot with my friends, and it just popped out with Mom. She was really shocked. Guess I better be more careful. What if I swore at a teacher?"*].

There are deeply important, take-away messages that kids and adults need to hear and internalize, the sand to the oyster. Crucial lessons in appropriate behavior, emotional maturity, and self-control. Mistakes happen. These lessons are much easier and cheaper to learn while kids are still young. Let's take advantage of these natural opportunities to work with mistakes as they occur, while the mistakes, and the kids, are small.

Teaching balance and boundaries takes time, more mistakes, and the willingness of adults to give more than a surface treatment to these errors. Diverting ourselves by looking through the wrong end of the telescope, or oversimplifying with a formulaic set of punishments and rules, undermines our ability to get a good result – today and tomorrow.

Building Integrity: Acknowledging Mistakes

I read the following example of integrity in action in my community newspaper. On a spring night in April 2006, three teen boys entered a suburban Toronto cemetery and overturned 170 headstones [I'm sure you realize that's *not* the integrity part]. A year later, those kids took out an ad in the community newspaper, admitting to the vandalism and extending apologies to the families whose gravestones were overturned, for the damage and grief they had caused.[33]

I consider that ad a huge act of integrity, on the part of both the kids and their parents. It doesn't matter that the idea for the

---

[33]*Etobicoke Guardian*, Jun 9, 2007

public apology most likely did not come from the kids, and was probably the idea of the parents or the court. Teens can do stupid things sometimes [adults, too!], but there is a huge power in apology and repair. Those kids were lucky, to have the guts to stand up and take responsibility for their actions, and fortunate as well, to have adults around them who insisted on accountability. I'm sure that was not easy, and likely very uncomfortable, for both the parents and kids.

The take-away points from this example are:

- **Insist on responsibility**, even if the damage was unintentional or accidental.

- **Don't punish excessively**. Use Jane Nelsen's 3Rs – Related, Reasonable, and Respectful – for best results.[34]

- **Mistakes are, unfortunately, normal. Responsibility and repair should be too.** Don't panic when mistakes occur and we can pave the way for responsibility, repair, and learning.

Going Forward: It's A Beginning

This brief overview of pitfalls and areas of insufficient support in our current systems points the way towards our next steps:

- We must strive to create, even if it must be legislated, safe, nonjudgmental environments in which children can grow and learn in peace.

---

[34] J Nelsen, *Positive Discipline* (New York: Random House, 2006)

- Laws are not a substitute for prevention. Effective systems must contain substantial efforts in both areas.

- Efforts should focus on bullies, targets, and bystanders, both adults and children. Everyone has a role to play in prevention, protection, and making amends when our efforts fall short.

- When there is a mistake, a problem, or a catastrophe, we should be able to rely on our laws [big and little] to help guide us to make appropriate repairs and restorations.

- For that to happen, we must frequently and systematically evaluate and change our existing laws, so that they are directly, reproducibly effective.

- With every mistake, problem, or catastrophe, we must realize that we have, *once again*, missed the boat on prevention. Each time, we must recommit and substantially increase our preventive vigilance, diligence, and effort. **There is no other solution.**

Armed with this knowledge, we can review the rules and laws in our homes, schools, communities, states, and provinces, and move forward to make them more bullying-specific, close loopholes, improve consistency, decrease the time between onset and resolution of bullying episodes, and make sure that the "little" laws in our homes and schools take us off the path of needing to rely so heavily on federally and provincially mandated "big" laws. And while we're waiting for the laws to catch up, adults and children must be fearlessly willing to step into our moral responsibility to protect one another from bullying.

10

Tools We Can Use

We've just looked at the big picture laws and structures that can help us reach our goals and attain consistency. While we're working to improve the laws, there is much we can do in the "small picture," right in front of us. Indeed, we must work on both tasks simultaneously. This chapter focuses in on the many simple things we can do every day to create and maintain welcoming, bully-free environments for our kids.

The responsibility for creating safe and respectful communities must be shared with everyone – adults and kids alike. We each have different roles. It's the adults' responsibility to "build" a respectful structure; it's the kids' responsibility to "play" within that structure, maintaining the standards set by the adults. And, as we've seen, we must *all* be willing to change both our perceptions and our actions, if we are genuinely determined to reduce bullying.

Woven into previous chapters of this book are many practical, results-oriented ideas. This chapter discusses some additional topics: birthday parties, stress handling, community volunteer activities. These are situations that don't even involve bullying. Or do they? We'll take a closer look.

These ideas share the same goal: We must work to level the social playing field for our kids. We need to break down some of the barriers that stand in the way of our kids making and maintaining casual, accepting friendships with one another. The harder it is to make friends and the more rigid the social groups [eg, you can only belong to one group at a time], the more desperately kids will fight to gain entry and the more they will bully other kids they perceive to be lower in the social hierarchy to strengthen their own standing. Being welcome in several social circles gives you options. When you're having a bad day with one group of friends, you can hang out with another group for a while – you won't be completely bereft of friends.

We're always going to like some people more and some less, have more in common with some than with others. **We don't have to be everyone's best friend or love everyone. We must, however, commit to tolerance and acceptance of others, more of a live-and-let-live attitude, and create more breathing space for kids and teens to develop their unique personalities and talents.**

We can make it easier for kids to be friendly with one another. We can insist that kids [and adults] be more accepting and less critical of others and change or adapt our existing structures and behaviors to serve that goal. Our lives and societies are much richer when we celebrate diversity, express curiosity about one another, and encourage everyone to reach their highest potential.

Support Healthy Social Groups And Friendships

1. **Look For Activities That Keep Kids Grounded In Respect For Self And Others**. This is where kids can find like-minded friends and supervising adults who actively value respect. For kids who don't have enough friends, or are having troubles with current friends, a new social sphere is a great way to bolster a child's confidence and sense of competence in another environment. Having even one good friend, who also values respect, is great protection from bullying.

   For every child, even bullies or targets, a respect-based activity provides a chance to connect with a new group of kids with different values, a chance to view her own actions through a new lens, and an opportunity to press the reset button. Joining a new sports team, a special interest group, or a girls' or boys' after-school program offers kids the chance to make new friends, to break down barriers between people and social groups, and to form productive working relationships with people they may not love but could learn to like or respect. Look for community or school programs like Girls' Respect Groups or Boys Advocacy And Mentoring that connect teens to preteens, giving preteens a place to ask their questions and teens the opportunity to share their experience and provide leadership, kindness, and guidance.

2. **Help Kids Build Self-Respect And Develop Their Own Internal Boundaries**. Whether it's your own child or a child in your class, you can help kids build self-respect and learn to be choosy about their friends. **Teach kids to stop chasing relationships with people who treat them badly**. Encourage the skill of moving in closer to friends on the days when friendships are kinder and more respectful, creating more distance on days when asked to exclude a third person [and speak up: *"No, I wouldn't do that to her"*]. Teach kids to monitor problematic relationships daily. If the relationship is abusive or demeaning, to your child or others, teach your child to back away from the "friendship" and give the other kid[s] a chance to change. If most of the relationship is "away days," maybe it's time to find other friends.

3. **Help Kids Fit Into A Peer Group And Make Friends.** Teach children how to nurture friendships. Read books together and discuss the "care and keeping of friends." Make sure kids have some, *but not all*, of the clothes and accessories of their peer group. This helps kids fit in and protects them from bullying, but adults and kids must find a balance. It's also a great opportunity to discuss shopping, the value of labels [both price and status], how to choose good quality clothing, buying on sale, etc.

4. **Teach Better Conflict Skills**. In addition to the friendship skills discussed in Chapters 7 and 8, be sure to teach kids how to have disagreements. Stick to the current issue, no name-calling, yelling, or threats, try to find a solution

agreeable to both parties, learn how to give and accept an apology [more on this later], take responsibility for your mistakes, work to change, and learn to release a grudge [girls and women, this means us!] and move forward. Keep the conflict small – between the original parties. Don't let it ripple out in a wave of gossip, bad-mouthing, and side-taking. *"I'm having a conflict with Chandra right now. We're trying to work it through"* is all that needs to be said.

5. **Respect And Play To Your Child's Personality Strengths**. It's not necessary to force your introvert to become the life of the party. Introverts are well served by their own sense of reserve and can be protected and grounded by having just one good friend. Extroverts can work on developing self-control and patience. Talk to your child. What personality type does he think he has? Talk about the strengths and weaknesses of both introverts and extroverts. Express confidence that your child will grow to know himself, be comfortable with his strengths, and learn how to shelter and support his weaknesses.

6. **Balance Cyberfriends With Face-To-Face Friendships**. Our kids' friendships will rely heavily on social networking, but it's not a replacement for, nor will it teach the skills of, face-to-face friendships. Help kids develop both aspects of today's peer relationships.

7. **Leave Room For Imperfection**. We're not perfect. Neither are our kids. Friendships and working relationships have the

imperfections and strengths of their human creators. Encourage your child to accept life – and other humans – with some imperfections. Don't hover over every aspect of your kids' relationships, but have a sense of the *"Oops, too far"* line and encourage your kids to recognize it and change [friends or behavior] before reaching that limit. That's good advice for adults too.

Plan Inclusive Parties & Social Activities

8. **Simplify Holiday Celebrations.** We have significantly ramped up our celebrations in North America in the past two decades. Birthdays, graduations, communions, religious holidays, and other rites of passage used to be fairly low-key, involving immediate family or school classmates only. Somehow these have become enormous events resembling weddings in their complexity, with dancing elephants, event planners, hundreds of people, and thousands of dollars. Weddings have escalated enormously too, until the recent economic crisis.

   While the intent may be good, it creates a huge opportunity for social exclusion. When the party's that special, it hurts more to be left out. Let's keep the spirit of celebration and the connection to family and friends, but let's return to simpler, more relaxed get-togethers.

9. **De-Emphasize Birthdays And Birthday Parties.** Birthday parties have become so overblown that they need their own discussion. It's a birthday, not a coronation. Our kids need

our time and good wishes, not a catered event for 120 to celebrate a one-year-old's birthday.

Yearly birthday parties used to be only for the very young. After early elementary school, only significant milestones were marked with a party. Celebration of coming of age is a part of many religions and nationalities, but this used to be quietly celebrated within the family or the religious community.

Many factors may have contributed to the explosive growth in party frequency and complexity. Working parents want to provide special celebrations for their kids, immigrants want to retain and keep their kids connected to traditional celebrations, population mobility results in people living far from their extended family, so they celebrate more often with friends, population mobility also makes it easier to hop on a plane to attend a birthday celebration, parents turn kids' birthday parties into convenient "adults, too" gatherings. There are many positive reasons why kids' parties have grown in size and scope. There are also some not-so-wonderful reasons. The sport of "competitive parenting" sometimes results in the perceived need to outdo the last party, causing a spiraling escalation of party costs and complexity.

If we can't return to the time of fewer or low-key parties, we can make our parties more welcoming to all and plan them with care that they don't lead to hurt feelings. This is especially important for younger kids. It helps teach the value of being friendly to everyone. By the time kids get to late middle and high school, they tend to have smaller groups of close friends, based on common interests, but if they've grown up in environments that value friendliness towards all, they won't be mean and rude to friends from earlier childhood, even when they're no longer close.

When planning parties, find ways to include the whole class or group in the celebration [eg, camp groups in summer] and avoid party formats that exclude most or some of the class. Don't put kids in the position of having to hide invitations that only half the class receives. Kids end up dealing with the bad situations adults create. Many teachers have told me how crushed kids feel to come back from lunch or recess and discover that their desk *doesn't* have an invitation sitting on it. Many schools are now encouraging kids to deliver party invitations outside of school. Banning invitations from school desks is a good idea, but does not fully solve the problem.

Yes, it is more expensive to have a larger birthday party that includes the whole class. **It's the price we pay for building inclusion.** The extra cost can be shared or reduced in several ways:

- Celebrate all October birthdays in the class on one day. Families contribute to a larger, combined party, outside of school, for all October celebrants and all their classmates.
- Send a cake to school for the whole class to share [check with your individual school about allergy-relevant concerns].

- Lessen the focus on gifts. Organize a "do good" community service activity for the whole class, then celebrate with cake and ice cream afterward.

- Have an all-out, individual birthday party every other year, inviting the whole class. This also reduces kids' expectations for a major party every year.

- Spread the party through the year. Parents can organize frequent, low-key activities for all or rotating subsets of the class – a movie, volleyball in the park after school with pizza [and veggies!], bowling, skating. Do it monthly – if a kid can't make it one time they can make it the next time. Reduce the fanciness, increase the frequency. Give all the kids a chance to hang out and get to know one another outside of school.

10. **Use The Same Approach To Graduation Celebrations And After-Prom Parties. Include The Entire Graduation Class**. Our kids have achieved something great – together – when they graduate from middle school or high school. Let them celebrate together too. Don't leave some kids out, don't make kids have to hide invitations or lie to friends about their after-prom or after-graduation plans.

There are Safe Prom organizations dedicated to giving high school kids safe, alcohol-free, driving-free alternatives to drunken and dangerous festivities. While the stated goal is keeping kids safe and reducing drunk-driving accidents, the secondary benefit is that it provides an inclusive social environment where all graduates may celebrate their accomplishments together.

The Safe After-Prom [or After-Grad] party is an overnight of food and lively arcade games in the school gym, with music and great prizes [computers, trips] given away up to the very last minute [7 am], to encourage kids to stay for the whole event. Participants typically must sign a pledge agreeing to stay all night, not to arrive drunk, not to drink while on school premises, and to turn their car keys in for the evening upon arrival.

11. **Plan Party Guest Lists**. Review guest lists with your child. Insist that the whole class be invited. Ask who's not on the list. If you have access to a complete class list, review it with your child. Discuss how the invitations will be delivered. This becomes a different concern as kids reach the teen years, where a party invite posted on Facebook can generate dozens – or hundreds – of unexpected guests faster than you can say *"My parents are out for the evening."* Then we'll want as small a party as possible! Encourage high school kids to have varying, small groups of friends over frequently. Make your home teen-friendly.

Make Newcomers Feel Accepted

12. **Welcome New Children Into The School And Community.** Our current efforts to welcome new children do not last long enough to be effective. It takes a minimum of three to six months for a child to feel connected to their new home, school, and neighborhood. At school, make it clear to the "old kids" that everyone is expected to introduce themselves, be

friendly to, and include the new kid – in classroom activities, at lunch, and at recess. Find classmates from the same neighborhood to walk home or ride the bus together.

Assign rotating "friend ambassadors" for four to eight weeks, to teach new kids the ropes, walk them to class, and introduce them to other friends and classmates. Student reporters can "interview and introduce" the new student, either to other classmates or in articles for the school newspaper. Highlight commonalities, shared interests, and the newcomer's special skills or talents.

Parents can reinforce the welcome if teachers send a message home so parents know there are new kids in the class. Invite new kids home after school and on weekends, to get to know everyone one-on-one. Connect to the new parents too.

This is another example of the multiplier effect that changing kids' behavior can have on our whole society. Teaching kids to offer this kind of sustained welcome to newcomers has direct applicability to adult life in our mobile, multicultural societies. We could also do a much better job welcoming new adult immigrants, helping them find meaningful work and educational opportunities, using their talents and prior training more effectively. When our kids grow up taking responsibility for welcoming newcomers, they will bring those attitudes and skills into their adult lives and workplaces. New immigrants who feel accepted by and embedded into their new surroundings overcome the temporary obstacles of language and cultural differences more easily.

13. **Apply Newcomer Tips To Current Students With Differences That Make It Harder For Them To Fit In.** Kids with learning disabilities or differences, less developed social skills, or physically evident differences are all at greater risk of being bullied. Adults must stand firm on the value of helping everyone, making a place for everyone, and especially *not* making a difference or disability the starting point for social humiliation.

14. **Rotate School Groups And Sports Teams**. This is an important tip for teachers to use even when there aren't any new students. Too often we let students choose their own project groups and sports teams, and the same students get chosen – *and not chosen*. Teachers and coaches can prevent this by stating that everyone must get a chance to work with everyone else and teams and groups are chosen by numbering off. This will support the making of new friendships and prevent team and group selection from becoming a popularity contest.

Value And Develop Emotional Competence

15. **Teach The Skills Of Emotional Intelligence [EQ]**. The skills of emotional intelligence are more important to success in life than "brain smarts." As the saying goes, *"IQ gets you hired; EQ gets you promoted."* Recent research backs that up. Kids with high levels of emotional self-control grow up to be adults

with more financial success, less substance abuse and criminal activity, and significantly better health than children with poor self-control.[1]

Here are the EQ skills, in summary:[2]

- **Self-Awareness**: Know your own emotions.

- **Emotional Control & Self-Management**: Wait your turn, delay gratification, reduce anxiety, self-soothe, recover quickly.

- **Self-Motivation**: Organize yourself and your emotions to achieve a goal.

- **Empathy**: Recognize the emotions of others.

- **Relationship Management**: Use your own emotional knowledge to guide your actions.

EQ skills are important life skills that also underlie and support bullying prevention. We must learn how to recognize, understand, and control our own emotions, as well as be able to recognize the emotions of *others* and use that understanding to guide our own behavior. The challenge: Adults must have good EQ skills in order to teach kids, or must at least be willing to [re]learn along with them.

16. **Control Your Stress**. **Stress management is a key supporting skill to successful bullying prevention**. When

---

[1] C Weeks, "For A Child, It's All About Control," *Globe And Mail*, GlobeAndMail.com, Jan 25, 2011

[2] D Goleman, *Emotional Intelligence: Why It Can Matter More Than IQ* (New York: Random House, 1997)

we live our lives at the very edge of our ability to manage our stress, it's too easy to cross the line into being a bully, without meaning to or realizing it. Stress management is important for both adults and kids. Most adults have poorly controlled stress – we see the downsides daily. For kids, the stakes are even higher for several reasons: (1) Kids have less life experience and fewer coping skills than adults, (2) Stress has taken on epidemic proportions in kids' lives today – the rates of anxiety and depression in girls have never been higher, (3) Long-term stress damages and rewires your brain, making it a lifelong weakness for kids who don't learn how to handle it, and (4) The poor example of adults is not helping!

Our ability to handle extra stress depends on how much stress we're already carrying. One day I almost drove through a stop sign. I stopped short but in time, without entering the crosswalk, and nowhere near touching the man on the sidewalk waiting to cross the street. As he crossed in front of my car, he gave me one of those in-your-face nasty looks, waving his hand, saying something I couldn't hear through my closed windows [it was probably for the best!].

Ordinarily, that wouldn't have bothered me. I have would looked at the guy and mouthed the word "*Sorry*" large enough for him to see it, or just ignored him and thought to myself, "*Guess he's having a bad day.*" That day though, I was suddenly so angry at him I could have jumped out of the car and grabbed him by the throat [I struggled to maintain my self-control and I did nothing.]

Later that evening, I was thinking about how uncharacteristically enraged I had felt for those few moments. I thought about how I'd been under a lot of strain for the past few months, helping out with three extremely ill relatives. I then realized it had just been that morning that I'd learned that my mother had been diagnosed with a serious illness needing surgery – relative number four [don't worry, she's fine now]. No wonder I was at the end of my rope! Things that wouldn't ordinarily bother you can flip you out when you have no reserve. It takes a commitment to handle our stress, plus some skill learning how not to act on our first [or second] impulsive reaction when we're pushed beyond our limit.

My Favorite Tips For Handling Stress. This could be a book unto itself, but here are some of the ideas that work best for me and the people I coach. Meditation, progressive muscle relaxation before bed, meridian tapping [look it up], deep breathing breaks for one minute every two or three hours, exercise [especially outdoors in summer], healthy eating, adequate sleep, gratitude journaling, helping others, relaxing with friends, laughing, and making the commitment not to "catastrophize" or rev your own emotional engines [reliving past problems or confrontations and driving your emotional temperature even higher] will all help. Learn how to recognize when you're near your limit and try not to hang out around people who push your buttons until you build back some reserve. If you can't avoid it, at least go in with the conscious intent to recognize incoming emotional missiles and not get triggered – and have an escape plan. Pick one or two ideas to start – everyone has unique needs and responds differently. Nobody does all these things perfectly, but when your life is stressful, consciously choose to do at least a few things that will improve your ability to handle stress.

17. **Teach The Skills Of Apology, Forgiveness, Accountability, And Repair.** Apologies are uncomfortable. Actually, it's the embarrassment of having made a big enough mistake that it requires an apology that causes the discomfort. Remember the words of philosophy professor Israel Knox? *"Wrongdoing is the gap between the standards we profess and the actions we perform."* The discomfort comes when we look in the mirror. As it should be. That discomfort, if you don't take it away, is that sand to the oyster, the uncomfortable stimulus to mind- and heart-opening growth.

People today view apology as weak. Nothing could be further from the truth. It takes strength to face yourself in the mirror and do the work needed to grow. Start when kids are young. It is a hard skill to learn late in life. Fortunately, adults can relearn as we teach our kids.

Let kids sit with the discomfort. Don't smooth the way. Let kids step into their age-appropriate responsibility to clean up the mess they created – a broken glass or a broken heart. With adult backstopping, *"Let's figure out what you can do to put this right," "What equipment do we need to clean up this broken glass?",* kids can develop their hearts, souls, and consciences, along with their bodies and brains.

Wait till the child is ready to apologize and make sure that the target is ready to receive the apology. It might seem easier to force the aggressive child to apologize immediately, but this typically results in a useless apology – meaningless to both the aggressor and the target. Give both kids a chance to cool down and prepare. Use a sticky note reminder to ensure it gets done by the end of the day. Tell the children to prepare themselves to be emotionally ready – to give or receive the apology – by then.

Remember, the work begins, not ends, with the apology. Apologies are worthless unless accompanied by genuine efforts both to repair the immediate damage and to prevent it from recurring.

The apology recipient has work to do too. Learn how to forgive and release a grudge. Forgiveness does not mean that you have to continue the friendship or that the transgression was "OK." Some actions are so hurtful they can damage a relationship permanently. Forgiveness is a gift we give *ourselves*, to untie the bonds that bind us to anger or sadness and allow us to leave the past behind, to move forward with peace and hope. Forgiveness can take time and practice, but it is a skill worth mastering.

18. **Teach Resilience**. This could also be a whole book. Kids with strongly anchored respect for themselves and for others are usually pretty resilient too. Teach kids how to walk it off when things don't go exactly as they hoped or planned. Help

kids be introspective about what part [positive and negative] they may have contributed to the outcome – *"Hmm, what did I learn from that?"* Help kids build from their strengths as they learn new emotional, social, academic, or physical skills to support their weak areas. Adults lead by example.

Upgrade Behavior – Adults And Kids

19. **Adults, Clean Up Our Own Act**. Kids will never listen to us if we're still swearing, gossiping, giving people the cold shoulder, and holding grudges. We must walk our talk.

20. **Pay Attention To Tone Of Voice And Body Language**. In addition to the words we choose, tone of voice and body language have a huge influence on the message. Words delivered with eye-rolling and sarcasm can mean exactly the opposite of the same words delivered with sincerity and eye contact. This applies to adults and kids.

21. **Be Flexible In Discipline [Adults]**. A *"Just say no,"* black-or-white approach will only encourage kids to sneak behind your back. Adults must develop some "shades of grey" knowledge to *live comfortably with the discomfort of raising teens*, aware enough to know that some risky behaviors [eg, sex, sexting, social networking via the Internet, drinking, smoking, drug use] may be part of the teen program. If we've done our job encouraging kids to know their own boundaries, we can expect them to make generally good choices. We can also expect some mistakes; see the next point.

22. **Don't Overreact To Mistakes.** Stay calm. Try to adopt an *"I'm glad this happened now"* approach and stay open to the learning opportunity the mistake creates [model it on the outside, even if your heart is racing]. Staying calm encourages – but does not guarantee – that kids will come to us when their problems are still small. It also encourages kids not to overreact and to think clearly when they run into problems, both face-to-face and online.

23. **Set Limits On Technology**. Keep the Internet connection in a public place. You will have to decide your family's policy for children using laptops with wireless connections. Have a family discussion to set appropriate limits: hours per day online, Facebook only *after* homework [good luck with that one in high school!], rules for taking a cell phone to school, rules for staying in touch electronically when out with friends.

Allow some compromise. When kids help make the rules, they are much more likely to follow them. Give your children incentives to show you their maturity. Make many opportunities for practice. Identify knowledge gaps and upgrade. [Here's one my family learned: When you're out and communicating via text message, the recipient – parent or child – must always say *"Got it"* so we know the message was received]. There should be reasonable consequences for mistakes, along with the opportunity to review and try again. Review and change the limits once or twice a year, as your children's ages and stages change.

Eventually, you want your kids to know how to set their own technology limits – to be able to decide that studying for an exam is best done *without* Facebook, but some homework is probably OK to do with friends chatting nearby. Our kids' brains are wired a bit differently than ours, but everybody's performance degrades with increasing distraction. Help your child learn to make appropriate choices – whether to be online *and* what's appropriate online conduct – when a parent *isn't* there.

You want your kids to be able to make these decisions *before* leaving your home for college and university or their first jobs. **You do not want to make all the decisions for your kids for 18 years, then send them out on their own, with no adults around, to struggle with these issues, unguided, in their dorm rooms and first apartments. I'm sure you realize this applies to every aspect of teen life, not just technological boundary-setting!**

24. **Create Independent Education Plans [IEPs] For Bullies**. This is a way to create a consistent approach to changing the bullying behavior of individual kids. We're beginning to see this trend in several states and provinces. Approach it as you would any IEP – for academic or emotional skill deficits. Identify the child's shortcomings and needs. Identify the needed resources. Make a plan with specific goals and deadlines. Involve appropriate resources and personnel.

IEPs need not be limited to schools. Parents, you can make your own IEP for your child's improvement at home. If your child has an IEP at school, meet with her teacher to ask what can be done at home to support the changes being made and the new skills being learned at school. Be persistent about specifics. Sometimes parents get a vague *"Just be encouraging of what we're doing here."* We need more. If your kid needs the structure of an IEP at school, the goals should be supported and reinforced at home. With gentleness, love, flexibility, and encouragement [that's the parents' goal].

If you don't get help from the school to develop your home-based IEP, make your own. Get a copy of the IEP document and start from there. Read, talk to other parents, and talk to professional coaches and counselors. Start with one or two ideas to support the school goals. Evaluate monthly.

Keep The Big Picture In Mind

25. **Commit Resources To Prevention. We must put money – and effort – into preventing bullying. If we only [or substantially] fund crisis situations, we will condemn ourselves to a rollercoaster ride from crisis to crisis.** Spend more money and time on activities for kids that foster friendships and common interests. If we reach kids early enough, they won't need adult remedial corporate anti-bullying activities disguised as team-building. Start early – preschool is not too soon! [Yes, there are wonderful team-

building exercises that do indeed foster working friendships and help organizations assemble the most talented teams for specific work assignments. I'm referring to the too-prevalent use of team-building exercises as a remedial Band-aid for dysfunctional work groups.]

26. **Stand Up And Support Those Needing Help.**

And

27. **Tap Into Kids' Creative Organizing Spirit & Abilities.** This story illustrates both points. The students at Central Kings Rural High School in Halifax, Nova Scotia, came to the aid of a grade 9 boy being taunted for wearing a pink shirt. First the boys and then every kid in the school wore a pink shirt, sending a loud message of support to the targeted boy – and an even louder message through the school and to their community: *"No bullying here."*

That was just the beginning – the idea spread like wildfire. Soon, 35 schools had students wearing pink shirts emblazoned with *"Real Men Wear Pink"* and eating pink mashed potatoes in the school cafeteria. Even the Premier of Nova Scotia wore pink in solidarity and declared the second Thursday at the start of each school year as Stand Up Against Bullying Day. As one student said, *"Wearing pink sends the message that we are totally against bullying and it's not something we approve of or accept here."*[3]

---

[3]"Nova Scotia Students Rebuke Bullies By Wearing Pink," *Toronto Star,* TheStar.com, Sep 22, 2007

That's the creative power of teen social networking at its best, used for community action and change.

28. **Pay It Forward**. In life, we can rarely pay back the people who've helped us and taught us. We can, however, pay it forward. No matter how down we are, there is always someone else who needs a helping hand. When you need help, you should be able to get it. And when you can give help, you should give it. We can always find a little time. Helping others is also one of the best ways to handle stress and ease depression.

    This is an important lesson for our kids. Adults teach children about care and empathy when we help others by giving the gift of our time. Teach children to help within the community by being alert to opportunities to build, deliver, decorate, paint, read, tutor, visit, teach, or coach. Look for ways for kids to share their unique skills and ideas. The act of extending our hand to others builds self-respect in the giver, generates gratitude in both the giver and the recipient, and helps us get to know people as individual human beings.

Equipped with these additional strategies, we can now use our intellectual and emotional understanding of bullying to select from a full toolkit of immediately usable, flexible ideas. We can work together to change and dismantle existing systems that encourage or enable bullying. We can ensure that our kids' homes, schools, and communities become kind-hearted, welcoming, bully-free zones.

11

Stop Bullying Now!
10 Action Steps

Let's step back, summarize, and simplify. We need to know what to do tomorrow. Every school and every community starts from a slightly different situation, and our choice of action items will be determined by our own current needs. We all need to bravely assess our strengths and weaknesses and work, with purpose, towards the big picture goal. We must stop staggering from emergency to emergency.

We need to look beyond the most obvious or first symptoms and dig deeper for the underlying causes and structures that enable bullying. We must look for connections and think complexly, about both the problems and their solutions. We must resist the temptation to slap a quick fix on the problem, usually a short-term punishment with little lasting effect. That said, the most effective things you can do are simple: (1) Pay attention and (2) Be willing to say *"Just stop it!"* when you see bullying in progress. That will handle about 80% of the problems.

Some bullying problems require a more nuanced approach. Intervene too quickly or with rules that are simplistic [eg, the "no snowballs" approach], and we risk disabling our kids – creating permanent victims who feel powerless to help themselves or who always look to someone else to tell them what's right. On the other hand, if we wait too long to intervene when we know that bullying is occurring, we risk permanent damage to all involved – the target, the bully, and the bystanders. When we look away, we ingrain long-term behavior and we ensure that kids' bullying – and adult bullying – will continue.

While there are many commonalities to the types and causes of bullying, there isn't a one-size-fits-all solution. We must select from the wide range of common tools available to us and apply them in unique combinations to address the specific needs of each issue we confront. This requires that adults pay attention, get involved, make adjustments, and participate in the continuing, low-level monitoring required *after* the problem is "solved."

We must reorient ourselves towards prevention, rather than punishment after the fact. Our goal is to spend much *less* time on bullying issues, but prevention is the *only* way to reach that goal. With prevention, we make the commitment to not let people or events get pushed too close to the edge of "sudden," but predictable, catastrophe.

Our biggest obstacle is overcoming our own inertia. It takes commitment and some effort to retune our eyes and ears, but the results speak for themselves. Reducing kids' bullying and increasing self-respect and respect for others will have an enormous, positive ripple effect on both kids and adults, in every aspect of our individual and communal lives.

With that in mind, there are action steps that we can all take. Identify the two or three areas where your environment needs the most work, review the action items from earlier in the book and from the big categories below, pick a few, and start from there. Evaluate your progress bi-weekly or once a month, then add another item to the list of goals.

10 Action Steps To Stop Bullying:

1. **Lead By Example**. Adults must speak and act with respect and courtesy towards one another and to kids, even and *especially* in times of conflict and disagreement. Don't call your kids [or your spouse] names when you're angry at them. Don't gossip about Aunt Anne on the phone, even when you think your kids aren't listening. We must hold ourselves to high standards and insist that children do the same.

2. **Focus On Prevention**. Start when kids are young and the problems are small. Identify issues before they become crises and don't let them build. Keep paying attention. Prevention requires persistence and consistency.

3. **Don't Tolerate Bullying**. Big or small, first time or repeated, bullying has no place in our homes, schools, or workplaces. There should be consequences for misbehavior and mistakes, even unintentional, if someone was hurt by bullying behavior. Focus on restorative consequences more than

punitive. Every time there's a bullying incident, it's our cue that we haven't focused enough on prevention and need to do more.

4. **Build Respect, Empathy, And Inclusion.** Look for activities that are inclusive and that break down the barriers between kids [reading buddies, chess club, Girls' Respect Groups, etc]. Promote acceptance of and curiosity about differences. We need to make space for people who do not look like us or think like us.

5. **Empower Bystanders**. We must create safe environments for our kids, where protection is the norm and mistakes are stopped in their tracks by the early, commonplace intervention of bystanders. We must insist that it is *everybody's responsibility to speak up and help out.* Our environments must demonstrably value and reward bystander action.

6. **Train All Adults.** Make sure adults look at bullying issues with the same eyes. Adopt consistent definitions of what constitutes acceptable and unacceptable behavior, and where to draw the line. Make sure new parents, teachers, and other adults entering the system are brought up to speed on common goals. Improve communication about potential problems between staff at school and between school and home.

7. **Monitor And Supervise**. This means *better* adult supervision, not more. Adults should be "on alert" early,

monitoring the warning signs and building blocks of rude behavior or bullying. Put yourself in places where you can observe kids' words and behavior – wander around the playground, periodically stand within earshot of their playroom. We need to intervene sooner, at the early stages. Intervene kindly [don't bully!] and don't enable the bully by looking the other way.

8. **Build Strong, Positive Leadership**. Make positive leadership opportunities available to adults and children. Watch for those kids with strong personalities and guide them away from bullying, into other avenues where they can exercise their personal power for the common good.

9. **Set Clear Standards For New Students And Groups**. Schools have the unique opportunity to graduate, and thus replace, a significant percentage of the student body every year – as much as 33% [wish we could do that in some workplaces!]. It's an opportunity to indoctrinate new students with the values of the school and our expectations for their behavior.

Take advantage of the opportunity. Use visiting days and the first week of school to advertise your standards and expectations. *"This is how we treat people here, even when you're angry at them or don't even like them. We are all expected to live by this behavior code and we will hold you to it."* This is just as important as having an excellent academic record or a full range of after-school activities. Set guidelines for after-school activities that all students must agree to, including *"the respectful, inclusive treatment of all participants or students expressing an interest in the group. The same courtesy and respect will be extended, as well, to our competitive opponents."* **And then we must live every day of the rest of the year acting in concert with those stated goals.**

10. **Develop Short- And Long-Term Strategies And Goals.** Write them down, review them monthly. Celebrate and make a big deal about accomplishing change. We must be willing to maintain our attention and sustain the effort to effect real change.

Next Steps: Moving Forward Together

Viewing the big picture, we can all see that bullying is not *someone else's* problem – it's yours, mine, and ours. There can be no more waiting for the magic anti-bullying program, anti-bullying policy, or anti-bullying law. We need to act *before* the "sudden" appearance of a serious problem that causes permanent damage.

Adult leadership is crucial – one word can have a huge impact, putting kids on a different path. Make corrections while they're easy and cheap. Failing to step in sets the stage and enables the next act of the drama.

We must become more mindful and sharpen our awareness of our unconscious contributions to bullying. We must stop turning our environments inside out to accommodate bullies and enabling bullies by looking away, making excuses, blaming someone else, and failing to intervene when our leadership is needed.

We can create safe, nurturing environments for our kids and ourselves, where the leadership of bystanders is encouraged, expected, and rewarded [for a while, until it becomes a permanent part of the culture and the reward comes from knowing you helped another human being who needed aid].

We must all take responsibility. We must all do our part, a little every day. We have different skills, individually and as a community. We need to help one another. *"Repair the world"* is a common theme in many religions. No single individual can complete the task, but all of us are required to contribute.

Our work continues from today. The challenge is how to take this knowledge and put it into action, with observable results and permanent improvements. **Our commitment to stop bullying must become ingrained in our culture**, not something that disappears after the cameras turn off, the bullying expert leaves the school, the students graduate, or the candlelight vigil ends. It's the little things, day in and day out, that make the difference. **Kids need to know that *every day* is Bullying Prevention Day**.

Let's Get Started.

Index

A

Apology, 1, 8, 26, 32-33, 51, 57, 58, 63-64, 66-67, 89, 116, 217, 236, 269, 290-291

B

Beane, Allan, 84
Beckham, Dylan, 8, 208
Birthday parties, 280-283
Brown, Gordon, 54-59, 93
Bully
  characteristics, 91-94
Bully, The Bullied, And The Bystander (Barbara Coloroso), 46, 83, 152, 156
Bullycide, 3, 5, 141
Bullying
  action plan for bully, 207
  action plan for bystanders, 115-119, 204
  action plan for target, 211-214, 216-222
  adult contribution, 6, 47-80
  and conflict, 30, 109, 158-163, 278
  and leadership potential, 93, 205
  and power, 29, 62, 83-84, 143, 152, 158
  and respect, 43, 165-202
  and sports, 15, 44, 53, 64-69, 154-155, 175, 178, 277, 286
  and the law, *ix*, 130, 233-273
  definition, 83-84
  definition for kids, 84
  invisible to adults, 22-23, 222, 230
  physical, 85
  relational, 87
  school, 38-42, 59-67
  school withdrawal, 224
  symptoms, 203-232
  unintentional, 206
  verbal, 85
Bystander, 5, 7, 14, 19, 43, 50, 54-58, 62, 82, 91, 103-119, 124, 141, 143, 165, 204, 223, 249, 273, 300, 302, 305
  characteristics, 103-119

C

Clementi, Tyler, *ix*, 4, 49, 75, 133, 157, 169, 237, 260
Coloroso, Barbara, 46, 83, 152, 156, 235
Columbine, 3-5, 36-37, 87, 90, 99, 100, 145, 240, 256-257, 264
Conflict resolution, *v, vii, viii*, 1, 7, 17, 29-30, 109, 158-163
Cutting, 213
Cyberbullying, 39, 85, 89, 121-149

D

Dating violence, 194-198
Dove Campaign For Real Beauty, 182

E

Emotional Intelligence (EQ), 286-287

F

Forgiveness, 32-33, 290-291

G

Girls' Respect Groups: An Innovative Program To Empower Young Women & Build Self-Esteem!, v, 200, 201

Girls' Respect Groups (GRG), *v, x,* 23, 79, 165, 193-194, 198-202, 277, 302
Graduations, 283
Grudges, 1, 11, 33, 279, 291

H

Harris, Eric, *ix,* 3

I

Independent Education Plan (IEP), 294-295
Intermittent Explosive Disorder, 25

J

Jeffrey Johnston Law, 245, 245-249

K

Klebold, Dylan, *ix,* 3
Knox, Israel, 13, 290

L

Leadership
adult, *xiv,* 7, 8, 10, 13, 14, 18, 64, 74, 93, 115, 117, 141, 147, 154, 169, 185-189, 190, 199, 205, 226, 229, 266, 277, 303-305
Logan, Jesse, *ix,* 137-144, 157, 201

M

Mean Girls, 180-181

N

Newcomers, 36, 94, 284-286, 303

O

Olweus, Dan, 83

P

Parent Education Network, *vi,* 30
Patterson, Dane, 240-243, 252-254, 258, 261
Prince, Phoebe, *ix,* 2-3, 14, 35, 37, 86, 90

R

Reality shows, 6, 69-76
Resilience, *v, viii,* 36, 66, 154, 168, 174, 177, 224
Respect (self-respect), 43-44, 57, 92, 108, 138, 165-202, 278, 297, 300
Rutgers University, 4, 260

S

School
bullying in, 38-42, 59-67
school community definition, 39-40
unique prevention strengths, 38, 40-42
Sexting, 137-143, 148, 157, 292
Stress, 56, 61-62, 102, 172, 179, 211, 213, 216, 220, 222, 264
Stress management, *v,* 7, 18, 111, 287-290, 297

T

Target, 14, 50, 54-58, 72, 82, 94-103, 126-127, 162, 165, 179, 211-214, 216-225, 251, 273, 277
characteristics, 94-103, 211-214
provocative, 95
Taunting, 45, 96, 97, 138, 151-154, 160, 227, 263
Teasing, 151-54, 160, 227, 263
Theno, Dylan, 98, 224
Title IX, 239-245, 253-254

W

Wesley, Dawn-Marie, *ix,* 111, 157

www.ingramcontent.com/pod-product-compliance
Lightning Source LLC
Chambersburg PA
CBHW060247100426
42742CB00011B/1668